SANCTUARY AND CRIME
IN THE MIDDLE AGES, 400–1500

just ideas

transformative ideals of justice in ethical and politcal thought

series editors

Drucilla Cornell

Roger Berkowitz

Kenneth Michael Panfilio

SANCTUARY AND CRIME IN THE MIDDLE AGES, 400–1500

Karl Shoemaker

FORDHAM UNIVERSITY PRESS

NEW YORK 2011

Library of Congress Cataloging-in-Publication Data

Shoemaker, Karl.
Sanctuary and crime in the middle ages, 400–1500 / Karl Shoemaker. — 1st ed.
p. cm.—(Just ideas : transformative ideals of justice in ethical and political thought)
Includes bibliographical references and index.
ISBN 978-0-8232-3268-0
(ebook : alk. paper)
1. Asylum, Right of—Europe—History—To 1500. 2. Law, Medieval.
I. Title.

KJ1010.S54 2011
345.45'632056—dc22

2010023925

13 12 11 5 4 3 2 1

First edition

Contents

Abbreviations

ACO	*Acta Conciliorum Oecumenicorum*
A Gu	*Alfred's Treaty with Guthrum* (ed. *Liebermann*)
Alf	*Laws of Alfred*
As [I–VI]	*Laws of Æthelstan* (ed. *Liebermann*)
Atr [I–X]	Laws of *Æthelred* (ed. *Liebermann*)
BL	British Library
CCSL	*Corpus Christianorum Series Latina*
CIC	*Corpus Iuris Canonici* (ed. Friedman)
CJ	*Codex Justininanus*
CL	*Corpus Legum ab Imperatoribus Romanis ante Iustinianum Latarum*
Cn [I–II]	*Laws of Cnut* (ed. *Liebermann*)
CSEL	*Corpus Scriptorum Ecclesiasticorum Latinorum*
C.Th.	*Codex Thedosianus* (Theodosian Code)
D	*Decretum* (ed. Friedman)
Dig.	*Digest of Justinian*
ECf	*Laws of Edward the Confessor*
Edg. [I–IV]	*Laws of Edgar* (ed. *Liebermann*)
Edm. [I–III]	*Laws of Edmund* (ed. *Liebermann*)
E Gu	*Edward's Treaty with Guthrum*
E.Th.	*Edictum Theodorici*
Gesetze	*Die Gesetze der Angelsachsen* (ed. *Liebermann*)
Hist. Eccl.	*Historica Ecclesiastica*

IRME	*Ius Romana Medii Aevi*
JECS	*Journal of Early Christian Studies*
JUST	*Rolls of the Itinerant Justices*
Leis Wl	*Leis Willelme* (ed. Liebermann)
LHP	*Leges Henrici Primi* (ed. Downer)
MGH	*Monumenta Germaniae Historica*
NA	National Archives (Great Britain)
Nov.	*Novellae*
PG	*Patrologia Graeca*
PL	*Patrologia Latina*
RDC	*Revue du Droit Canonique*
RHD	*Revue Historique du Droit Français et Etranger*
Robbins	Robbins Civil and Religious Law Collection, Berkeley, California
Wl Lond	*William I, Writ for London* (ed. Liebermann)
X	*Liber Extra* (ed. Emile Friedman)
ZDR	*Zeitschrift für Deutsches Recht und Deutsche Rechtwissenschaft*
ZSS GA	*Zeitschrift der Savigny-Stiftung für Rechtsgeschichte, Germanische Abteilung*
ZSS KA	*Zeitschrift der Savigny-Stiftung für Rechtsgeschichte, Kanonistische Abteilung*
ZSS RA	*Zeitschrift der Savigny-Stiftung für Rechtsgeschichte, Romanistische Abteilung*

Prologue

In its medieval form, sanctuary law granted a wrongdoer who fled to a church protection from forcible removal as well as immunity from corporal or capital punishment. The fugitive might be required to pay a fine, forfeit his goods, perform penance, or go into exile, but almost without exception his body and his life were to be preserved. Laws carving out sanctuary protections appear in every major medieval legal tradition. Fourth-century Roman law recognized sanctuary, ensuring that it was part of the legislative traditions that medieval Europe received from Rome. Ecclesiastical canons reiterated it, backing sanctuary with the Church's spiritual authority. In the early Middle Ages, a host of royal legislative commands repeated it, mooring sanctuary to images of pious and benevolent kings. In later medieval England, sanctuary traditions were incorporated into the routine administration of royal law, providing a resolution to all sorts of felonies until Tudor reforms all but abolished the privilege. In many cities on the European continent, sanctuary remained a central feature of feuding, exile, and dispute-resolving processes until the sixteenth century.

In the sixteenth century, the thousand-year-old legal practice came under increasing political and juridical attack. Roman lawyers, scouring the classic Roman law texts, argued that sanctuary rights belonged to the prerogative of secular sovereigns and could be restricted in the interest of the "*res publica*." Even the papacy participated in the restriction of sanctuary rights, promulgating in 1591 a bull that lengthened the list of crimes that no longer qualified for sanctuary and conceded a role for laymen in forcibly extracting fugitives from churches. The role of canon lawyers in the death of sanctuary is complex, and began in thirteenth-century attempts to reconcile ecclesiastical privileges like sanctuary with an emergent conception of deterrence-oriented criminal law. These thirteenth-century canon law doctrines had a lasting impact and were even conspicuously cited by Henry VIII in his move against sanctuary during his divorce with Rome in the 1530s. But the attack on sanctuary was not limited to Protestant lands. François I of France, for example, issued legislation that abolished sanctuary in 1539. Sanctuary's early modern abolition was closely tied to the emergence of juridical discourses that stressed the necessity of uninterrupted territorial sovereignty and deterrence-oriented understandings of punishment. Sanctuary, which had once been an important expression of medieval sovereignty and which had been integrated into the administration of criminal law in medieval common law and Roman-canonical jurisdictions, was recast as a nuisance that responsible lawmakers must be careful to restrict or abolish altogether.

I began this study attempting to understand how every major European legal tradition could recognize some form of protection for criminals who fled to a church. Why was allowing respite to a criminal who fled to a church considered an appropriate response to wrongdoing? How could such a legal practice flourish in European legal traditions for more than a millennium? And given that sanctuary survived for so long, why was it suddenly abolished throughout Europe in the sixteenth and seventeenth centuries? When did the sanctuary protections that had been transmitted from the late Roman Empire into every major medieval European legal tradition begin to seem inappropriate, even dangerous, so that a once-honored legal practice came under vociferous attack from secular and ecclesiastical quarters? To answer such questions, this study seeks to reconcile the history of sanctuary law with the general history of medieval criminal law and to relate the abolition of sanctuary to the emergence of a new understanding of criminal law and punishment at the dawn of the early modern era.

My initial investigations yielded two surprises. First, no general book-length study of medieval sanctuary law had been produced in English for nearly a century. The bulk of scholarship on medieval sanctuary, having been produced on the continent, has tended to treat the Roman-canonical tradition to the exclusion of the English common law tradition. Concomitantly, despite some fine article-length treatments of sanctuary law within the English legal tradition, there has been no sustained attempt to situate English sanctuary law within the broader picture of medieval Europe. Second, the sizeable literature on sanctuary law produced by historians has led to remarkably uniform conclusions. According to the standard accounts, protecting criminals who sought refuge in churches was an unhappy necessity for peoples without strong centralized governments, whose kings and churchmen could not sufficiently suppress private violence or regulate public vengeance. In this literature, sanctuary is considered a crutch; healthy legal regimes do not need it. It struck me early in my investigations that the people who actually lived under a regime that honored sanctuary laws probably did not, however else they may have understood sanctuary protections, regard those laws as evidence of an inadequate legal order or as mere placeholders serving until modern legal reforms could set things aright. Because the history of sanctuary has not yet been integrated with the history of criminal law, sanctuary has generally been treated as antithetical to criminal law practices in medieval Europe. Yet, sanctuary thrived for more than a millennium not because of its utility in an age of barbarity but because it accorded with medieval conceptions of pious sovereignty and ecclesiastical intercession and dovetailed with a range of medieval penal practices that were understood to be legitimate in their own right.

All research on the history of medieval sanctuary law must start with Pierre Timbal's monumental *Le droit d'asile*, published in 1939. Timbal's book begins by describing sanctuary practices in ancient Egypt and ends nearly five hundred pages later by cataloguing sanctuaries for criminals that still existed in Malabar, Tahiti, and, according to Timbal, in America in the "région du Missouri." In between, Timbal executed a breathtakingly rich account of sanctuary law from the Roman Empire through the abolition of sanctuary in sixteenth-century Europe, although for the most part he left Anglo-Saxon and English common law sources to the side. My own interpretation of medieval sanctuary law differs from Timbal's, but his achievement deserves more recognition than it has received among Anglophone scholars.

That almost seventy years had passed since the appearance of the last comprehensive monograph on medieval sanctuary, and almost one hundred years since the last such book appeared in English, gave me little pause, at least in the beginning. As my research deepened, the vast "untilled soil" I thought I had found proved to be as much a liability as an opportunity to contribute to the field of medieval legal history. It also helps explain the ambitious chronological scope of this study. Under any circumstances it would have been necessary to examine sanctuary law within the Theodosian Code because a great deal of early medieval legislation must be understood against the backdrop of late imperial Roman law and its transmission into Western Europe, but I found that the history of sanctuary law in the late Roman Empire had not been treated very thoroughly in English-language scholarship. As a consequence, I had to examine closely both the context of that imperial sanctuary legislation and its incorporation into the Theodosian Code (AD 438), which was such an important model for legislation in early medieval Europe.

While very few extant sources delineate how sanctuary law was practiced in medieval Europe before the thirteenth century, nearly every medieval legislative source—ecclesiastical or secular—announces some form of protection for criminals who took sanctuary. That some medieval legislative texts are preoccupied with sanctuary is not altogether surprising, given the indisputable role of ecclesiastics in drafting even so-called secular legislation in the early Middle Ages. Still, this calls for explanation. Although it may have been self-evident that Christian houses of worship should be free from violence and bloodshed, why would churchmen have been so eager to place themselves between feuding enemies or to thwart royal justice? And why would kings heed the message contained within the early medieval *Leges* that good kingship was bound up with respect for sanctuary law? In other words, what did sanctuary mean in the medieval world?

The available sources create certain unavoidable imbalances in research of this scope. The English plea rolls, which provide a largely continuous view of the administration of criminal law in England from the end of the twelfth century, offer a unique glimpse into the place of sanctuary in everyday administration of criminal law in England and show that the common law of sanctuary was distinctive in a number of ways, including the almost unlimited access to sanctuary for all types of felons and the administrative linkage of sanctuary with exile practices. On the other hand, while late medieval canon law sources reveal little about the administration of sanctuary in Roman-canonical jurisdictions, they do reveal an emergent tension between sanctuary and canon law conceptions of punishment. In regard to sanctuary practices outside late medieval England, Timbal did unearth some sources showing the disposition of sanctuary cases in fourteenth- and fifteenth-century royal French law, but the most detailed and quotidian view of medieval sanctuary is found in the records of the early English common law. There are reasons to suspect that the late-medieval English experience with sanctuary was not altogether different from that on the contemporary Continent, though English sanctuary practice was likely the most administratively disciplined in Europe. Still, considerable gaps in the record make it difficult to draw firm conclusions. In medieval Italy, both civilian jurists and canonists agreed that some form of sanctuary should protect at least some criminals, but evidence of sanctuary's actual administration is scarce. Surviving papal sources allow us only glimpses of sanctuary in practice on the European continent in the fourteenth century and thereafter. Fourteenth-century papal registers, for instance, show an expectation that sanctuary be respected in places as distant as Majorca and Bratislava. Yet the papal curia was unlikely to create a record in instances where the sanctuary privilege was respected, and thus the sources sometimes offer more evidence about exceptional cases than they do about the routine administration of sanctuary laws within canon law. Because of the abundant sources, the latter portion of this study is tilted toward the English common law. Where comparative evidence is available, it has been incorporated so that the picture might be somewhat rounded out to the extent possible, but the most detailed picture of how sanctuary law was successfully integrated into late medieval governance is provided by common law sources, and this book reflects that fact.

This book represents the accumulation of more debts than I can ever repay. The greatest of my intellectual debts are owed to my teachers at the University of California, Berkeley. I count myself fortunate to call Philippe Nonet my teacher, and I join a long line of his students when I acknowledge his generosity and grace as a teacher and friend. Laurent Mayali deserves special thanks for his patient guidance and support as I first began to work with medieval Roman and canon law sources. The late Tom Barnes shared his wealth of knowledge concerning English archives and the history of English law. David Lieberman has been an unfailing source of moral support over the years and taught me to think like a legal historian. Marianne Constable provided valuable insights throughout the life of this book, and her own work served always as a model to me for what a legal history project could be. I accumulated earlier debts at Cumberland School of Law in my home state of Alabama, where Professors Trisha Olson, Tom Berg, Andy Klein, David Smolin, and R. George Wright encouraged me to pursue a life in legal scholarship rather than one in law practice.

Mark Antaki, Roger Berkowitz, and Shai Lavi were my graduate school colleagues at Berkeley, and they remain friends. The friendship and thinking they shared is often missed and never matched. Others who have read this manuscript in whole or parts are Tom Green (who I am sure read more drafts than he cares to remember, but whose insights were invaluable), Patrick Wormald, William Courtenay, Rob Meens, Sherri Olson, Sam Collins, Michael Kulikowski, Martha Newman, Hugh Thomas, Sophie Peralba, William Jordan, Jennifer Culbert, David McDonald, Bill Reese, Lee Wandel, Patrick Gudridge, Elizabeth Allen, Richard Ross, Alison Frank, Fran Hirsch, and Brett Sheehan.

Various chapters of this book were presented at the University of California, Berkeley; Fordham University; the University of California, Irvine; Bard College; the Institute for Advanced Study, Princeton; the American Bar Foundation; and the University of Wisconsin–Madison.

Financial support for the initial research that forms the basis of this book was provided by the University of California, Berkeley, and by a generous fellowship from the Robbins Collection (Boalt Hall School of Law). Support for archival research in England was provided by the North American Conference on British Studies Dissertation Year Fellowship. The book was completed thanks to support from the University of Wisconsin–Madison and a wonderful year spent at the Institute for Advanced Study, Princeton, under the auspices of the National Endowment for the Humanities.

I also want to express deep thanks to Merilyn Shoemaker, Doug Shoemaker, and Blaine Sessions. Finally, my greatest debts of gratitude are owed to Ayten Kilic, Emma Shoemaker, Juliette Shoemaker, and Aksel Shoemaker (who arrived only a few months before the appearance of this book). Though none of them has read it, this book would not have been written were it not for them.

SANCTUARY AND CRIME IN THE MIDDLE AGES, 400–1500

Introduction

Although every medieval legal tradition offered criminals who fled to a church respite from corporal and capital punishment, in the sixteenth century kings, parliaments, and popes reached the common conclusion that the privileges that protected sanctuary seekers presented a major obstacle to good order, and the thousand-year-old legal practice was abolished or drastically restricted throughout Europe. With remarkable unanimity, scholars since the eighteenth century have looked approvingly upon the abolition of a practice that, according to their critique, had allowed respite to the guilty and unnecessarily infringed upon the proper reach of sovereign jurisdiction.[1] On account of sanctuary, "the strong, the swift, the premeditating murderer cheated the gallows."[2] Moreover, in the opinion of one eighteenth-century scholar, sanctuary law was "pregnant with an infinite deal of evil and mischief" because "the very act of persons betaking themselves to sanctuary always implied the commission, and even the confession, of their respective crimes."[3] In short, sanctuary was an "error . . . costly to the civilized community, in that wrongdoing was protected."[4] From its infancy, the science of criminology has agreed. The eighteenth-century penal reformer Cesare Beccaria concluded that "places of asylum invite to crime more than punishments influence against it."[5] By the early modern period, not only had sanctuary come to be identified with impunity for criminals, but it also was thought to promote more crimes.

Just as detrimental in this view was sanctuary's infringement upon the province of the sovereign and its laws. "Within the borders of a country there should be no place independent of its laws," and "to multiply such places of asylum is to create so many small sovereignties . . . where laws have no say."[6] Such a practice "seriously interfered with the administration of justice."[7] When sanctuary was finally abrogated, "we may see more clearly from what a fruitful source of outrages we are freed by the laws obtaining in all cases their natural and uninterrupted course."[8] The prevailing conceptions of sovereignty led to a general agreement that sanctuary was an offense against rational and evenhanded state administration.

The abolition of sanctuary consequently became a hallmark of progress. In the modern age, "under a due administration of Justice," sanctuary can only be "simply and constantly mischievous."[9] Said one late-nineteenth-century writer, "the more the administration of laws improved, and the less imperfect was the system of laws which they had to administer, the fewer the instances of resort to sanctuary."[10] Indeed, if due process and a fair trial were guaranteed, "sanctuary was a public nuisance."[11] Its "final abolition was a measure calculated to advance the interests of justice and morality in the land,"[12] for "with the advent of a well-organized judiciary and even-handed justice, sanctuaries and asylums became places of escape rather than refuge."[13] The triumph of the rule of law, then, rendered sanctuary undesirable, even detrimental.

Of course, sanctuary was not always portrayed as an unmitigated evil in historical accounts. In an often-quoted passage, Henry Hallam nostalgically conceded:

> But in the rapine and tumult of the middle ages, the right of sanctuary might as often be a shield to innocence, as an impunity to crime. We can hardly regret, in reflecting on the desolating violence which prevailed, that there should have been some green spots in the wilderness, where the feeble and the persecuted could find refuge.[14]

As another nineteenth-century writer admitted, "the sanctuaries of medieval Christendom may have been necessary remedies for a barbarous state of society."[15] In the words of a third, a compromise "in all rude ages," sanctuary "substituted as judge or arbitrator, learning for ignorance, coolness for patience, impartiality for prejudice . . . and . . . mitigated the ferocious punishment."[16]

Writing in 1930, the French legal historian Gabriel Le Bras found sanctuary to be an instrument particularly suited to the needs of medieval and ancient societies. Without "a universally competent public justice, where neither the general peace nor protection of the individual was well assured, and where common respect for sacred things preserved certain edifices and certain districts from acts of violence," sanctuaries flourished.[17] At the end of the decade, Le Bras' student Pierre Timbal published *Le droit d'asile*, which remains the foundational historical work on medieval sanctuary. Timbal reached conclusions quite similar to his mentor. "Strong political power assured the order and restraint of asylum; but periods of anarchy saw its utility develop."[18] Consequently, in the "chaos of feudalism," where political power was weak and juridical control almost nonexistent, sanctuary law "reached its apogee."[19] While Le Bras and Timbal liberated sanctuary law from the historical narratives that celebrated the end of sanctuary as a triumph of enlightened legal reforms, both scholars continued to cast sanctuary as an instrumental response to weak legal orders.

Studies of sanctuary law in England also cast sanctuary in instrumental terms. Charles H. Riggs, examining the Anglo-Saxon legal tradition, called sanctuary "one of the most effective instruments the times provided for bringing men to submit to the law" in the face of incomplete or disordered political authority.[20] In his account, royal and ecclesiastical authority in early medieval England found sanctuary law a beneficial means of bringing wrongdoers who could otherwise perpetuate the blood feud or easily stay beyond the reach of weak authority under "the weight of royal and ecclesiastical pressure . . . to compound for wrongdoing."[21] Local communities, too, saw that sanctuary provided injured parties monetary compensations, which the kin of a slain or injured party presumably preferred to judicially imposed punishment.[22] Although Riggs disagreed with Timbal over the extent to which religious sensibilities can explain the prevalence of sanctuary laws in early medieval Europe, he agreed with Timbal that sanctuary law was a particularly attractive tool of weak political orders and feuding cultures.

Some recent article-length treatments of medieval sanctuary have offered a way beyond the functional commitments of the older scholarship. Gervase Rosser has argued that sanctuary law provided temporal and ecclesiastical authority a site where it was possible to exploit "the strength of feeling in the neighborhood group" for venerated places.[23] By carving out this space "inside the framework of public authority," sanctuary allowed communities "relief from an excess in government" and room to settle disputes locally.[24] Although other evidence suggests that medieval communities sometimes found the obligations imposed upon them by sanctuary law to embody "excess in government," Rosser's key insight is that sanctuary flourished not only in periods of relative disorder and violence but also in periods of relative stability and strong governance. Besides substantiating some of Rosser's conclusions, William Jordan's provocative essay on sanctuary in medieval England notes that "it is inappropriate to read the medieval history of sanctuary from the early modern assault on it," helpfully recognizing the extent to which early modern juridical accounts of sanctuary have set the parameters of the historical accounts.[25] While Rosser and Jordan focus on sanctuary's social history, Richard Helmholz helpfully set sanctuary law within its internal juridical context, showing how it is fertile ground for exploring the manner in which medieval canon lawyers developed rules to administer the privilege over time. He also pointed out that the demise of sanctuary cannot be explained as the result of church-state jurisdictional competition.[26] Recent essays by Trisha Olson have also correctly stressed the conciliatory aspects of medieval sanctuary law, situating sanctuary practice within penitential discipline in the central Middle Ages and helpfully reminding us of the theological commitments that undergirded medieval sanctuary practices.[27]

Taking up the challenge of this recent sanctuary scholarship, I attempt to deepen our understanding of sanctuary law's vitality in the Middle Ages. This will require answering several questions: What conditions of thought allowed sanctuary to be an acceptable response to wrongdoing in the Middle Ages? How, for instance, could a grant of sanctuary to a murderer be seen as an appropriate alternative to the repressive sanctions or blood feud that might otherwise have followed? Why did this specific institution, imbued with its own set of rituals and procedures, stand in such obvious propriety in that world?

In its earliest instantiations, medieval sanctuary rested on twin pillars. It was, on the one hand, intimately connected to the penitential discipline of the early Christian communities and provided ecclesiastics with an opportunity to perform intercession on behalf of fugitive criminals, an obligation that was often articulated in early Christian sources. But sanctuary also received sanction in Roman law. As early as the 390s, imperial legislation sought to regulate who could claim sanctuary in churches and under what conditions. Although sacred groves and temples sometimes offered protection to fugitive slaves and criminals in the ancient world, the particular confluence of Christian intercessory practices and sanctuary in churches seem to have required unprecedented imperial attention to sanctuary's legality at the end of the fourth and beginning of the fifth centuries.

The sanctuary legislation promulgated by the Roman Empire provided a blueprint for early medieval peoples who were not particularly wedded to Roman institutions of criminal law. Even so, the blood-feud practices that thrived in the early Middle Ages likewise presented more than a few opportunities for bishops and saints to provide reminders of their spiritual and political power through intercession conducted on behalf of sanctuary seekers. By the later Middle Ages, however, a number of ecclesiastical voices had taught kings that sanctuary protections were an emblematic feature of pious kingship; the lessons were well learned and occasionally implemented with more enthusiasm for sanctuary than the papacy found commendable.

By the twelfth century, the link between sanctuary, penitential discipline, and feud resolution had weakened. The church still defended sanctuary, but it defended it primarily as one of its own jurisdictional prerogatives, not as an avenue to spiritual redemption or the peaceful settlement of disputes. In becoming a jurisdictional privilege, sanctuary law was reconstituted as an aspect of administrative processes aimed at crime control. In this regard, Angevin kings, in part building on the legislative attempts of their Anglo-Saxon predecessors, were better able to domesticate sanctuary within the administrative structures of royal law than any other contemporary European monarchies. The English common law's success in domesticating sanctuary actually lengthened the life span of sanctuary law in late-medieval England by partially insulating English sanctuary law, at least for a time, from the intellectual currents that took root within medieval canon law and that contributed to sanctuary's eventual demise. New priorities that late-medieval canonists set for criminal law eventually came into irreconcilable conflict with sanctuary law and gained purchase in Europe, including within England. Sanctuary, which had occasioned very little criticism from secular or ecclesiastical corners for several centuries, was finally branded by canon lawyers, Romanists, and English common lawyers alike as an "invitation to delinquency." The articulation of a new set of priorities for criminal law set sanctuary in direct tension with good governance, and what once had been a routine and appropriate resolution to a criminal act was roundly denounced by church and crown.

I

THE FOUNDATIONS OF SANCTUARY LAW IN LATE ANTIQUITY

1

Authority, Intercession, and Penance

In the late 390s, commenting on a scene in Vergil's *Aeneid* in which Greek soldiers had turned Juno's temple into a repository for captives and war booty, pagan author Servius Grammaticus explained that the Asylum of Juno was a temple "from which no one can be dragged out to punishment."[1] With this allusion to the protections ordinarily afforded runaway slaves and criminals within the temple, Servius highlighted the violation perpetrated by the looting soldiers. In two remarks appended to his commentary, Servius further elaborated that fugitive criminals could only hope to find respite in those temples to which sanctuary rights had been granted under imperial law and he claimed that sanctuary laws were originally established by the sons of Hercules in Athens and later imitated by Romulus in Italy.[2] Whatever their opinion regarding what Romulus might have copied from the Greeks, late-fourth-century Roman emperors would have approved Servius's assertion that sanctuary protections were valid only if recognized by imperial law. Perhaps because he was a pagan, Servius did not feel compelled to remark that Christian churches also served as sanctuaries for criminals, but had he done so, he might have noted that claims of sanctuary made in Christian churches had begun to attract considerable attention at the imperial court in the 390s.

In the last decade of the fourth century, Roman emperors issued several edicts that asserted imperial authority over claims of sanctuary in Christian churches and attempted to restrict the protections for fugitive slaves and debtors in those churches. It is difficult to know how successfully these edicts were enforced throughout the Roman Empire, but within the first three decades of the fifth century the imperial court reversed course and issued a series of edicts acknowledging that Christian churches possessed a relatively expansive right of sanctuary and that bishops had a duty to offer aid to fugitive criminals. Later, these edicts were included in the *Codex Theodosianus* (438) and *Codex Justinianus* (535), and there they determined to a large extent the legislative framework of sanctuary in the Roman-canonical tradition for the next millennium.

Servius's remarks went to the heart of issues swirling around the right of sanctuary in the late Roman Empire: the historical provenance of the practice and its amenability to imperial regulation. While Servius recalled the myth that Romulus copied sanctuary from the sons of Hercules, another cherished Roman myth asserted that Rome owed its birth to the establishment in its hills of a sanctuary that sheltered murderers and thieves from surrounding tribes.[3] Imperial legislation, issued in 386 and included in the Theodisian code in 438, even permitted fugitive slaves to take sanctuary beneath statues of Roman emperors.[4] Such myths and legal practices render more poignant Augustine's opening salvo in *The City of God*, which criticized pagan Romans who fled to Christian churches rather than pagan worship sites for protection from Alaric's restless troops in 410.[5] The refusal of Alaric's soldiers to plunder Christian churches, according to Augustine, revealed both the hypocrisy of Roman pagans and the superiority of Christian practices over pagan traditions.

Early ecclesiastical councils also displayed a keen awareness of Rome's ancient sanctuary traditions. An episcopal council held in Ephesus in 431 asked: "If even worldly princes decreed in their laws that whoever would flee to their statues should be unharmed, how much more should those who are received into the protection of the immortal heavenly realm remain uncondemned?"[6] Repeated in a canon passed by a council held at Mâcon in 585, this rhetorical question, like Servius's comments, implied a close association between sanctuary's history and its legal force.[7] Servius located sanctuary's legality in Roman history and imperial authority; early Christian writers, on the other hand, located the legitimacy of sanctuary in the claims of the Christian religion and episcopal authority. Neither was completely wrong.

The cultural resonances of sanctuary law within the late ancient Roman world were too deep and too wide to be identified with any single source. Rather, pre-Christian customs, imperial legislation, ecclesiastical decrees, and patristic apologetics all played important roles in shaping and justifying the sanctuary practices that appeared in imperial Roman law and early canon law. Christianity, therefore, did not have a monopoly on the modes of thought that made granting sanctuary to a fugitive a morally intelligible, praiseworthy act. Nor did imperial authority. The sanctuary protections expressed in imperial Roman legislation rested on foundations that encompassed imperial policy and ecclesiastical practices.

Because histories of sanctuary law have tended to honor the polarity expressed by Servius and Augustine and have located the origins of sanctuary exclusively in either imperial authority or Christian sensibilities, it is necessary to reassess the foundations of sanctuary law in the late Roman Empire in order to identify the multiple legal, social, and theological sources that reflected and shaped the practice.[8] Establishing the context of those sources will set the stage for examining how the transmission and reception of sanctuary law into early medieval legal traditions allowed the practice to become deeply rooted in European legal traditions and flourish until the sixteenth century. Examining the emergence of sanctuary law in the late Roman Empire will also provide an important context for assessing the juridical debates among Roman, canon, and English common lawyers that decided the ultimate fate of sanctuary law just over a millennium later, at the dawn of the early modern period.

THE HISTORIOGRAPHY OF IMPERIAL ROMAN SANCTUARY LAW

Since the early modern era, scholars have presumed that they faced an exclusive choice in identifying sanctuary as either a pagan custom or a distinctively Christian innovation. Originally at stake in this choice was the legitimacy of sanctuary law itself; if sanctuary could be shown to have a pagan pedigree, its pervasiveness in the legal traditions of the ancient and medieval church could be condemned. On the other hand, if sanctuary could be historically grounded in the legal authority of Christian emperors or the law of the church, its legality might be better secured.

According to seventeenth-century Catholic historian and theologian Louis Thomassin (1619–95), ancient sanctuary law could be traced to a "usage . . . of the pagan temples," but reason demanded that in Christian Rome "our churches were . . . equally respected and honored with the same immunities."[9] To this argument, Thomassin appended a legal-historical claim, asserting that sanctuary received its first valid legislative sanction under Christian emperors. Relying without citation upon a text many scholars had already suspected was a forgery, Thomassin claimed that Emperor Constantine had promulgated an official right of sanctuary immediately after his conversion to Christianity.[10] If Constantine's establishment of sanctuary law could not be firmly attested, Thomassin continued, then sanctuary was certainly granted a foundation in positive law by Emperor Honorius in the late fourth century. Here, Thomassin cited evidence that in 399 episcopal emissaries from Carthage petitioned the emperor to recognize sanctuary rights in churches.[11] Believing that no pagan sanctuaries could claim such a secure foundation in positive law, Thomassin concluded that the sanctuary practices of fifth-century Christianity were unpolluted by pagan legal practices.

The lawyerly mode of thought that Thomassin employed was not coincidental. He was following arguments that canonists had formulated in defense of sanctuary privileges in the previous century. For example, Italian jurist Jacobus Menochius (1532–1607) acknowledged that sanctuary privileges could be found among pagan peoples, but then, echoing the Ephesian council of 431, asked, "if even the *ius gentium*" recognized sanctuary, "how much more should these immunities be bestowed upon the churches of God?"[12] Sanctuary, Menochius asserted, was ultimately grounded "in the pontifical law, which in itself is also called the divine law."[13] Menochius saw sanctuary privileges as expressions of divine law, whereas Thomassin located sanctuary's origins in the positive legislative enactments of Christian emperors, but both deemed the pagan precedents for sanctuary law inconsequential because sanctuary's origins were juridical, not historical. Sanctuary, in their view, remained legitimate because they understood it to be a product of Christian sovereign authority.

Many civilian-trained jurists, particularly those in the Protestant tradition, disagreed. The late imperial legislative approval of sanctuary signaled to these civilian jurists that sanctuary laws were simply an element of imperial prerogative.[14] Thus, in their view sanctuary law did not participate in immutable principles of divine justice or papal authority. What the emperor granted, the emperor could take away. Some civilians also took an impish delight in pointing out that, according to the Gospels, Jesus had violently expelled moneychangers from the temple. If even Jesus had been willing to expel wrongdoers from a holy place, should not secular judges be able to do so?

Thus, for some early modern Protestant commentators, the recognition of sanctuary rights in pagan temples was by no means an argument in favor of honoring those rights. Just as the seventeenth-century Dutch jurist Antonius Mattheas found it regrettable that medieval sanctuary laws had been "transferr[ed] from paganism to religion,"[15] Samuel Pegge (1704–96), an English antiquarian, denounced ancient "Christian leaders, from whom we might expect the best" for recklessly "transferring all of the privileges and immunities of the Heathen temples . . . onto the Christian churches."[16] Sanctuary laws consecrated in the ancient sources, Pegge continued, were born from a pagan propensity for "blind reverence and devotion" and rested upon "a mistaken and ill-judged veneration for fabrics, and altars, and the saints."[17] Regardless of what ancient Roman and canon law had sanctioned, argued Pegge, sanctuary was inflected with pagan habits of worship and should not be included among proper Christian institutions.

While the tone of the debate over the provenance and legitimacy of sanctuary tempered in the following centuries, its basic structure remained much the same. For example, nineteenth-century scholar Aemilius Richter argued, "The church stepped into the place of the temple, asserting for itself those [immunities] that had been enjoyed [by heathen temples]."[18] For historians who viewed sanctuary as a practice Christianity borrowed from others, it remained only to determine precisely which ancient peoples had originated the practice. Sanctuary's origins were sought alternatively among the Egyptians,[19] Greeks,[20] or "Semitic" peoples."[21] Meanwhile, other nineteenth- and twentieth-century scholars continued to maintain the Christian origins of sanctuary law. Although sanctuary "was already known in pre-Christian antiquity," wrote Paul Hinschius, its medieval form grew up from "the soil of the Church and not immediately from heathen conditions."[22] "The right of asylum of Christian churches," concluded another author, "thus owes its origin to the custom of the faithful, to the pious sentiments of the Christians, who saw in the sacred places a refuge where they could shield themselves from unjust and arbitrary vexations."[23] Pierre Timbal also saw medieval sanctuary as an outgrowth of the moral commitments of early Christianity. "One might say," he suggested, that it "was recreated by the practice of [episcopal] intercession," whereby bishops actively petitioned secular courts for leniency and mercy on behalf of wrongdoers who had fled to Christian churches.[24] Sanctuary, in this view, emerged out of a spirit of Christian charity and pastoral care.

The scholarly skirmishes outlined above might suggest that interpretations of sanctuary among early modern jurists and historians were largely predetermined by confessional or professional biases and that there was no room for a middle way. But not all Protestant jurists were entirely opposed to sanctuary, and not all Catholic scholars insisted on grounding sanctuary in divine law or denied its place within imperial or royal prerogatives. Even Martin Luther may have approved of sanctuary in principle, according to a treatise tentatively attributed to him that appeared in Latin versions in 1516 and 1517.[25] Tracing precedents in the Bible and Roman law for European sanctuary laws, the tract called for stricter sovereign regulation (but not abolition) of sanctuary. Whether or not Luther was the author of the sanctuary treatise, whose earliest printing was not attributed to him, it was at least plausible in the early sixteenth century that he had written a text tolerant of sanctuary at roughly the same time he was publishing his Ninety-five Theses. Qualified approval of sanctuary also was essentially the position that Hessian jurist Nicolaus Mylerus von Ehrenbach espoused in the seventeenth century. In his view, sanctuary, properly regulated by the sovereign, provided a desirable mitigation of the occasional harshness of penal laws.[26] The possibility that sanctuary had pagan roots did not trouble Mylerus. He simply argued that sanctuary law was grounded in earthly sovereignty (not in canon or divine law) and urged close secular control over what sorts of crimes were eligible for sanctuary. His position was not unlike that of Dutch Catholic jurist Zeger Bernhard van Espen (1646–1728) who conceded that sanctuary privileges were within the purview of the secular prince. Although useful when circumstances called for the sovereign to display discretion and benevolence, sanctuary protections, Van Espen wrote, should be restricted or denied by the prince as the needs of the social order dictated.[27] Thus, while some scholars and jurists continued to favor more extreme viewpoints, by the early modern period canon and civilian jurists alike began to adopt a middle position: Sanctuary was a legitimate institution if properly regulated and kept firmly within the control of secular power.

The juridical middle ground happened to reflect legal and political reality in the early modern period. For instance, in the 1520s Henry VIII of England had asserted the prerogative to extract fugitives from churches when circumstances warranted and François I of France claimed the same prerogative in

1537.[28] Before the century ended, the Church itself, in a papal bull Gregory XIV issued in 1591, had reasserted the primacy of ecclesiastical judges with respect to removing fugitives from churches, but also carved out a list, largely agreeable to civilian jurists and secular rulers and drawn primarily from civilian legal sources, specifying crimes that no longer warranted sanctuary protection.[29] In each of these three instances, imperial Roman sanctuary laws provided powerful, though contested, evidence concerning sanctuary's legitimacy.

The historiography of late antique sanctuary law reveals how jurists and historians continued fighting the battles that had resulted in the abolition of the privilege in the sixteenth century. Even in the twentieth century, when early modern confessional conflicts had somewhat abated, scholarly accounts of those origins mirrored in important respects the juridical debates of the early modern period. One striking result has been a tendency of legal historians to seek the historical origins of sanctuary in officially promulgated legal codes. Like early modern jurists, modern legal historians scoured Roman legal sources and continued to give them primacy over other historical evidence that sanctuary was grounded in preexisting social practices and customs. As a consequence, the historical origins of sanctuary are still largely associated with its positive legal recognition by Roman emperors.[30]

Thus, not only were the sanctuary protections that proliferated in medieval legal traditions traced to "the first statutory recognition of sanctuary"[31] by Christian emperors who first gave it positive juridical effect,[32] but a misleading dichotomy also was sometimes smuggled into the debate, presenting historians the self-imposed choice of granting medieval sanctuary law either a Christian or a pagan pedigree. Seeking an answer in legislative texts, and preoccupied with the legislation of Christian Rome, these scholars turned their focus away from the social practices and theological commitments that granted sanctuary an intelligible place in the ancient and medieval worlds. Such narrow interpretations neither engage with sanctuary's historical significance nor recognize how deeply rooted sanctuary was in the legal and social order. Indeed, to moor sanctuary's historical origins to its legislative recognition in the late empire is to demand more of imperial legislation than its contemporaries probably did.

There are recent exceptions to this tendency. In certain respects, Anne Ducloux's reexamination of sanctuary's late antique *naissance* avoids a rigid choice between ancient paganism and Christianity.[33] Instead, Ducloux contends sanctuary originated in a broad-based late Roman "ferveur populaire" to which both the church fathers and imperial legislation reacted—with authoritative concessions in favor of sanctuary.[34] Sanctuary, thus, was ultimately grounded in a substructure of pagan popular "*mentalités*."[35] "*L'héritage païen*" that Ducloux finds for sanctuary was tolerated and, in turn, amalgamated into the moral sensibilities of the church fathers and the authority of imperial legislation at the beginning of the fifth century.[36] More recently, Harald Siems has left undecided the question "whether asylum in late antiquity derived from the intercession-right of the bishops, or from the sacredness of places, or from . . . the heathen temple."[37] Because evidence exists for each position, argues Siems, the roots of sanctuary cannot be hermetically confined within ecclesiastical teachings, popular pagan practices, or the legislative enactments of the empire.[38]

Despite these recent exceptions, historical treatments of sanctuary law have transformed early modern legal and political debates over sanctuary's legitimacy into historical questions about its origins. For this reason alone, a reexamination of the historical origins of sanctuary law in the late Roman world is necessary. Late imperial legal texts play such an important role in the emergence of legal traditions in the early medieval world that the same reassessment will also provide insights into the transmission of sanctuary law into early medieval Europe. In addition, it will prepare the ground for examination of the juridical debates among Roman lawyers, canonists, and English common lawyers that surrounded the abolition of sanctuary in the sixteenth century.

THE FOUNDATIONS OF SANCTUARY IN PATRISTIC THOUGHT: INTERCESSION AND PENANCE

At first, early Christianity did not invoke the inviolable sanctity of the house of God to justify the sanctuary privileges it claimed. Instead, the episcopal duty to intercede on behalf of the accused and condemned and the penitential discipline administered by the churchmen served as the initial intellectual foundation for sanctuary. In fact, the notion of sacred spaces developed rather slowly within early Christianity.[39] As Richard Markus argues, in the early years of Christianity, the revered shrines, temples, and groves that abounded in the ancient Mediterranean world were generally associated with pagan forms of worship.[40] For example, when discussing the erection and dedication of church buildings, Augustine remarked that God dwelled within Christian believers themselves.[41] In regard to Christian sanctuary claims, John Chrysostom advised, "When you take refuge in a church, do not seek shelter in the place, but in the spirit of the place. The Church is not wall and roof, but faith and life."[42] It is possible to overstate the claim that early Christianity was not amenable to notions of sacred space. John Chrysostom and other patristics portrayed churches as important spatial buffers against the spiritual contagion of theatres and pagan worship sites.[43] But an explicit link between Christian sacred space and the protection of fugitive criminals was somewhat slow to develop.

Although Ambrose of Milan has been credited with developing a notion of the inviolability of Christian churches,[44] early Christianity's clearest intellectual accommodation to that notion occurred when the saints' cults matured and relics and tombs contributed to a Christian sacred topography.[45] In regard to sanctuary legislation, it was only in the fifth century that an episcopal council (in this case a Gaulish council) linked sanctuary protections to "reverence of the place."[46] In the late fourth century, on the other hand, Christian authors had not explicitly cited the sanctity of the physical confines of a church in claiming that a criminal who took refuge in a church should enjoy protection from violent seizure. An intriguing piece of evidence survives in the twentieth Sirmondian Constitution. The text, which purports to have been issued in 430 by Theodosius II and Valentinus, apparently grants a form of sanctuary protection to fugitives who flee to "bishops or priests or deacons in the street or field or any place" on the grounds that "*in sacerdotibus ecclesia constat.*"[47] The authenticity of the text has been questioned,[48] and neither Theodor Mommsen nor Clyde Pharr included it in their respective editions of the Sirmondian Constitutions,[49] but it suggests an understanding of sanctuary protections that was not wholly dependent upon the physical confines of a church.

The assumption that Christian churches deserved heightened respect was not absent in Christian writings before the early Middle Ages. Orosius recorded that when Alaric stormed Rome in 410, he commanded his troops that "if anyone fled into the basilicas of the holy apostles Peter and Paul, these, first of all, were to be granted security and inviolability."[50] Augustine opened *The City of God* by recounting the actions of barbarian armies who pillaged heathen temples but, "for the sake of Christ,"[51] refused to slay those who ran to Christian churches. Elsewhere, however, when presenting a sustained defense of Christian sanctuary protections, Augustine, did not point directly to the sanctity of the church building. Rather, he looked to the intercessory duties of churchmen and penitential discipline, two concepts inextricably bound up with the practice of sheltering fugitives in Christian churches.

Intercession

In intercession, churchmen petitioned secular courts on behalf of "those wrongly oppressed by force" and "afflicted widows, or despoiled orphans."[52] The duty to give aid to orphans and widows had ancient support in sacred texts, and the Council of Sardica (present-day Sophia) around 343 had echoed biblical injunctions that urged special protection for "orphans and widows."[53] But Christian charity was also understood to require bishops to attempt to gain leniency or even clemency for malefactors tried before imperial magistrates. An early Christian text attributed to St. Clement admonished the church at Corinth: "Let us intercede for those who fall into any transgression,"[54] and the Sardican Council instructed that even "persons . . . who on account of their crimes have been sentenced [before imperial courts]" should receive intercession.[55]

Christian intercession had roots in the New Testament. Paul's First Epistle to Timothy exhorted that "supplications, prayers, intercessions, and giving of thanks, be made for all men."[56] That these "prayers [and] intercessions" also should be made for "kings and for all that are in authority"[57] was a striking inversion of the hierarchy of temporal social statuses in the Roman Empire, overturning the classical image of an influential nobleman interceding graciously on behalf of his unfortunate client before a magistrate. Despite the inversion, Paul's remarks are testimony to the immediate intelligibility of intercession within the social order of the Roman world. Indeed, intercession was a category Paul used to characterize salvation: "For there is one God, and one mediator between God and man, the man Christ Jesus."[58] As early Christian theology raised intercession to the level of a divine attribute of Christ, intercession for sanctuary seekers became a defining task for bishops and saints alike. What was in principle a duty for all Christians, by the fourth century became a practice primarily associated with bishops, who were expected to use their status and influence on behalf of those in danger of losing life or limb in Roman courts.[59] Intercession on behalf of the accused and condemned came to be seen as one of the primary duties attached to episcopal office.[60]

A striking account of the theological foundation for the duty of episcopal intercession comes to us in an early fifth-century epistle of Augustine. Macedonius, a Christian and a Roman magistrate commissioned to administer justice in the wake of Donatist unrest in North Africa, had written to his friend and mentor Augustine raising three objections to the intercessory activities of bishops who appeared in his court to plead for leniency on behalf of admitted criminals. First, "if sins are so strongly prohibited by God," a bishop seeking leniency or impunity for a wrongdoer appears to approve wrongdoing. Second, Macedonius insinuated that bishops who sought clemency for a wrongdoer should also share equal culpability with the one who had sinned. Third, he questioned the prudence of intercessors and the sincerity of supplicants since "all sins appear more excusable when the one who is guilty promises [his own] correction." For these reasons, Macedonius expressed to Augustine his grave doubts about whether intercession even "came from [Christian] religion."[61]

Augustine carefully turned each objection on its head. As he explained, not only was intercession a proper part of the Christian religion, but it also happened to be an expression of divine mercy that worked toward the eternal betterment of the wrongdoer and the intercessor alike. The intercessor did not approve wrongdoing when he sought mercy for a criminal. To the contrary, "the more the vice displeases us," the more zealous should be the bishop's intercession because "we do not want [the wrongdoer] to perish while the vice remains unamended." Without effectual intercession the wrongdoer might "end this life in punishment" only to find that punishment "does not end with this life." In Augustine's view, intercession aimed to turn the wrongdoer from his sin so that he might live free from it, while secular punishments only injured or killed the body without purging the soul. Unlike the secular magistrate, the intercessor aimed to "free the man" from the sin.[62] Finally, Augustine reminded Macedonius that intercession did not confer impunity. Christians had disciplinary methods of their own, methods superior to punishments imposed by secular judges. "We remove sinners from the society of the altar" so that through repentance, they may be able to please the one (God) they have offended. Indeed, argued Augustine, truly penitent sinners punish themselves. Hence, the one who repented sincerely did nothing other than ensure that his wrongdoing did not remain unpunished. Far from impeding punishment, concluded Augustine, intercession actually facilitated a more profound form of correction than imperial justice.[63]

Augustine's account of intercession reveals a current of thought prominent in early Christian writings: Intercession presumed the spiritual primacy of sin over crime. While patristic writers did not sharply distinguish "crime" (*crimen*), "sin" (*peccatum*), and "wrongdoing" (*male factum*)—terms canon lawyers were still trying to untangle in the late Middle Ages[64]—they tended to locate the seriousness of a wrongful act in its character as an offense against God. That it was also an offense against the earthly prince or community of men was secondary. First and foremost a separation of man from God, sin was more than a violation of a command; it was a breach of the relationship between God and a sinner. Theologically speaking, a sinner "had not merely done wrong . . . but had fallen into corruption" and was no longer in communion with God.[65] In ecclesiastical thought, sin's priority over crime radically diminished the importance of secular punishments. Thus, John Chrysostom could ask, "What good results when a secular judge executes a man?" Whereas secular authorities destroyed wrongdoers, Christian practices secured their redemption.[66]

Patristic writers provided the theological blueprint for intercession, justifying the practice and rendering it an episcopal duty. This patristic justification of intercession, in turn, helped insure that intercessory practices remained a key component of episcopal activity in the early Middle Ages. There was as well a crucial social component of intercession that placed episcopal intercession against the backdrop of late Roman aristocratic practices. But before this important point of continuity between the late empire and early medieval Europe can be examined more fully in Chapter 2, the theological justification of intercession must be related to another concern of the early church—penitential discipline.

PENITENTIAL DISCIPLINE

Augustine's letter to Macedonius justified intercession on the grounds that it led to ecclesiastical discipline rather than the brutal finality of imperial justice. Ecclesiastical discipline was forward-looking. In the words of St. Cyprian, "through penance all sins can be dissolved for him who would in whole heart return to God."[67] Penance, then, was the ecclesiastical discipline imposed upon sinners so that through "sorrowful groans" and a contrite heart they might be "admonished . . . instructed and prepared for the future."[68]

In the early years of Christianity, the doctrine of penance had not yet received a clear or systematic articulation.[69] Debates arose, for instance, over the number of times a Christian might undergo penance. Some held that a Christian could only undergo penance once in a lifetime. Others insisted that confession and penance had to be performed publicly. Moreover, there was as yet no agreement on the formal procedures for administering penance, whether done privately or openly. Nonetheless, penance, broadly understood as a means of "effecting pardon . . . through reconciliation" of the sinner with God, was an integral part of the practices of late antique and early medieval Christianity,[70] sufficiently fixed within the intellectual landscape of early Christendom that patristic writers could claim that penance and the intercession that facilitated it were superior to secular sanctions.

At each step in his justification of intercession, Augustine relied upon penance so firmly that intercession's propriety rested almost solely upon the opportunity it gave a sinner to repent through ecclesiastically administered penance. If, by his crime, the sinner had primarily offended God, then penance provided an opportunity for the sinner to reject wrongdoing and to begin living righteously, renewing his standing before God and, by extension, within the community of the faithful. In this view, the imposition by the secular authorities of a corporal or capital punishment upon a criminal might prevent such reconciliation.

Within Christian doctrine, it was Christ's Atonement that ultimately made the sinner's reconciliation possible, but penance was an expression of the Atonement writ small. The conciliatory aspects of penance, as well as the sundering character of sin, were reflected in the actual application and oversight of penance by early bishops. Once secured from the secular courts by intercession, the wrongdoer would typically be temporarily segregated from other Christians and their rituals as he was gradually restored to the Christian community.[71] He placed himself within the tuition of the church, submitting himself, in principle at least, as a member of the body of Christ and subject now to its discipline and oversight.

SANCTUARY IN A CHURCH AS THE PLATFORM FOR INTERCESSION AND PENANCE

From the standpoint of early Christianity's own canons, intercession and penance went hand in hand with extending shelter to those who fled to a church. Sanctuary was explicitly tied to ecclesiastical discipline as early as the Sardican Council (c. 343). Convoked by Emperors Constans and Constantius II at the urging of Pope Julius, the council was not ecumenical because many Eastern bishops refused to attend. Its primary purpose was to settle doctrinal conflicts arising out of the Arian difficulties.[72] The council, however, also chastised bishops who were perceived to be failing in their obligations to intercede on behalf of criminals and those who sought their protection, ordering:

> But since it happens often that those who suffer injury, or who for wrongdoing are condemned to exile or to the islands, or those, in fact, incurring any sentence, flee to the mercy of the church, these are to be aided and indulgence is to be petitioned without delay.[73]

The canon did not purport to institute a new practice. Rather, it recalled bishops to their existing obligations and assumed that sanctuary belonged to a constellation of practices that involved episcopal intercession. The Sardican canon also preserved an ambiguity present in many of the ancient sources concerning precisely where sanctuary belonged in relation to penance and intercession. At times, it appears that sanctuary was justified because it enabled intercession and penance. At other times, the obligation to provide sanctuary was cast broadly enough that it encompassed intercessory and penitential practices.

This ambiguity also existed in patristic sources that linked intercession to the sanctuary protections sought by fugitives to a church.[74] Augustine, for example, wrote of a man who "fled to the church at Hippo and there, as fugitives are accustomed, was expecting his troubles would end through our intercession."[75] In 398 or 399, Augustine had interceded on behalf of a man named Fascius, who feared that he might be subjected to corporal punishment for a debt of sixteen silver *solidos* and "hastily ran to the succor of the holy church."[76] Augustine apparently helped arrange for the repayment of Fascius's debt and asked his congregation to stand as surety for Fascius if he was subsequently unable to repay it.

Although it is not clear whether Fascius owed his debt to a private creditor or to the public fisc,[77] and the texts that come down to us do not clarify the matter,[78] the public or private nature of the debt would have been relevant. Emperors Theodosius, Arcadius, and Honorius had issued a law in 392 that asserted debtors should be dragged out of churches if they failed to satisfy their public debts.[79] It is the earliest extant imperial legislation concerned with sanctuary in churches. Six years later, in 398, Honorius and Arcadius issued another law asserting that both public and private debtors who had fled to a church could be forcibly removed if they, or their ecclesiastical defenders, failed to satisfy their obligations. It is not possible to know whether the 398 law had been transmitted to North Africa by the time Augustine interceded for Fascius.[80] Augustine made no mention of any imperial enactments that may have governed the matter, though the outcome of his intercession fairly accorded with the imperial policy contained in those laws.[81]

Augustine again did not mention imperial law several years later, around 415, when he interceded against a tribune on behalf of Victorinus, who had fled to the church at Hippo after an unspecified dispute with his family. As Augustine described the affair in a letter to bishop Novatus, a tribune came to the church while Augustine was away and intended to extract Victorinus.[82] The tribune presented a document, ostensibly from the Count of Africa, which ordered the removal of the fugitive from the sanctuary, but Victorinus prudently remained in the church until Augustine returned. At that point, the tribune appeared at the church in the presence of Augustine and read the purported order from the Count of Africa. Because Augustine doubted the authenticity of the document, which the tribune would not let Augustine handle or read and which had not even been deposited in the municipal archives, he continued to protect Victorinus.[83]

This instance of intercession and sanctuary is noteworthy for two reasons. First, the tribune's attempted fraud implies that a valid order from the Count of Africa may have resulted in the removal of Victorinus. Second, these events may have taken place after the promulgation of an edict that forbade forcibly removing a fugitive from a church. There is no evidence that he did so, but one might expect Augustine to have justified his intercession before the tribune by reference to imperial law.

The law in question, published April 1, 409, comes to us via the Theodosian Code. The text of the law, which primarily concerns a heretical sect called the *Caelicolae*, exists only in a corrupted and partially unintelligible state.[84] That Augustine did not invoke such a law has led some scholars to contend that the edict of 409 probably did not originally include a provision in favor of sanctuary seekers, and the tribune's apparent assumption that an order from the Count of Africa could secure the removal of a sanctuary seeker supports this view.[85] Moreover, had Victorinus been under a judicial sentence, for which there is no evidence in Augustine's account, Augustine's intercession may have been in contravention of a 398 imperial law forbidding intercession for those who had already been convicted.[86] In any event, Augustine continued to protect Victorinus against the tribune.

The imperial legislation that may have governed these cases may not matter much. One need not refract Augustine's conduct on behalf of fugitives through the lens of imperial legislation regarding sanctuary law (assuming it was known or perceived to have any applicability at all).[87] Augustine did what Christian bishops had already been doing for decades, interceding on behalf of those who fled to them or their churches for protection against criminal prosecutions and debts. In the case of Fascius, he simply interceded with the creditors, ensured that Fascius did not encounter physical coercion, and secured payment of the debt (with a promise of reimbursement to the new guarantors). His own duties as bishop obligated Augustine to intercede between fugitives and imperial officials, and it was not exceptional that he fulfilled them.

Other early Christian figures fit this model. In 372, Basil interceded on behalf of a widowed noble woman who had fled to his church in Caesarea and hid herself there in order to avoid marriage to a local official. Basil is reported to have protected her even though he was eventually made to answer before an imperial magistrate for doing so. Gregory of Nazianzus related the episode in a panegyric composed in honor of Basil's pious courage against worldly power, which Gregory described as "laying down the law for us all in such matters."[88] That debtors and criminals might behave as the widow had was no objection; they deserved ecclesiastical aid as well, all the more so if they needed to repent of some misdeed.

The ecclesiastical duty Basil and Augustine carried out was well understood even before the Council of Sardica pronounced it, and it was expressed in acts of episcopal intercession throughout the last half of the fourth century. Of course, not every act of intercession or claim of sanctuary was successful. Admittedly ambiguous sources suggest that in 350 Emperor Constans may have been dragged from a small Pyrenees church by his enemies and killed.[89] Some six years later, in the midst of the Arian controversies, Bishop Athanasius reported being chased from his church in Alexandria, and he was subsequently arrested in a church while saying a mass.[90]

Such violations of churches and outrages against bishops have led some historians to emphasize that sanctuary did not enjoy legality at the end of the fourth century.[91] After all, episcopal protection of fugitives would not gain notice in imperial law before 392[92] and would not actually gain imperial approval before the first decades of the fifth century. Only in 432 would outrages committed within churches against fugitives or their ecclesiastic protectors explicitly warrant severe secular penalties.[93] Thus there is evidence to support historians' claims.[94]

From the standpoint of the ecclesiastical sources, however, it is not clear how important sanction in imperial law was for fourth-century churchmen who protected sanctuary seekers. Augustine and other high-ranking churchmen certainly demonstrated some knowledge of legal procedure in imperial courts, but the outcomes of cases where bishops attempted intercession seem to have depended more on the dynamics of personal power, political advantage, and popular opinion than on the pronouncements of an imperial edict.[95]

THE FALL OF EUTROPIUS

Perhaps no case illustrated the dynamics at work better than the fall of Eutropius in 399. Eutropius was a eunuch who began life as a slave and was eventually taken into service by an officer of the imperial court where he gained the favorable attention of Emperor Theodosius.[96] After Theodosius died, Eutropius became the close attendant to Emperor Arcadius, Theodosius's son, and assumed the role of grand chamberlain.[97] Involved in intrigues of the highest order, Eutropius was able to disenfranchise and exile his most important political rivals.[98] Early in 399, Eutropius even arranged to have himself named Roman consul. The fragility of his position as consul became clear early in his tenure. That same year, a revolt broke out in Phyrgia after Eutropius refused a request for promotion and funds from Tribigild, a Gothic military commander in the employ of the empire. When Tribigild threatened to bring the revolt to Constantinople, Gäinas, another Goth entrusted with protection of the capital city, refused to send his army out to meet Tribigild unless Eutropius was removed from power. When the wife of Arcadius backed Gäinas, Eutropius ran from the palace to the Church of St. Sophia where Chrysostom was bishop, having been elevated at the insistence of Eutropius just two years before. Ancient authors took considerable delight in pointing out that Eutropius, who formerly had arranged for imperial edicts that restricted the scope of intercession and sanctuary protections in order to disadvantage his political enemies, was himself forced to claim sanctuary.

Chrysostom's own account of his role in Eutropius's sanctuary claim is preserved in two homilies, both of which framed Eutropius's fall as an example of the fleeting glory of this world—"the vicissitudes of human affairs"—and the mercy and steadfastness of the church.[99] "The Church," noted Chrysostom, "which you treated as an enemy, has opened her bosom to you."[100] According to Chrysostom, officers sent from the imperial court had come to capture Eutropius, but his flight to the altar, where he clung "quivering," had saved him.[101]

Chrysostom tells his readers that he did not linger on the misery of Eutropius to reproach him or to gloat over his misfortunes, but rather to induce compassion in his flock. Chrysostom was aware that some within his congregation had been roundly criticizing him for sheltering Eutropius and that the army was clamoring for the former consul to be executed. Nevertheless, he presented the church's protection of Eutropius—which he likened to a caring mother sheltering a frightened child under her cloak—as a demonstration of the church's merciful strength. Even though Eutropius had "cut off the right of refuge" in the church to his enemies, it was appropriate that the church protect him. Chrysostom even suggested, in a phrase that has caused some consternation to historians of sanctuary, that the flight of Eutropius to the church was in violation of the very laws Eutropius had sponsored.[102]

As noted already, a triad of imperial laws issued between 392 and 398 had successively forbidden sanctuary to public debtors,[103] Jews pretending to be Christians in order to gain protection from criminal charges or debts,[104] slaves,[105] and other kinds of public functionaries.[106] The laws issued in 397 and 398 appear to have been generated by Eutropius and his questor[107] and may have been part of a series of laws issued in 398 aimed at disadvantaging a political rival named Timasius. Timasius was exiled, and his wife Pintadia fled to the Church of St. Sophia, where she was protected by the intercession of Bishop Nectarius.[108] The laws Eutropius had aimed at his foes appear in passages scattered throughout the Theodosian Code (438) and the Justinian Code (535).[109] Chrysostom, however, did not look to imperial law to guide his actions. He simply performed his episcopal duties and took the opportunity to display the power of the church and its bishops.

Emperor Arcadius had already made an impassioned plea on behalf of the eunuch to his soldiers, who had gathered at the palace "shouting, leaping, and brandishing spears," urging Arcadius to avenge the insults done to his imperial majesty by Eutropius.[110] According to Chrysostom, Arcadius reminded his soldiers, by "shedding tears," of the hallowed place to which Eutropius had fled. When Chrysostom recounted the emperor's intercession on behalf of Eutropius, he also succeeded in calming the outrage of his congregation, who also shed "streams of tears" as Chrysostom spoke.[111] "A few days ago the church was besieged: an army came, and fire issued from their eyes, yet it did not scorch the olive tree; swords were unsheathed, yet no one received a wound," he continued.[112] Sanctuary provided opportunity for Eutropius to see the truth of life's fleeting glory and for the church to demonstrate that it was strong enough to protect even its most unpopular enemies against a fearsome army.

Chrysostom's efforts and the glory redounding to the church were somewhat diminished a short time later. After apparently escaping from the St. Sophia, Eutropius was captured, exiled, and eventually killed. Some ancient writers reported that he had been captured with the church's complicity inside the Church of St. Sophia,[113] but Chrysostom insisted that Eutropius was captured only after he secretly escaped the protective confines of St. Sophia.[114] In either case, the church's right of sanctuary, administered through one of its leading bishops, had played a role in political intrigues of the highest order in the late empire.

CONCLUSION

At the end of the fourth century, prominent churchmen justified sanctuary protections upon the twin foundations of episcopal intercession and penitential discipline.[115] In some of the early Christian sources, such as the Sardican canons, one might plausibly reverse the relationship, and assert that intercession was justified because it rested, in part, on the act of bestowing sanctuary. Conceptually, the practices remained distinct, however, and the duty to intercede extended beyond sanctuary seekers. While penitential discipline applied to all sorts of sinners, not just sanctuary seekers, sanctuary highlighted the opportunity to discipline supplicant wrongdoers.

By tying sanctuary to intercession and penance, early Christianity articulated a form of discipline and order that was grounded in the commitments of Christian theology rather than the interests of imperial governance. Early

Christian sources give very little indication that the protections offered to fugitive criminals required imperial approval. Glancing ahead, it is interesting that that some jurists in the late medieval and early modern periods, as well as the historians who followed them, would dedicate so much energy to grounding sanctuary law in the authority of imperial legislation. Early Christianity did not.

The patristic view of sanctuary and punishment might suggest a significant rift between the sensibilities of early Christianity and the Roman Empire. Patristic writers sometimes portrayed the matter just this way: "The concerns of public office are alien to the Church. One administers great dread, the other clemency and mildness."[116] Sanctuary, by this account, would seem to emblemize the special role of bishops and churches as buffers against the harsh law of the emperor. But it is important not to overplay the grounding of intercession and sanctuary in distinctively Christian sensibilities. Aspects of the sanctuary protections bishops offered in the late Roman Empire would have been familiar outside a specifically ecclesiastical context. The following chapter examines sanctuary within the context of traditional forms of patronage in the ancient Roman world.

2

Roman Aristocratic Traditions, Imperial Penal Law, and Sanctuary

Despite its theological aspect, the sanctuary protection offered by Christian churches was not entirely inconsistent with the aristocratic Roman traditions of intercession and clemency. Nonetheless, historians have assigned sanctuary a more contested place within the history of Roman penal law, citing three successive imperial edicts issued in the last decade of the fourth century to restrict sanctuary, and assuming that Roman penal traditions were antithetical to practices like sanctuary, which shielded wrongdoers from punishment. According to Timbal, "the rigorous justice of Rome, inspired by a principle of public interest, could not admit asylums, which . . . impeded the arrest of an accused or the punishment of an admitted criminal."[1] Such concerns with unimpeded justice, Timbal suggested, were heightened in the later empire by mounting fiscal difficulties and the threat of barbarian invasions. Thus, the resistance toward sanctuary privileges manifested in late imperial legislation has been generally understood as grounded in long-standing Roman traditions. As a result, the eventual concession of sanctuary laws in the imperial legislation of the Christian era appears to be a privilege wrested by an increasingly powerful church from an ever-reluctant empire.

There is evidence, however, that imperial resistance to sanctuary privileges was episodic and not based on a fundamental tension between ecclesiastical sanctuary and Roman penal traditions. Over a century ago, Theodor Mommsen noticed that sanctuary "was first vigorously limited or, in fact, eliminated" only late in the imperial era.[2] As Mommsen knew, the imperial court regularly conceded sanctuary privileges to temples in conquered Greek provinces.[3] For instance, Livy described the privileges of a temple at Delium, "which the Greeks call an asylum."[4] Tacitus said that Rome did not know such a "shameful" custom, but he appears to have been exaggerating.[5] Instead, the evidence shows that Roman traditions were more than merely indulgent toward sanctuary customs.[6]

Although ancient Roman law did not grant automatic protections to those who sought refuge in temples, it did recognize a tradition whereby fugitive slaves could seek respite from angry masters by embracing the feet of a statue of Romulus in Rome.[7] Early in the imperial era, this protection was extended to slaves who embraced the feet of a statue of Caesar.[8] Even in the Christian era, as late as 386, the ancient rules granting protection to fugitives who embraced statues of emperors were reiterated.[9] Tacitus reported that a Roman soldier accused of treason could avoid arrest by embracing the sculpted eagle that represented his legion.[10]

Even more significant was the importance Roman penal law gave to certain intercessory and supplicatory traditions. As far back as the republic, Roman courts had granted a condemned criminal the procedural right to call on influential friends (if he had them) or the general public (in the *provocatio ad populum*) either to secure leniency or to remove his case to another judge for reconsideration before execution of the sentence.[11] In Mommsen's view, the *provocatio ad populum* was historically linked to the constitutional principle that the right to try and impose punishment on citizens rested with the people, not the patricians. Despite fairly sustained criticism of this and other facets of Mommsen's account of the *provocatio ad populum*, Roman criminal procedure clearly did provide the opportunity for spectators and supporters of an accused to voice their own views in a criminal proceeding.[12]

Like the church, Roman law had its own, albeit procedural, form of intercession available to the accused. In the penal law of the republic, after a malefactor had been condemned before a magistrate, he could plead for the *intercessio* of any other Roman magistrate, who could then invoke *intercessio* and quash punishment. The intervening magistrate could even remove the case to his own court.[13] In historical scholarship, this process has been treated as a form of "constitutional limitation" upon the power of the state to punish in that each magistrate could check the inequities of the others.

Intercessio, however, was not only a legal practice, but was also a quasi-institutionalized supplication procedure.[14] It was rooted in the network of patronage and clientage that determined the order of Roman society and allowed that one's fate before the penal law could be determined by the influence of friends or patrons.[15] Cicero noted "noble" and "powerful" men whose mere presence could change the outcome of suits against their dependents.[16] If an unfavorable final sentence was handed down, writing letter after letter to secure a pardon "was an obligation of one's power to the degree one had any."[17] Although the outright sale or purchase of influence or pardons might incur censure, a patron's intercession was a recognized and accepted aspect of Roman criminal law.[18] It was against the backdrop of these legal and social practices that Constantine in 318 enacted a law forbidding magistrates to object if a party wished to remove a case to from their jurisdiction to an episcopal court. "If any person should desire him to transfer his case to the jurisdiction of Christian law and to observe that kind of court, he shall be heard, even though the action has been instituted before the judge, and whatever shall be adjudged by them [the Bishop] shall be held as sacred."[19] Christian bishops in the late empire were given an analogous version of the intercessory role elite Romans had long enjoyed.

The dynamic of intercession and supplication was part Roman private life as well. The younger Pliny (died circa 112 AD) wrote to his friend on behalf of a former slave:

> Your freedman, whom you said angered you, came to me and fell prostrate at my feet. . . . He wept much, and entreated me much, even with silent cries. In sum, he gave me faith in his repentance. Truly, I believe him to be emended, since he feels himself to have transgressed. You are angry, I know; and I know as well that you are angry with merit; but clemency is all the more praiseworthy when the cause of anger is most just. . . . Allow for your indulgence. Do not torment him, nor even yourself. For when a man of such gentleness [as you] becomes angry, you torment yourself.[20]

While the influence of Stoicism is seen plainly in his cautions against anger, Pliny was invoking an aristocratic ethos and his exhortations were hardly idiosyncratic. A magistrate applying penal law would not have understood his own position any differently. The exhortation to extend clemency invited a demonstration of magnanimity; in Pliny's remarkable assertion, "clemency is all the more praiseworthy when the cause of the anger is most just."

According to other traditions of authority in the ancient Mediterranean world, a praiseworthy ruler "took the edge off his justice" and demonstrated his magnanimity "with a certain indulgence toward offenders,"[21] which Diogenes, the author of the ancient treatise *On Kingship*, thought was a hallmark of a great king.[22] In one of the earliest Christian references to intercession, St. Clement exhorted believers to hearken to the tradition of "pagan kings" who sometimes, "when a period of pestilence occurred, followed the advice of oracles and gave themselves up to death, in order to rescue their subjects by their own blood."[23] Intercession was grounded, not in one particular religious or legal tradition, but in a larger frame of ancient aristocratic traditions that honored patrons who interceded on behalf of their dependents.

Because aristocratic intercession might protect criminals, imperial legislation targeted such intercession in the same manner that it initially targeted sanctuary in churches. An edict of 399 doubled the penalty of any "persons who for cause of tax fraud" fled to the protection of a high-ranking official or ex-official.[24] An edict of 362 had aimed to punish "certain decurions [who] had fled to the homes of the powerful" for protection from their municipal obligations,[25] and in 383, an imperial edict had recalled to their duties decurions who "had fled to the offices of the various provinces" seeking shelter from their public obligations.[26] The frequency with which the empire legislatively singled out those who put "themselves under the protection of powerful persons or institutions and with their help escaped their legal duties" indicates that the protections offered by the powerful were commonplace and not necessarily exclusive to bishops and churches.[27]

When John Chrysostom was forced by some momentary political difficulties to flee Constantinople for Cappadocia, he met there a powerful matron who told him, "If you run into trouble . . . flee into our protection."[28] As she possessed a secure keep, Chrysostom would not have failed to see that his hostess was offering him protection in much the same way that he, as bishop, could shelter within his church those who fled from imperial sanctions.[29] Indeed, despite the penitential thrust of his own defense of sanctuary protections, Chrysostom might have understood the protection he bestowed on fugitive wrongdoers such as Eutropius to be of a kind with the protection offered by his own benefactor.

The connection between power and protection was still evident in the minds of the fifth-century writers who praised Alaric, a Visigoth and occasional sacker of Rome, for his "order that fugitives to the churches of Saints Peter and Paul were to be kept secure and inviolate."[30] Whether the order was an instance of political calculation or piety or simply a literary trope later authors employed to glorify the church, it is significant that Alaric's actions were made to conform to ancient traditions of noble forbearance.

Other late imperial sources tied grants of sanctuary with accession to political power. Emperor Constantine was widely regarded throughout the early medieval period to be the quintessential Christian legislator, a reputation created and confirmed by an apocryphal series of "Ten Laws" that Constantine was said to have promulgated in the days surrounding his baptism.[31] Scholarly tradition traces these laws to a text forged sometime in the mid-sixth century, though recent research suggests that it may have been forged in the fifth century,[32] or even in the late fourth century.[33] According to the "Ten Laws," on the fifth day after his baptism Constantine declared, "In whatever place a church has been built or consecrated, this shall obtain: whatever guilty person flees to it shall be defended."[34] Because it is widely known as a forgery, historians of sanctuary have almost systematically disregarded the text. Yet, it was influential, being reproduced in numerous manuscripts of the early medieval period, where its image of the sanctuary-granting emperor in the late Roman Empire was transferred to the medieval imaginary.[35]

The point is not to find prefigurations of Christianity in the ancient world or to find pagan sensibilities in Christianity, but to show that sanctuary protections resonated within broad cultural and legal contexts in the ancient world. They were intelligible on terms that were not wholly dependent on the theological justifications of the church. Granted, the intercessory traditions of antiquity were not entirely syncretic with the intercessory duties of bishops in the courts of the Roman Empire. Ancient intercessory practices invited the ruler to demonstrate his *benignitas* as a characteristic of a noble life. In contrast, by the fourth century, Christian intercession was not justified in terms of worldly benignity; rather, it was as an actual end of punishment. As a consequence, the justifications for intercession were displaced from the earthly sphere into an eternal beyond. When the Roman Empire began promulgating legislation regulating sanctuary protections at the end of the fourth century, however, it did so in a context that extended beyond the practices of the Christian church to an older and wider set of elite social practices and political traditions.

The legislation the empire promulgated in the last decade of the fourth century and the first third of the fifth century shaped the rules that governed sanctuary in Europe until the sixteenth century. In certain respects, the importance of that legislation even grew after the decline of the empire as written modes of lawgiving were adopted by European kings in the early medieval period. It is necessary, therefore, to examine the initial promulgation of sanctuary legislation in the last years of the Roman Empire before tracing its transmission and reception in the Middle Ages.

ROMAN SANCTUARY LEGISLATION: THE THEODOSIAN CODE

As Gabriel Le Bras warned, late Roman sanctuary legislation and the scholarly interpretations it has spawned try "*la patience des érudits.*"[36] Much of the extant evidence comes to us through the Theodosian Code, which is particularly unsuited to the task of sorting out the precise moment in which the empire officially recognized the right of sanctuary. Scholars, however, have tended to assume that codification of the sanctuary privilege in the laws of the late empire is somehow more secure evidence for the legitimacy of sanctuary than other sorts of evidence that point to a long-standing and thriving social practice. In this respect, they expect more of the legislation than its issuers did.

The *Codex Theodosianus* was not promulgated until 438, four decades or more after many of the historical instances of sanctuary found in the patristic sources. There also were at least three imperial laws concerning sanctuary issued in the 390s that were not accessible in the codified form they received in 438, i.e., organized into topical books and rubrics, arranged chronologically, and, in many cases, edited. Only the particular tasks put to the compilers of the *Codex Theodosianus* in the decade leading up to 438 made those pronouncements resemble generally applicable laws intended to bring a uniform sanctuary policy upon the empire. The contexts of the pronouncements and the petitions that prompted them do not appear in the code at all.

As a rule, imperial edicts were copied, transmitted and posted in public places within a short time after they were issued.[37] Given this system of notification, it is difficult to know how much of the content of the imperial edicts regarding sanctuary was familiar to bishops, laymen, and provincial officials in the last decades of the fourth century and early years of the fifth century. Theodosius II, at least, seems to have thought many imperial laws were not widely known or understood because he stated this as a reason for commissioning his code.[38] Just as we know very little about how pronouncements were received and interpreted by bishops and other churchmen, we do not know much about how the imperial officials and private actors who pursued sanctuary seekers understood their own position, though bishops who confronted them occasionally attributed hesitancy to the imperial officials. Late-fourth-century bishops offered intercession and sanctuary to fugitives within ecclesiastical and aristocratic traditions that did not explicitly claim any sanction in imperial law. When these bishops, like all good patrons, exercised their power on behalf of supplicants, imperial law was, at most, one more thing to be navigated in the exercise of this power.[39]

All the legislation regarding sanctuary that has survived in the *Theodosian Code* contemplated a preexisting and implicitly lawful practice. The first extant imperial law (October 18, 392) to address sanctuary was meant not to preempt or eliminate, but merely to restrict, the practice of protecting fugitives in churches, singling out public debtors:

> Public debtors, if they presume that they might flee to churches, should either be extracted from their places of concealment, or the bishops who are proved to hide them should be exacted [for the debts of the fugitive]. . . . [H]ereafter, no debtor shall be defended by clerics, or else those clerics who presume to defend them shall satisfy their debts.[40]

The imperial authorities, having perceived rampant avoidance of customary municipal and financial obligations, sought to protect the means of revenue collection. The wording of the edict implied that other categories of criminals could take sanctuary without imperial restrictions.

Even as it applied to public debtors, however, the edict was by no means a frontal assault on the sanctuary practice as a whole. Because those debtors were simply commanded to repay their debts, their exclusion from sanctuary would not, without other considerations, implicate corporal or capital punishments.[41] One of the primary ecclesiastical concerns, protection of wrongdoers from the finality of execution, was not immediately at issue. The church's own stance toward sanctuary, moreover, required that fugitives, insofar as they were able, satisfy their monetary debts before entering the protection of the church.[42]

Augustine himself helped to arrange payment of at least one sanctuary seeker's debt.[43]

Repetition of imperial edicts on important matters, though not altogether unusual in the Theodosian Code, can signal persistent problems. In June of 397, the emperors Arcadius and Honorius addressed sanctuary in churches again:

> Jews accused of any wrong or plagued by debts who feign to wish joining themselves to Christian law, so that by fleeing to churches they might be able to avoid their crimes or the weight of their debts, should be denied entry and shall not be received until after they have returned all their debts or, their innocence demonstrated, they have been purged.[44]

While imperial sanctuary legislation continued to show a concern with debtors, this legislation was aimed specifically at Jews. It cast sanctuary as a privilege that protected only those who already professed the Christian religion. Patristic writers, on the other hand, generally spoke of Christian sanctuaries as open to all men. No one, in their view, was to be denied the possibility of joining or rejoining the community of the faithful, even those who only feigned interest in Christianity to reach safety. Just as sanctuary might afford an opportunity for repentance, it might afford a chance for true conversion as well.[45] The edict of 397, however, forbade sanctuary to Jews accused of criminal acts until they had proven their innocence. Patristic writers and early canon law had never made innocence a condition for respite in a sanctuary.[46] On the contrary, patristic writers assumed that the fugitive required penitential reconciliation or conversion.

In 398, a third sanctuary edict further restricted the sanctuary privilege to exclude others fleeing public or fiscal responsibilities:

> If, after this, anyone flee to a church who is a slave, handmaiden, public debtor, procurator, purple dye fish collector, or, in the end, anyone involved in public or private accounts . . . they shall be recalled to their former lot . . . even as if by forcible seizure.[47]

In the late fourth century, the Roman Empire had allowed decurions, a particular class of municipal officials, to take clerical orders if they disavowed their customary inheritance along with the municipal responsibilities it entailed. In reversing such allowances, the sanctuary legislation of 398 painted a picture in which such abdications of social responsibility, whether from a pious wish to serve the church or a desire to avoid the onerous fiscal duties imposed upon decurions by the empire, were becoming widespread. The edict of 398 also targeted sanctuary for runaway slaves, which would continue to be a subject of legislation in both the late empire and the early Middle Ages.

The first three sanctuary edicts that appeared in the Theodosian Code carved out categories of fugitives who should not benefit from sanctuary protection,[48] and the tone of this legislation has suggested to some historians that sanctuary was a tolerated custom that became legitimate when—but only when—it finally received explicit approval in imperial legislation.[49] Such a view fails to take into account how much force customary practices could have in the late empire. Gaius had already equated what is done by "tacit consent" with *ius* in matters of property.[50] Paulus, in the early third century, had even asserted that custom had greater force than written law.[51] Written laws themselves might fall into desuetude and lose their vitality.[52] Although Emperor Constantine made it plain that written laws trumped customs (which he conceded were *non vilis auctoritas*), this rule did not render custom any weaker than written enactments, which, according to imperial jurisprudence, could also be trumped by subsequent pronouncements.[53]

The classic studies of sanctuary were suspicious of sanctuary's customary force on the grounds that only "superstitious fear" or "Christian sentiments," but not law proper, prevented fugitives from being dragged from churches in the decades before sanctuary became "juridically protected" in imperial legislation.[54] In this view, only explicit recognition of the protection in imperial law, coupled with the promise to punish those who breach sanctuaries, secured the privilege fully. Yet the first imperial laws to address sanctuary merely set about clarifying the scope of a valid practice.

The difficulties with using the Theodosian Code as historical evidence for the origins of a Christian sanctuary practice are compounded by the fact that the surviving narrative sources from the late fourth century are both ambiguous and contradictory about the imperial laws governing the sanctuary privilege. Chrysostom thought Eutropius had been behind a law forbidding sanctuary protection to fugitives,[55] as did fifth-century church historians Socrates Scholasticus and Sozomenus.[56] If such a law ever existed, one possible implication would be that Eutropius had actually overturned some prior, but no longer extant, legislative recognition of sanctuary in churches.[57] It is not clear what Chrysostom, Socrates, and Sozomenus were referring to, but no blanket prohibition on sanctuary enacted by Eutropius, or even a fragment of such a law, is extant. On the other hand, these writers may have been referring to one of the other laws from the time of Eutropius that, as previously discussed, restricted the scope of intercession and sanctuary but did not forbid the practices altogether.[58]

Complicating the matter even further, Zosimus recorded that Eutropius had been dragged out of the Church of St. Sophia "in violation of a law which guaranteed asylum in churches."[59] Although Zosimus may have only meant that, in his opinion, the custom of sanctuary in churches had the status of imperial law, his remark has caused considerable consternation to scholars. Martroye, especially, has taken Zosimus to mean that Eutropius, soon after his rise to power, was himself behind some long-lost enactment that formally respected the right of asylum in churches.[60] This would mean that within a brief span of time, Eutropius sanctioned sanctuary and then officially restricted access to it, all in laws that are not extant.[61] Martroye's speculation, while entirely circumstantial, is not necessarily without grounds. Contradictory edicts emanating from the same imperial court are not unheard of,[62] and Eutropius himself apparently issued contradictory rules in other areas of law. For instance, a law he had enacted in 397 contradicted established legal principles by rendering the children of convicted traitors eligible for punishment along with their fathers. Despite recent attempts to rehabilitate Eutropius's reputation as an administrator,[63] he did issue laws designed to deprive his enemies of property and amass their goods to himself, in contradiction of established legal precedents.

Sozomenus thought that Eutropius's legislation forbidding the right of sanctuary was effaced from the records after his fall.[64] Effacement of legal enactments after the fall of a high-ranking official was a known convention in the Roman world. Donatists in North Africa thought that the death of Stilicho entailed suspension of laws he had promulgated, so it is possible that Eutropius had issued sanctuary legislation that was subsequently lost.[65] There is also evidence that the compilers of the Theodosian Code changed the method they employed when collecting texts dating after 398.[66] For the post-398 texts, the compilers stopped relying on municipal archives and worked only from the central archives in Constantinople. It is merely a conjecture that some texts from Eutropius's tenure could have been lost in this way. As slender a reed as that is, nearly contemporary narrative evidence suggests the possibility of both the recognition and the abolition of sanctuary rights in legislative enactments of the late 390s that are no longer extant.[67] Of course, the question is not nearly so vexing if one takes the view that sanctuary was a lawful practice before the promulgation of an edict authorizing it or a code to give that edict a home.

The scholarly quest for the first officially posited law to legitimate sanctuary in the Christian empire is hindered by a lacuna in a law promulgated in 409. The law, which appears in Book 16 of the Theodosian Code, is primarily an imperial denouncement of an obscure heretical sect and a call for return to the proper Christian faith.[68] The surviving text of the law is corrupted and unintelligible in parts. It does not appear initially to have anything to do with sanctuary protections at all, but it concludes that churches were to be spared harm in any conflict between heretical sects and Christians: "We order, therefore, that no person who is harmful to the churches . . . or to lead away the . . . of anyone, with Our regulation that is faithful and devoted to God."[69]

Mommsen, following Godefroy, was able to supply the textual lacuna with a passage from the *Codex Justinianus* (1.12.2; in the rubric dedicated to sanctuary protections) that shared language with the corrupted Theodosian text.[70] The Justinianic text, dated also to April 1, 409, reads: "By a faithful and devout precept we ordain that no one be permitted to drag away those who have fled to sacrosanct churches."[71] Reading the lacuna in the Theodosian Code through the lens of the Code of Justinian gives us some idea of what the compilers of the Justinian corpus expected when they edited the 409 edict. It is not an entirely secure method for reconstructing the Theodosian Code, but it is perhaps the best effort we can supply. In this case, the Justinianic sanctuary text has little to do with the concern for heretics displayed in the original Theodosian text. Scholars studying sanctuary have remained chary of crediting the edict of 409 with constituting sanctuary in the empire.[72] Their hesitancy stems from a search for a secure foundation in positive law for sanctuary, since, in the words of Martroye, the reconstructed edict of 409 does not permit us "a certain proof of the legal sanction of the right of asylum."[73] The law of 409 is both less troubling and less important if one accepts that sanctuary protections were lawful in the empire without explicit recognition in imperial legislation.

The quest for "certain proof" of an imperially endorsed sanctuary right has also been confounded by a law from 419 not included by the compilers of the Theodosian Code. It comes to us through the Sirmondian Constitutions, published by Jacques Sirmond in 1631 from early medieval Frankish manuscripts. As a legal text, it expresses much of the same hyperbole and literary flourish as the Theodosian Code. "It is fitting that humanity, which was known even before Our times," began the law, "should temper Justice." "Therefore," it continued, "the sanctity of ecclesiastical reverence shall apply to the space of fifty paces beyond the doors of the church. If anyone should hold a person who goes forth from this place [the church building], he shall incur the criminal charge of sacrilege."[74] The remainder of the text reiterated the right of priests to intercede in court on behalf of accused criminals, showing again the close connection between sanctuary and intercession in Roman law.

The law from 419 gave a justification for sanctuary that earlier imperial pronouncements had not:

> For when very many people flee from the violence of cruel fortune and choose the protection of the defense of the churches, when they are confined therein, they suffer no less imprisonment than that which they have avoided. For at no time is an egress opened to them into the light of the vestibule.

This text clearly implies that the sanctuary protection previously enjoyed within the walls of churches was legitimate; for reasons of *humanitas* and good order, it simply needed to be spatially extended outside the walls of the church building.

Although this text sometimes has been considered the earliest legally secure instance of sanctuary law, in part because it explicitly made violations of sanctuary punishable under penal law,[75] the fact that the compilers of the Theodosian Code did not include this law has led some to consider it an early medieval forgery.[76] Elizabeth Magnou-Nortier has argued, relying largely on the location and date of the surviving manuscripts, that all the Sirmondian Constitutions, including Constitution 13 on sanctuary, were fabricated at Lyon in the reign of Charles Martel.[77] The internal evidence of the Sirmondian Constitutions, however, points to their authenticity. As many as thirteen of the laws in the Sirmondian manuscript provide the original form of laws that were subsequently edited in the Theodosian Code.[78] However, Sirmondian Constitution 13 is not one of them. This suggests at least three possibilities concerning the absence of Sirmondian 13 from the Theodosian Code: (1) the compilers of the code knew of that sanctuary law but rejected it (perhaps as superfluous); (2) the compilers failed to unearth the text; or (3) it is an early medieval forgery. Magnou-Nortier has argued the constitution regarding sanctuary is an eighth-century forgery, and attempts to show that the provision of Sirmondian Constitution 13 extending sanctuary protections fifty paces outside the church walls was actually borrowed from a canon of the 681 Council of Toledo, which she finds to be the first instance of regulating the space outside a church for purposes of sanctuary law.[79] Other fifth-century imperial legislation, however, shows a similar concern with regulating that space (only without designating precise distances), so there is no reason to think that the Toledo council originated the concept.[80] That the compilers of the Theodosian Code dismissed the constitution of 419 as superfluous also seems unlikely, for they included five texts under the rubric for sanctuary law, regardless of potential contradiction, policy change, or repetition. It seems most likely that the compilers simply overlooked the law of 419. Their task, after all, was not to establish the historical moment at which sanctuary was instituted in imperial law. The project of compiling and issuing the Theodosian Code derived from imperial concerns with shoring up and projecting the authority of imperial law.

Late-imperial legislative texts cannot be treated like a modern legal code.[81] To be sure, the compilers of the Theodosian and Justinian codes knew how legal practices could be instituted or abolished through legislation. But the Theodosian Code was an expression of sovereignty, not a source of authority. In the late empire, the task of the lawgiver was not so tightly bound up with modern understandings of legitimacy that we must search for the origins of sanctuary in an official legal text. An imperial lawgiver could employ edicts to restrict an existing customary practice without feeling compelled to locate the authority of the custom itself in an official statute. Hence, the absence of any edict that can be identified with certainty as sanctuary's official founding did not present a meaningful problem (until the modern age).[82]

Nonetheless, two successive imperial edicts of 431 and 432 are often identified as the most secure moment of legalization for sanctuary.[83] Following the general principles of sanctuary laid out in the constitution of 419, they linked sanctuary to clemency, episcopal intercession, and benign sovereignty. The space in which the sanctuary protection operated was again regulated and extended outside the church walls, and the obligations incurred by those who sought sanctuary were spelled out as well. The edict of 431 was the most comprehensive and detailed regulation of the sanctuary privilege known to the fifth century. Anyone entering the confines of the church was protected. Also, any house, courtyard, or bath falling within a delineated buffer space was so privileged.[84] As for those seeking sanctuary: No one was to eat or sleep within the temple or at the "sacred altar" itself; persons who brought weapons to the church and would not relinquish them after being warned by the bishop were to be expelled by force, but any other attempt to remove a refugee by force was subject to a capital penalty.[85]

In 432, another edict declared, "any slave, who seeks out a church without any weapon will not be sent away before one day [has passed]."[86] In the meantime, clerics were to work to insure that the "master grant indulgence to the slave for his sins" so that "without any lingering spirit of ire," the master might lead the slave away.[87] The wrongs of a slave did not ordinarily concern the public criminal jurisdiction of Rome, allowing masters wide leeway to discipline their recaptured slaves. Although the rules pronounced here do not look terribly different from the protections granted to slaves who fled to statues of Caesar, the conciliatory thrust of the edict and the prominent role given churchmen reflected ecclesiastical sensibilities. The early Middle Ages would see these rules adopted and adapted in European legal traditions, and the conciliatory role of clerics would become increasingly important for both secular and ecclesiastical law in the medieval period.

The real importance of these last two edicts was their timing. They came early enough to be included in the Theodosian Code of 438. In turn, the Theodosian Code, or shorter recensions of it, would be widely transmitted into the legal traditions of the early Middle Ages. Imperial edicts of 451 and 466, which added further regulations to the scope of the sanctuary protection, were gathered only by compilers of Justinian's corpus.[88] In the sixth century, Justinian also issued legislation restricting the scope of sanctuary. But despite Justinian's own efforts, the empire was irreversibly divided by the sixth century and the influence of Justinian's sanctuary legislation was limited almost entirely to Byzantium in the centuries immediately following its promulgation. Only in the later medieval period, when jurists in Italy revived the study of Roman law, did Justinian's legislation restricting sanctuary have any impact on medieval Roman and canon law in Western Europe. In 535, a *novella* of Justinian had proclaimed that "the precincts of the sacred shall not be open to homicides, adulterers, or *raptores virginum*."[89] Another edict of the same year had excluded "violators of the Christian faith" from sanctuary.[90] The quintessentially imperial justification for these restrictions was that they were "useful and necessary to the *Respublica*."[91] In part because such restrictions were not known in European legal traditions until the end of the medieval period, homicides made up one of the most commonly recognized categories of sanctuary seekers in the Middle Ages. In fact, many barbarian laws named homicides as especially worthy of sanctuary. In addition, the invocation of the public interest as grounds for these restrictions, crucial for juridical debates of the early modern period, was virtually unintelligible in the early Middle Ages. Crime and sanctuary in European law would not be explicitly evaluated in terms of a concept of public interest for almost one thousand years. Meanwhile, the Theodosian edicts of 431 and 432, which lacked any of Justinian's later restrictions on homicides and such, were highly influential in the transmission of sanctuary legislation into early medieval law.

CONCLUSION

The sanctuary practices that emerged from late antiquity into the medieval period did not have roots in one exclusive tradition of thought. Rather, sanctuary drew on meanings embedded deeply in both ancient aristocratic and Christian traditions concerning wrong and punishment, sin and penance, and kingship and grace. Each of these traditions would help shape sanctuary in the early medieval period, but sanctuary would also be transformed by early medieval feuding practices, patterns of pious kingship, and modes of legislation.

II

THE EMERGENCE OF SANCTUARY LAW IN THE EARLY MIDDLE AGES

3

Reassessing Early Medieval Sanctuary Legislation

"This infamous cleric, both accused and judged, escaped from the custody of the *missus* to the church, which he should not have entered until after penance, and which he entered against the law."[1] These words were written in the name of Charlemagne around 801–802 in a letter admonishing Alcuin, the abbot of the Basilica of St. Martin in Tours, whom both Charlemagne and Bishop Theodulf of Orléans held responsible for granting the fugitive cleric sanctuary "against the law." Although most likely drafted by an imperial scribe, perhaps one knowledgeable in law, the letter has been said to offer a glimpse of Charlemagne's personal anger over the incident.[2] Alcuin's provocative response also survives: How can it be said "that a guilty sinner should not be received by the Church?" "If sinners cannot enter the church, perhaps there may not be found a priest who can say mass in it."[3]

At the heart of this exchange lay a disagreement over the scope of the right of sanctuary in churches within the Carolingian empire. Bishop Theodulf, a Visigoth who had fled to Tours from his native Saragossa in order to escape Muslim incursions, would have denied sanctuary to convicted fugitives who had not yet completed their judicially imposed penance. Theodulf had Charlemagne's support in this dispute. Alcuin, on the other hand, would have granted shelter to fugitives regardless of crime, prior conviction, or pending penitential sentence. The crime for which the cleric had been convicted is unknown, as is the ultimate resolution of the case. Nevertheless, that an English-born abbot, a Spanish-born bishop, and the Frankish emperor (through his scribes) should marshal passages of the Theodosian Code, Irish and Frankish canon law collections, and Visigothic and Salic royal law in a dispute over sanctuary law, makes a striking statement about the place of sanctuary in the early medieval world.

The dispute also demonstrated a significant degree of continuity between the Carolingian and the late Roman empires with regard to sanctuary law. Early medieval legal traditions were replete with references to sanctuary, and neither Charlemagne nor Theodulf questioned the validity of the right of sanctuary itself.[4] By the early ninth century, a host of early medieval sources supported the proposition that a fugitive who reached the confines of a church should be protected. Of course, many of these sources were modeled explicitly on the rules transmitted in the Theodosian code, but in the early Middle Ages, episcopal synods had contributed a growing body of legislative materials that announced sanctuary protections for fugitives and specified punishments for those who violated churches by dragging fugitives out.

Despite the disagreement between Alcuin and Charlemagne about the precise legal relationship between penance and sanctuary, early medieval legal sources show that penance continued to be an important aspect of sanctuary law, as it had been for such leading figures in the early church as Augustine and Chrysostom. Intercession likewise continued to be in important component of sanctuary law, as it had been for both ecclesiastics and aristocrats in the late Roman Empire. Finally, Alcuin's intercession against Charlemagne and Bishop Theodulf showed that Carolingian rulers, much as their Roman predecessors, struggled to bring sanctuary to heel within official legal processes. Similar attempts can be seen in Anglo-Saxon sanctuary legislation.

Though remaining linked to intercession and penance, early medieval sanctuary was also intimately connected to social contexts that historians generally treat under the rubric of blood feud. Thus, it is possible to see evolutions in the relationship between sanctuary law, ecclesiastical intercession, and the feud. The constellation of dispute-resolving procedures that obtained in early medieval legal traditions, including the blood feud, altered the shape of the sanctuary laws that had been received from Christian Rome in important ways. While the following chapters examine the relationship between feud and sanctuary more closely, the present chapter concerns the textual traditions that underpinned the transmission of sanctuary into the European Middle Ages.

REASSESSING THE HISTORICAL TRADITION OF SANCTUARY LAW

A long scholarly tradition has imagined medieval sanctuary laws as a makeshift response to a politically fragmented and lawless world. Charles Riggs, writing in 1963 but building on a much older historiography, portrayed Anglo-Saxon sanctuary law as a functional response concocted by politically decentralized and weak kingdoms seeking to shore up social order.[5] Unlike the older historiography, Riggs recognized that sanctuary law was a key component of medieval dispute resolution, rather than a practice that simply undermined the authority of the law. Still, such a functional approach fails to appreciate that sanctuary law was itself a vehicle for both kings and ecclesiastics to express social and political power.

The legal texts produced by and for some of the most powerful early medieval monarchs articulated protections for murderers and thieves who fled to churches because it was an important aspect of kingship to recognize such protections. For the same reason, many instances of sanctuary legislation can be connected to moments of conquest and political transition, and medieval traditions (sometimes apocryphal, but perhaps no less telling on that account) attached to Constantine, Clovis, Charlemagne, and William the Conqueror associated pious and noble kingship with the capacity to be a sanctuary-granting and sanctuary-respecting ruler. Hence, while historians have often understood sanctuary protections as a sign of—or functional response to—political weakness, I argue that sanctuary laws actually signaled certain kinds of political strength.

Identifying sanctuary as an important expression of power, however, does not fully explain how sanctuary law fit so easily into the various royal and ecclesiastical legal traditions of early medieval Europe. In the extant memorials of early medieval royal and ecclesiastical lawgiving, it is difficult to find a legislative text that does not contain some mention of sanctuary protections. Part of the explanation for this is that intercession and penitential discipline had become firmly embedded in early medieval penal traditions through mimicry of Roman legislative examples, in particular, the Theodosian Code. Sanctuary, however, was also closely linked to revenge and compensation practices typically oriented toward the blood feud that were not officially part of imperial Roman law or canon law but figured prominently in early medieval legislation.

That the Church was strong enough to interject its sanctuary privilege into the world of the blood feud has been viewed as one of the early medieval church's triumphs in a world rife with private violence. What is more remarkable than the fact that sanctuary protections sometimes served to arrest violence is that many legal texts presented sanctuary as one of several platforms upon which lawful violence might be brought to a peaceful and honorable conclusion. More than simply a normative restraint on violence or symbol of kingly power, sanctuary protections were a crucial part of the rules of the larger game of wrong, response, and resolution.

To the extent that medieval legal traditions speak of crime and punishment, they seem committed to the view that breaches might be restored, wrongs righted, feuds resolved, and sins atoned. It is for this reason, and not simply for expediency, that the majority of penal clauses in early medieval legislation speak in conciliatory tones (except when dealing with strangers and outsiders). They rarely rely on the kinds of coercive and bloody sanctions that early modern European law codes embraced in hope of deterring offenders. Medieval penitential practice, the paradigmatic example of conciliatory sanctions, intersected with sanctuary law at many points, as did feuding, ritual hostage taking, and legislatively prescribed composition payments, all of which were grounded in a strong conciliatory ethic. Sanctuary drew its intelligibility not from its role in checking "medieval barbarity," but from its accord with deeply seated medieval understandings of wrong, punishment, and resolution.

There are important limits to what can be said about early medieval sanctuary law. We can say next to nothing about how, if at all, medieval legal texts were applied in actual cases until well into the ninth century, and even then the evidence is very thin. Because written law served a different purpose in the early Middle Ages than it does today, only some early medieval legislation is intelligible as statute law in the modern sense. As Patrick Wormald observed, "the puzzle is that much is not."[6]

Producing written laws was an important task of early medieval kings. Bede, in the eighth century, famously described the written laws that Æthelbert produced (in English) in the early seventh century as done "*iuxta exempla Romanorum*," possibly referring to the Frankish examples (which were Latin).[7] A great portion of the written law that comes down to us from the early medieval continent is the product of Frankish scriptoria from which copies were circulated. Few early medieval law codes circulated in forms conducive to judicial consultation. Moreover, some legislation, particularly that of Frankish provenance, was left undated, leaving considerable uncertainty about dates of issuance and provenance. Even the Franks, whom Bede viewed as exemplary legislators, allowed successive versions of legislation to survive and circulate alongside newer recensions.[8] Before the ninth century, many law codes were appended to nonlegal material in books too large and poorly ordered to be practical. Also prior to the ninth century, written legal material subjected to any level of organization invariably reflected ecclesiastical interests, a fact that helps explain the survival of so much legislation relevant and favorable to sanctuary protections.[9] Moreover, not until the ninth century do we find the production of law books for the purpose of handy reference. The evidence that survives from before the ninth century indicates the symbolic importance of written law and the continuing influence of the Theodosian Code in early medieval Europe, but tells us very little about how sanctuary protections actually operated.

SANCTUARY LEGISLATION: TRADITION AND AUTHORITY

By the late fifth and early sixth centuries, the Roman Empire's political center of gravity had shifted eastward to Constantinople. At the same time, barbarian *gentes* encroached steadily upon the sphere of influence of Rome and of classical Roman law in the western empire. By 507, Clovis, king of the Merovingians and a convert to Christianity, had united significant portions of Gaul under Frankish rule through marriage and a succession of military victories. The heirs of Clovis and, to an even greater degree, their Carolingian successors established such hegemony in the wake of the Roman Empire that "the Carolingian period and the role of Frankish political expansion and cultural imperialism have taken their place in the historiography of most European countries as an essential phase in those countries' historical development."[10] For Wormald, Frankish legal traditions sound "the first chords of the anthemic arrogance that would one day give western Europeans mastery of the world."[11]

Some of the most important early medieval developments in law, and specifically in sanctuary law, can be traced to the filtering of Romano-Christian sources through Frankish political and legal traditions. That Carolingian texts sometimes spoke antagonistically of Rome does not negate the importance of Roman legal traditions as a source for Frankish law. Other Frankish legal texts, especially Merovingian productions, owed much to Roman law and to officials with Roman administrative backgrounds.[12] Sanctuary protections were a key part of this Romano-Christian inheritance, and can be found in the written laws of the Franks, Visigoths, Lombards, Burgundians, Alamans, Bavarians, Frisians, Saxons, and Anglo-Saxons.[13]

In the earliest confirmation of sanctuary protections from a Frankish source, an ecclesiastical council convened by King Clovis at Orléans in 511 declared, "If homicides, adulterers, or thieves flee to a church we establish that what the ecclesiastical canons decree and the Roman law establishes shall be observed; . . . no one may drag them out."[14] The rules of the Theodosian Code were distilled to their simplest form: Fugitive criminals should receive protection if they reached a church. The ecclesiastical legislation given at Orléans in 511 went a good deal further in protecting sanctuary rights than did other, almost-contemporary legislation in the seventh-century Visigothic adaptation of the Theodosian corpus or in the Roman-inspired Burgundian laws. Edicts promulgated by Justinian in the eastern empire in the 530s specifically excluded homicides and adulterers from sanctuary in churches, but codes produced in western Europe did not.[15] The Theodosian Code, and not Justinian's corpus, mattered in Italy, Gaul, and Iberia in the early Middle Ages, and there was no explicit exception for murderers in the Theodosian sanctuary rules. Visigothic kings eventually supplied an exclusion for homicides in their adaptation of Theodosian laws, but some medieval traditions, including the English common law, never did.

Clovis's council of 511 was not alone in invoking the precedents for sanctuary in the Theodosian Code. The nearly contemporaneous Burgundian laws stated that slaves who sought sanctuary for homicide were to be protected "since the Theodosian law in book nine given at Antioch permits no one to abduct an unarmed slave from a church."[16] Likewise, the earliest versions of Visigothic law replicated truncated but faithful statements of rules found in the Theodosian Code and grouped them in roughly the same order that they were found in the Theodosian Code.[17]

With respect to sanctuary legislation, secular authority sometimes relied on ecclesiastical authority and vice versa. The *Pactus pro tenore pacis*, a sixth-century Frankish text, used the phrase "as agreed among the bishops" to place royal sanctuary protections squarely within the canonical tradition of sanctuary law.[18] On the other hand, Pope Gelasius (492–96), simply recalled the Roman laws governing sanctuary when he wrote to a certain Bishop Boniface about a fugitive slave who refused to come out of a church,[19] and an ecclesiastical council held at Orléans in 549 affirmed sanctuary privileges with the phrase "as it is held written in the ancient constitutions," a reference to the Theodosian Code.[20]

As the imprint of Rome is evident everywhere in early medieval legislation, from laws regarding property to general patterns of legislative texts,[21] it is hardly a surprise that the earliest sanctuary rules in sub-Roman legislation owe obvious debts to the Theodosian Code.[22] An eighth-century collection known as the *Lex Baiuwariorum* began, "First of all, Moses of the Hebrew nation explicated in sacred letters the divine laws."[23] After tracing a line of ancient lawgivers that included the Athenian and Spartan legislators Solon and Lycurgus, the largest portion of the prologue highlighted the crucial importance of Rome as a legislative model in the early Middle Ages:

> Numa Pompilius, who succeeded Romulus in the kingdom, first gave laws to the Romans. Then, when the people were no longer able to bear the seditious magistrates, they chose the *decemviri* to inscribe the laws, who set forth the Twelve Tables translated into the Latin tongue. . . . Then Caesar began to institute laws, but was killed before he could. New laws were begun by Emperor Constantine . . . but they were mixed up and disorganized. Afterwards, Theodosius II, in a manner similar to Gregory and Hermogenius, set forth a code of constitutions from the time of Constantine under a special title for each emperor which he called by his name, the *Theodosianus*.[24]

This all-star cast of historical lawgivers was actually lifted from a passage in Isidore of Seville's *Etymologiae*.[25] As Bede's observations about written law and the Roman (Frankish) example have already demonstrated, the appeal of the Roman lawgiving tradition was far-reaching, extending to the farthest flung regions of Europe that had contact with Roman political culture.[26]

BIBLICAL PRECEDENTS FOR MEDIEVAL SANCTUARY LAW

Roman models were most often copied, but the figure of a lawgiving Moses loomed large. Nevertheless, scripture offered only ambiguous precedents to early medieval readers interested in sanctuary law. Deuteronomy recorded that the ancient Israelites were divinely commanded to build six "cities of refuge" after crossing into Jordan. But these cities of refuge were to be sanctuaries only for unintentional homicides. Yet the distinction between unintentional and intentional homicide was largely alien to sub-Roman legal traditions, which tended to place more emphasis on whether the slayer or slain was freeborn or slave than on the slayer's intentions. Other passages from the Old Testament that dealt specifically with fugitives to the altar in the temple, had they been read as controlling legal precedents, would have suggested a more restricted sanctuary practice than prevailed throughout the traditions of early medieval Europe. For instance, the Pentateuch recorded the divine command concerning one who slays with guile: "Thou shalt rip him from mine altar that he may die,"[27] and King Solomon ordered Joab to be slain even though "he caught hold on the horns of the altar."[28] These examples were certainly not unknown to Carolingian scholars, for many Old Testament motifs, especially those relevant to models of kingship, were readily employed by early medieval writers.[29] But aside from some biblical glosses, Old Testament texts concerned with fugitives to the altar had little or no impact on medieval sanctuary law. For example, ninth-century Carolingian scholar Rabanus Maurus (a student of Alcuin) linked the Old Testament cities of refuge with Christology and penitential discipline.[30] The main lessons he took away from Deuteronomy's description of the cities of refuge was that the three trans-Jordan cities designated as refuges were not actual places but were allegories for "faith, hope, and charity"—abstract nouns to which all Christians should flee. Further, Rabanus interpreted the stipulation that fugitives to the cities were permitted to return safely to their homes after the death of the High Priest as a rehearsal for the Atonement.[31]

Of the few legal texts that reveal an awareness of the biblical precedents for sanctuary law, one of the more widely known was an Irish canonical collection from the end of the seventh or beginning of the eighth century.[32] This collection even employed the heading "*De civitatibus refugii*," a clear nod to the biblical terminology, rather than the conventional Roman circumlocution "*De his qui ad ecclesiam confugiunt*" to designate sanctuary rules.[33] The sanctuary rules themselves are structured around snippets from relevant biblical texts, with patristic texts and canons as ancillary support. Alcuin, in the dispute over sanctuary with Theodulf and Charlemagne, relied on this Irish collection to establish that sanctuary was sanctioned by divine law, though he did not specifically acknowledge it in his letter. Even so, Alcuin emphasized contemporary canonical rules and did not dwell on the restrictive character of the Old Testament cities of refuge.[34]

In Anglo-Saxon legal literature, King Alfred included a vernacular rendering of the selected passages of Mosaic law, including passages that addressed cities of refuge and a divine command to rip intentional homicides from the altar, in the famous prologue to the laws that took his name.[35] In Alfred's prologue, the Hebrew term for "cities of refuge" was translated by the Anglo-Saxon word *friðstowe*, denoting a place to which one might flee.[36] Although *friðstowe*, in turn, came to signify the protections that might be gained by flight to a church, the substance of the sanctuary rules included in the Laws of Alfred (discussed in following chapters) was much more beholden to ecclesiastical law and Anglo-Saxon blood-feud norms than to scriptural prescriptions about cities of refuge. Of course, the purpose of Alfred's prologue was not to import ancient Hebrew law into England. As David Pratt has demonstrated, Alfred's prologue was part of a larger program aimed at reorienting Christian kingship and lawgiving.[37] But it is also clear that the Old Testament precedents deployed did not play a significant role in shaping early medieval sanctuary law, even where Alfred was careful to maintain some degree of continuity with earlier Anglo-Saxon sanctuary practices in the sanctuary provisions of his law code.[38] The sanctuary rules that appear in Anglo-Saxon legislation have little relation to the Mosaic precedents in Alfred's prologue, probably, as we will see, because sanctuary was integrated so closely with Anglo-Saxon feuding and dispute resolving procedures, whose legitimacy was not dependent on Old Testament models.

The drafters of early medieval sanctuary legislation did not seem to give much consideration to the New Testament either. Later, the image of Christ scourging moneychangers and chasing them from the temple in Jerusalem during Passover would provide Roman lawyers with ammunition against sanctuary.[39] But in the early medieval era, the legacy of imperial edicts and church canons, as well as the compatibility of sanctuary with early medieval feuding practices, mattered much more than biblical examples for the transmission of sanctuary law.

CONCLUSION

Early medieval legislators did not need to reach for authoritative precedents when they encountered sanctuary laws in the Old Testament. Early medieval citations to imperial and ecclesiastical legislation were claims to a Roman-Christian tradition in which grants of sanctuary to supplicant wrongdoers were clearly appropriate. Meanwhile, the reach of sanctuary privileges inherited from Rome and disseminated throughout medieval Europe steadily expanded, as early medieval sanctuary laws were endorsed from many quarters and in many voices. Sanctuary rules appeared in the canons of ecclesiastical councils at the initiative of kings, in royal legislation at the initiative of churchmen, and sometimes in forms drawn directly from Roman imperial sources.

Legal and textual traditions, however, tell only part of the story. The lines of transmission by which the written laws and unwritten norms of sanctuary were adopted will show just how ingrained the practice was in the social, religious, and political dynamics of early medieval Europe. Sanctuary was not simply copied from the Theodosian Code. As the following chapter shows, sanctuary law also served as a marker of political authority and Christian identity. Moreover, the intimate connection between the blood feud and sanctuary that emerged in some medieval legislative traditions would be important to sanctuary's domestication in the later Middle Ages (taken up in Part III).

4

The Transmission and Reception of Sanctuary Legislation in the Early Middle Ages

Inspired by a prevailing impulse to find what was primordially and authentically "Germanic" (as opposed to Roman) in early medieval law, nineteenth-century legal history searched for "native" sanctuary practices that could be traced to pre-Christian European customs.[1] As subsequent, devastating critiques of the concept of "Germanic law" have largely dissolved these kinds of inquiries,[2] it has also become clear that sanctuary protections almost always make their way into Frankish and Anglo-Saxon laws through ecclesiastical, not native, influence. In Visigothic legislation, sanctuary rules appear in the earliest recensions as a result of direct textual borrowing from the Theodosian Code. Clovis, who apparently oversaw the promulgation of sanctuary laws by an ecclesiastical council late in the last year of his life (511), probably also had authorized completion of the *Lex Salica*, which did not contain any provisions for fugitives who sought protection in churches. Instead, the compilers of the *Lex Salica* may have understood sanctuary to be an issue handled by the legislating that went on in ecclesiastical councils, although early medieval legislators were not always attuned to this sort of labor division. Sanctuary protections articulated in the *Decretio* of Clothar I (d. 561) and in the *Decretio* of Childebert II (d. 595) were folded by Carolingian scribes into later recensions of the *Lex Salica*.[3] Similarly, the earliest versions of the Alamannic law (the so-called *Pactus Alamannorum*), traceable to Clothar II,(d. 629) do not contain the references to protections for fugitives who fled to churches that later versions (the so-called *Lex Alamannorum*) do.[4]

King Æthelbert's seventh-century Kentish law code, produced within two decades of Augustine's Christian mission to England in 597, announced the compensation owed for theft of royal property, church property, clerical property, and for breaching the peace of the church, folding prohibitions on violence within churches into secular compensation practices. In light of the Salic and Alamannic evidence, some historians have speculated that the pride of place given to ecclesiastical concerns in Æthelbert's code, and the code's valuation of a bishop's wergild above the king's indicate later, ecclesiastically inspired interpolations.[5] Although Bede considered these clauses to be part of Æthelbert's original laws, nearly one hundred and fifty years separated Bede from Æthelbert, leaving ample time for scribal interpolation. Still, Patrick Wormald, who credits promulgation of Æthelbert's law to the king and his *sapientes* and not to Christian missionaries, argues that the first clause is placed exactly where and contains exactly what one should expect, given its early-seventh-century origins, and was not inserted at a later date.[6]

Hence, the evidence does not allow strong inferences about the existence of pre-Christian sanctuary practices among the Franks, or any other early medieval people. It does suggest, however, a widespread expectation that royal legislation should contain sanctuary provisions. Sanctuary protections were important to the symbolic program of early medieval legislation, because, like all written legislation in the early Middle Ages, they signaled that a king "had joined the Franks and Romans in the ranks of civilized" peoples."[7]

The reception of sanctuary was not a simple mechanistic transfer of Romano-Christian texts into early medieval legislation. Granted, some medieval law codes simply adopted wholesale the sanctuary rules found in the Theodosian Code. But the language and context of early medieval sanctuary legislation and practice reveal that sanctuary had become integrated with other aspects of early medieval law and society. By tracing the transmission of sanctuary laws into early medieval Europe, it is possible to see the emergence of sanctuary law as a symbolic marker of a lawful Christian people and as an important feature of feud practices.

What historians can say about sanctuary law before the tenth century largely concerns how it developed in Carolingian and Anglo-Saxon legal traditions. Most of the surviving sources document Carolingian culture and

Carolingian modes of producing legislation, though there are notable similarities between Carolingian and Anglo-Saxon legislative traditions.[8] Because Anglo-Saxon legislators paid considerable attention to sanctuary and to the blood-feud, the story told here will eventually move westward across the channel in the tenth century. There, it will illustrate how Anglo-Saxon sanctuary law fit into a relatively strong regime of royal governance that sought to subject both feuding practices and sanctuary protections to royally administered processes.

DIRECT RECEPTION FROM THE THEODOSIAN CODE: SANCTUARY FOR SLAVES, DEBTORS, AND CRIMINALS IN THE EARLY MIDDLE AGES

As in imperial Roman law, debtors and fugitive slaves occupied a significant place in early medieval sanctuary law. In this regard medieval sanctuary law shows the firmest imprint of the Theodosian Code. But that is not to claim that the Theodosian Code, or medieval legislation that copied it, was consulted and applied in actual cases or that social practices conformed to its administrative imperatives. Still, the legal texts are important evidence of what at least some thought a written law should contain about sanctuary claims.

The legislation from medieval peoples having the closest historical experience with Roman administration tended to be the most faithful in reproducing the sanctuary rules of the Theodosian Code.[9] A text known as the *Edictum Theodorici* provides a helpful example of the borrowing common in the earliest sub-Roman legislation. There is no scholarly consensus concerning the dating and attribution of the *Edictum.*[10] Savigny followed Carl Ritter, an early modern editor of the *Edictum*, in dating it to around 500 and attributing it to the Ostrogoth king Theodoric the Great, who held power in Italy at the end of the fifth century.[11] This was also the view of Frederick Bluhme, who edited the *Edictum Theodorici.*[12] Nevertheless, it may be that the *Edictum* should be placed in Gaul and attributed to Theodoric II (d. 466), making it the oldest surviving piece of sub-Roman legislation.[13] It has even been argued that the *Edictum* was actually the continuation of a legislative program undertaken by Theodoric II's father, Theodoric I (d. 451),[14] and that Magnus of Narbonne, a Roman prefect sent to Visigothic Gaul, had a hand in producing the *Edictum* sometime around the year 460.[15] This might account for the heavily Theodosian content of the *Edictum.*

The content of the sanctuary laws in the *Edictum* offers some slight evidence about the legislation's provenance. Cassiodorus described an Ostrogothic sanctuary practice related to commutation of the death penalty and island exile that does not correspond with the *Edictum*'s provisions for sanctuary.[16] This apparent discrepancy may suggest against Ostrogothic provenance, but there is no firm basis on which to make a judgment.[17] In any case, the provisions for sanctuary found in the *Edictum* were distilled more or less directly from the Theodosian Code. Fugitive slaves and debtors figure prominently in both.

According to chapter 70 of the *Edictum*, any slave who fled to a church should receive a promise of impunity from his master. That promise was to be mediated by a priest, demonstrating that the intercessory role of bishops, already well developed in the fourth century, was transmitted into sub-Roman traditions through royal legislation as well as ecclesiastical practices. Once the promise was exacted, the slave was to be returned immediately to his lord.[18] Thus, the rule followed more or less directly the path laid out in the imperial edict of 432 and preserved in the Theodosian Code.[19]

According to the *Edictum*, if, despite the master's promise, a fugitive slave remained unwilling to come out of the church, then the churchmen ("*archdiaconus . . . vel presbyter atque clerici*") were required to compel the fugitive to return to his master, or the master was to be repaid by the church from "other property"[20] This way, the master could receive value for that property that "he would have been able to seize if it was outside the church," but that instead was "lingering in hiding within the church."[21] Here, the rule struck a fairly simple compromise between the proprietary interests of the slave owner and the tutelary interests of the church. Churchmen, through their intercessory role, were able to assume the privileged social status that attached to protecting supplicants from powerful pursuers. Like the Theodosian Code, the rule gave no meaningful guidance for cases in which the master refused the substitute payment or the church was unwilling or unable to make it.

In chapter 71 of the *Edictum*, the direct borrowing from the Theodosian Code continued:

> If on account of a public debt someone has run to any church whatsoever, let the archdeacon compel the debtor to go out of the church . . . : If the archdeacon is unwilling to do this, let him pay back the debt with-

> out delay from out of the substance that the fugitive carried to the church. Unless this is done, it is determined that the archdeacon shall settle the [fugitive's] debt, for this is greatly in the public interest.[22]

The rule parallels those for fugitive slaves. It protects the same interests and presumes the same intercessory role for archdeacons. The obligation placed on clerics to repay the debts of the fugitives they protected was similar to a pronouncement in 466 of Emperor Leo that was later included in Justinian's code.[23] Augustine had repaid the debts of fugitives in such a manner early in the fifth century.[24] As in cases involving fugitive slaves, no guidance was given for cases in which creditors and churchmen were unable to come to terms.

Chapter 125 of the *Edictum*, however, pronounced harsh penalties for violently dragging any fugitive out of a church: "If someone has dragged men from churches, that is religious places, or attempts to carry someone away violently, he shall be punished capitally."[25] Again, the rule had a basis in the Theodosian Code.[26] In fact, it is not surprising that the legislative texts produced in the waning days of the Roman Empire, perhaps by a Roman prefect for Romans in barbarian-ruled provinces, followed closely the examples set out in the Theodosian Code.

The situation in the early sixth-century Visigothic *Breviarium Alarici* is no different. There, an abridgement of Theodosian Code 9.45.4 ordered protection for all unarmed fugitives. In addition, an *interpretatio* appended to the *Breviarium* explained that breaches of sanctuary could be punished with death and that the ecclesiastical buildings that surrounded a church were protected space. The *interpretationes* scattered throughout the *Breviarium* have generated considerable debate among historians, but they were probably juristic commentaries on the Theodosian Code itself produced in Gaul in the late fifth century, certainly after the Theodosian Code and before, or contemporaneously with, the *Breviarium*.[27]

As late as the seventh century, when Visigothic kings were well established on the Iberian peninsula and legislating in autonomous and relatively sophisticated terms, the Theodosian Code continued to shape the sanctuary provisions of the *Lex Visigothorum*. "Let no one dare to drag anyone violently from a church, unless the fugitive should wish to defend himself with weapons," the *Lex Visigothorum* commanded.[28] Its second provision absolved anyone who killed an armed fugitive who attempted to defend himself.[29]

Both rules follow the sanctuary provisions found in the *Breviarium* of Alaric and the Theodosian Code. They may even be traceable to the legislation of King Euric (466–85).[30]

The third and fourth chapters concerned with sanctuary in the *Lex Visigothorum* are from a slightly later date than the first two and probably belong to legislation of King Leovigild (568–86).[31] The third provision delineated the penalties for anyone who violated a church by violently dragging his slave or debtor from the altar. Those of high social station were required to pay one hundred *solidos*, those of lower station thirty. Those who could not pay at all were to be whipped, repaying by their bodies what they could not pay with money.[32] On this point, the *Lex Visigothorum* departed from the capital punishment threatened for breaching sanctuary in the Theodosian Code and in the earlier *Breviarium Alarici,* employing instead graded composition payments, which were ubiquitous in sub-Roman penal legislation. The fourth chapter restated the general rule that fugitives to a church should not be dealt with violently and reiterated the pivotal role of churchmen in exhorting the pursuer to grant indulgence to the "debtor or guilty one," echoing 9.45.5 of the Theodosian Code.

The *Lex Visigothorum*, however, departed from a trend in other early sub-Roman sanctuary legislation by explicitly removing homicides from the protection of the church and from the intercessory efforts of churchmen. Unlike the sixth-century Frankish ecclesiastical councils, but much like Justinian's own policies, Visigothic law did not protect homicides who fled to churches to the same extent it protected slaves and debtors. According to *Lex Visigothorum* 9.3.4, homicides, "who deserve to be killed," were not to be protected by the church but were to be treated by rules governing homicides prescribed in a separate provision of the *Lex Visigothorum*.[33]

The provisions dealing with homicides in general, and those who fled to churches in particular, were located in Book 6 of the *Lex Visigothorum* (hereinafter *LV*). Homicides who fled to churches, according to a rule promulgated in the reign of King Chindaswinth,[34] could not invoke sanctuary protections because although "many laws have been enacted" for the punishment of crimes, many "do not fear to act wickedly against divine precepts." Rather, they "place themselves in the protection of the churches of God." But because "wickedness should never go unpunished," lest men be encouraged to act in even more wicked ways, "every homicide shall be punished." Yet, despite its seeming readiness to do so, the *LV* stopped short of denying all protections to a sanctuary-seeking homicide. According to the *LV*, fugitive homicides could not be forcibly removed from the church without the permission and oversight of a priest and could not be killed after exiting the church. Instead, the homicide's eyes were to be plucked out so that his sight would be destroyed and he would be made "a terror to others."[35] This innovation on the rules inherited from the Theodosian Code stands alone in early medieval sanctuary law in that it specifically allowed a sanctuary seeker to be mutilated and it explicitly linked the denial of sanctuary with the necessity of exemplary punishments. Otherwise, in its broad contours the *Lex Visigothorum*, like the *Edictum Theodorici*, followed the Theodosian Code.

Early Frankish legal texts also echoed the basic sanctuary rules laid down in the Theodosian Code regarding slaves who fled from their masters. Thus, "slaves deserting their lord and having fled to a church," should, after they were "excused, be returned immediately."[36] The co-called *Capitularia Merowingica* of Clothar, which was later included in Carolingian recensions of the *Lex Salica*, followed the basic pattern but delineated sanctuary protections for criminals as well as slaves. Just prior to stating the general rule concerning fugitive slaves, Clothar's decree said: "No one should presume to extract a thief or any other guilty one from the atrium (porch) of a church."[37] If a church did not have an atrium, then an *arpennis* of land surrounding the church should be protected ground.[38] In addition, the Frankish legislation prohibited the use of fraud or force in inducing a fugitive to come out. Like the Theodosian legislation, Frankish law presumed that the master's oath and the slave's return would be overseen by a churchman.

Other legal texts produced in the orbit of Frankish hegemony offer a similar legislative picture. For example, in the *Leges Alamannorum*, a master was to show "fear of God, and pay honor to the church" by seeking the "priest of the church" before making any attempt to recover his fugitive slave from the church by force.[39] After the master spoke with the priest, the Alamannic law directed that he should "ask that the slave be returned to him." But only if the master gave "a legitimate surety that the slave's wrong will be laid to rest"[40] could "the presbyter return the slave to his master in peace."[41]

The church's canons regarding fugitive slaves were also largely in agreement with the rules set out in the Theodosian tradition. The First Council of Orléans proclaimed:

> If a slave who has fled to a church for any wrong whatsoever has received a promise [of impunity] from his master regarding the matter, it is determined that he return immediately to the service of the lord. . . . If a slave [receiving such a promise] is unwilling to go out of the church to his lord, let him be seized.[42]

That rule likewise accorded with the position that Pope Gelasius (492–96) had taken in a case involving a slave who had taken refuge in a church. Because the slave proved "unwilling to go out of the church" despite an oath guaranteeing impunity to the slave, Gelasius directed that the slave "return quickly to his lord." If the slave still "pertinaciously" refused to be restored to his master, Gelasius allowed him to "be returned against his will."[43] The strong degree of accord shown by ecclesiastical councils, papal letters, and royal legislative sources demonstrates the direct and lasting impact of Roman law on the sanctuary legislation of the early medieval world. That portions of the Gelasian epistle found their way into Gratian's *Decretum* in the twelfth century further cemented the close relationship between Roman and canon sanctuary law in the later Middle Ages.[44]

In sum, the sanctuary rules that appear in the early medieval *Leges* bear the heavy imprint of the rules governing sanctuary in the Theodosian Code. Because the appearance of written law in early medieval Europe generally depended on Roman models, that should come as no surprise. But beyond the form that sanctuary rules took in the *Leges*, the transmission of Roman legal texts does not fully account for widespread reception of sanctuary within early medieval social and religious practices.

INTERCESSION AND SANCTUARY

The Roman rules that appear in early medieval legislation show not only the influence of imperial Roman law but also the pervasiveness of the intercessory ideal of the church inherited from late antique cultural forms. The return of slaves who received promises of impunity, the ejection of armed fugitives, and the requirement that churchmen satisfy the debts of fugitive debtors who were unwilling to exit the church all exemplified this ideal. At the same time, the rules placed bishops, archdeacons, and even ordinary churchmen between the sanctuary seeker and his pursuers, envisioning that churchmen were to arrange repayment of the fugitive's debts, oversee the master's oath of impunity, insure the subsequent return of the slave, and permit the removal of an armed fugitive from the church. Although intercession had been an important facet of late antique aristocratic ideals of patronage, Augustine's defense of intercession and sanctuary gave the practice a Christian theological aspect, which sub-Roman legislative traditions tended to stress even while extending sanctuary to others besides fugitive slaves or debtors.

The *Lex Visigothorum* contained a typical provision showing the role churchmen were expected to play in sanctuary cases. "Let no one presume to touch those who have fled to a church or the doors of a church," began the royal law, "but let the pursuer seek out the presbyter or deacon in order to receive recompense."[45] It then fell to the "representative of the church [to] intervene before the pursuer," urging him to "grant forbearance and . . . indulgence" to the wrongdoer.[46] Over the following centuries, church canons echoed these pronouncements. Canon 39 of the Council of Mainz (813), which was included in many later canonical collections, including Gratian's *Decretum*, exhorted churchmen "to strive to obtain the life, members and peace" of wrongdoers who fled to a church.[47]

Narrative sources offer a window into the relationship between priestly intercession and sanctuary laws that the *Leges* do not. The most fruitful narrative source for sanctuary in the early medieval period is *Libri Historiarum X* (hereafter, *Ten Books*) of Gregory of Tours. Though he was preoccupied by the ethical order of the world and questions of retribution, mercy, punishment, and justice, Gregory was not concerned to engage in a direct discussion or explication of Frankish or canonical legislative texts. He never presented legislative texts as instruments for maintaining the world's ethical order. Divine grace was to perform this task. Consequently, while we do not find in Gregory's writings direct reference to the Roman or Frankish sanctuary laws, the ethical world presupposed in those sanctuary laws is recognizable in Gregory's accounts.[48]

Gregory's *Ten Books*, for instance, suggests that he knew something about how sanctuary claims were supposed to be resolved, particularly when they presented opportunities for ecclesiastical intercession. In the fifth book, Gregory reported that a male and a female slave fled together to a church in order to be joined in marriage without the permission of their lord, a man named Rauching.[49] Shortly afterward, Rauching arrived at the church objecting to the marriage and seeking the return of his slaves. At the church, Rauching was confronted by an unnamed priest who boldly told him:

> You know the respect due to the Church. . . . You will not be able to receive your slaves back unless you give faith regarding the permanence of their union; likewise, you must promise in return [for getting them back] that they shall remain free from all punishment.[50]

Rauching considered this for some time, then "placed his hand upon the altar and swore an oath" that the two slaves would never be separated.[51] Though Gregory did not state so, the priest's requirement that Rauching swear an oath that the slaves would be "free from all punishment" accorded fully with the Roman, canonical, and Frankish legal texts already discussed.

In demanding that Rauching also respect the marriage of the slaves, however, surviving legal texts seem to indicate the priest exceeded his authority. A rule in the *pactus legis Salicae* allowed masters to prohibit marriages of their slaves.[52] Furthermore, church councils did contemplate that slaves might flee to a church in order to wed and deferred to the rights of masters. According to a council held at Orléans in 541:

> If slaves, under the hope of joining in marriage, flee to the protection of a church, believing that by this they will be able to be married, by no means grant them license and clerics shall not defend the marriage. For the marriage is polluted. On account of religious order, those who married without legitimacy, intermingling in unseemly union within a sacred place, are suspended from the communion of the church for a set time. Concerning this we decide that the slaves shall be returned separately to their parents or their own lord with a promise of excuse. Afterward, if liberty is conceded by their parents and lords, and if they are willing, they may be joined in proper union.[53]

The priest in Gregory's account, on the other hand, wrested from Rauching an explicit promise that the slaves' union would be honored.

Upon returning to his estate, Rauching had the newlywed slaves buried alive together. According to Gregory, the cruel lord then remarked, "I have not broken my oath since those two will not be separated for all eternity."[54] A short while later, the priest who had initially interceded on behalf of the unfortunate lovers "ran quickly to the place, and upbraided Rauching," finally coercing him into having the two dug up. "The boy was extracted alive, the girl, however, was found suffocated."[55]

To judge by canonical sources, the penalties for such conduct should have been severe. According to the Fifth Council held at Orléans (549):

> If a lord, unmindful of his oath [sworn in regard to the sanctuary seeker], is shown to have gone beyond that which he swore, so that [the slave who] was to receive forbearance is later proved to have suffered any punishment whatsoever for the wrong, that lord, who was unmindful of his oath, shall be suspended from the communion of everyone.[56]

In fact, this rule only repeated in slightly altered form a pronouncement made by the First Council of Orléans in 511, which had punished masters who violated such oaths by "separation not only from the communion of the church and all clerics, but from the company of Catholics."[57] In Gregory's account, none of these penalties was imposed upon Rauching, and Gregory did not even suggest that they should have been. He merely noted, "this was the sort of outrage Rauching delighted in,"[58] and employed the sanctuary violation to foreshadow Rauching's eventual demise by remarking, "His death was a fitting and well-deserved end to the life which he lived; but about this I will tell you later."[59] As elsewhere in Gregory's narrative, what mattered was immanent divine justice, not potentially applicable royal or ecclesiastical laws.

Gregory may not have cited legislation, but he still stressed the intercessory role of clerics. Another such case involved Gregory himself. In the later years of the sixth century a royal treasurer named Eberulf took refuge in the Church of St. Martin in Tours, where Gregory served as bishop. After Eberulf had apparently refused to become Queen Fredegund's paramour, the scorned queen accused him of murdering King Chilperic and making off with some portion of Chilperic's treasury. King Gunthram, Chilperic's brother, consequently swore to destroy Eberulf and his offspring "down to the ninth generation," causing Eberulf to take up permanent residence in the sacristy of the church.[60]

In Gregory's telling, Eberulf and his entourage of "young women and his man-servants used to come in through the sacristy entrance and stand gaping at the frescoes on the walls or pry about among the decorations on St. Martin's tomb, all of which was a desecration of religious feeling."[61] Ever protective of the blessed memory of St. Martin, Gregory was vexed by the disruptions caused by Eberulf. Then Gregory had a dream. "I saw myself," said Gregory as he later related his dream to Eberulf: "in this consecrated building, celebrating the sacred rite of Mass. . . . Suddenly I saw King Gunthram rush in exclaiming, 'Drive out this enemy of my family! Rip this man from the sacred altar of God!' "[62] In response, "I turned to you [Eberulf] and I said, 'Grab hold of the altar cloth, you miserable wretch.' " At the same time, "I spread my own hands wide and pressed my chest against that of the King," crying out:

> Do not eject this man from the sacred church, neither endanger your life, lest the excellent Saint Martin . . . pierce you. Do not destroy yourself by your own javelin, because if you do this, you will lose both this present life and eternal life.[63]

But in Gregory's dream, Eberulf was able only to hold the altar cloth feebly (*non viriliter*) and eventually relaxed his grip altogether. And thus, the dream ended.

After Gregory recounted his dream to Eberulf, the sanctuary seeker responded, "Your dream is true. What you saw accords exactly with what I intended to do." He explained, "I had decided that if the king ordered me dragged out of this place, I would with one hand grasp the altar cloth and with the other my unsheathed sword. First, I would have killed you and then I would have begun to kill as many clerics as I could find."[64]

In Gregory's account, Eberulf did nearly everything wrong while taking sanctuary in the church. From the outset, the disruptive gawking of his entourage in the heart of the St. Martin's church demonstrated Eberulf's own lack of respect for God's church and the town's patron saint. At no point was Eberulf portrayed as a grateful and humble recipient of divine protection. Moreover, Eberulf was not shown confessing his sins or submitting to penance. Eberulf relied on the protections of the sacred relics and altar cloth only as a coward's insurance, not out of piety.

Even without directly mentioning sanctuary laws, Gregory presented an account that is intelligible in light of extant Frankish legislation and resonated within the ethical world implied by sixth-century sanctuary legislation. In his dream, Gregory warned King Gunthram of the penalty for violently seizing Eberulf from the altar, but he invoked neither the death penalty prescribed by the imperial Roman law,[65] nor the spiritual death declared by several ecclesiastical councils.[66] Instead, Gregory made St. Martin himself an agent of divine protection. As for Gunthram's quarry, Gregory never invoked the legislation that disqualified armed fugitives from sanctuary. For the world in which Gregory lived, the rules of Roman law received into Frankish traditions may have confirmed an already-understood ethical order, but they were not the force that shaped that order.

An additional detail of Gregory's account is obscured in English translations. In Gregory's dream, King Gunthram exclaimed, "*evellite homicidam a sacro Dei altario*!"[67] (Rip this murderer from God's sacred altar!). Knowing scripture, Gregory was aware of the parallel between the words he put in Gunthram's mouth and the divine command recorded in Exodus: "*ab altari meo evelles eum ut moriatur*"[68] (Rip him from my altar that he may die). Because in the Old Testament passage the fugitive was taken out and slain, Gregory's successful defense of Eberulf thus highlights the sharp divide between the vengeful God of the Old Testament and the New Testament "age of Grace" embodied in the interceding bishop.

Some early medieval sanctuary legal texts even made sanctuary and intercession almost coextensive:

> If some unfortunate wretch[69] crosses paths with a bishop or presbyter or a deacon, either in a city street or in a field or any other place, we order that they be detained or abducted by no one, *because in priests the Church consists*.[70]

This rule, included at the end of an edict attributed to emperors Theodosius and Valentine, did not appear in the Theodosian Code, and its authenticity has long been doubted. The strange position of the rule, appended to an edict that was entirely concerned with protecting clerics from criminal accusations, allows room for doubts. Jacques Godefroy, a leading seventeenth-century historian and jurist, also found the Latin style of the text incongruous with imperial legislation and suggested, with some hesitation, that it had Gaulish ecclesiastical provenance.[71] The liberalizing tendency of the rule, moreover, accords more with the tenor of sanctuary protections articulated in Frankish church councils. Despite its questionable provenance, the edict possessed undoubted authority in the centuries following the dissolution of the Roman Empire in the west. It was included in an important manuscript tradition and enjoyed wide circulation.[72] The association of the priest's body with the church for purposes of granting fugitives sanctuary signaled the extent to which clerical intercession was the cornerstone of the sanctuary privilege in early medieval legal traditions.

By the ninth century, some Carolingian legislation suggests that there were limits on the extent to which churchmen could intervene on behalf of criminals. According to the Herstal capitulary issued by Charlemagne in 779, "Homicides or others who according to the laws ought to be put to death, if they have fled to a church, they are not to be excused, neither are they to be given food."[73] This rule, which harkened to the Visigothic restrictions on sanctuary for homicides, was more constrictive than earlier Frankish sanctuary legislation. A more elaborate early ninth-century rendering of the capitulary was designated by its nineteenth-century editor as the "*Forma Langobardica*" because it circulated in this form in several early and mid-ninth-century Italian manuscripts. There, it stated: "Concerning homicides and other malefactors who according to the laws or in order to keep the peace ought to be killed: no one shall permit them to enter his church to be excused; and if the fugitive has entered against the will of the pastor, then the pastor shall not give him any food, nor permit anyone else to give him food."[74] Although in the surviving sources it was rare for churchmen to block the entry of a homicide, neither version of the capitulary allowed laymen to prevent a fugitive homicide from entering a church or to remove him after the fact. Nor did the legislation assume that churchmen would forcibly remove him, rather than starve him.

Judging from other nearly contemporary Carolingian sanctuary legislation issued under Charlemagne, a homicide who took sanctuary was to be tried under a guarantee that he would not be executed or maimed for his misdeeds (*concedatur ei vita et omnia membra*). After making amends to the extent he was able (subject to judicial discretion), the criminal could be exiled (again subject to royal discretion).[75] The Herstal capitulary, by limiting the ability of clerics to feed fugitives, provided a marginal limit on the intercessory faculties of clerics. Hunger would eventually prompt the fugitive to submit to royal process and exile.

Sometimes such limits on intercession were welcomed by clerics who did not relish the confrontations and extra duties it entailed. When St. Cuthbert asked to be buried at remote Lindisfarne in England, we are told in his *Life*, he noted (with prescient awareness of his saintliness) that the presence of his body in the cathedral would induce an "incursion of fugitives and evildoers of every sort" seeking protection. "You would," he is reported to have said to the monks gathered at his deathbed, "often find it necessary to intercede with the powerful ones of the time, and also endure much labor on account of the presence of my body."[76] We might be justly suspicious of whether Cuthbert ever uttered these words, but the concern put in the dying saint's mouth suggests that the obligation to intercede on behalf of sanctuary seekers was not always eagerly embraced by clerics.

SANCTUARY LAW AND MEDIEVAL CHRISTIAN IDENTITY

"Jews, if criminals or debtors, who flee to a church and convert to Christianity shall be absolved from all debt and guilt."[77] So began an anonymous early medieval *summa* of Roman law, the so-called *Summa Perusina*, regarding the imperial edict of 392 forbidding sanctuary to Jews.[78] Imperial Roman law had specifically excluded Jews who "feign[ed] to wish joining themselves to Christian law."[79] This gloss, by indicating that sincerely converted Jews would be admitted to the sanctuary protections of the church, emphasized what was implied in the Roman legislation: Jews making actual conversions (*Christianus factus fuerit*) would receive sanctuary protection, just like other Christians.[80] The *Summa Perusina*'s articulation of the sanctuary privilege shows more than the manner in which Roman rules were received, interpreted, and expanded in the medieval world. It suggests an intimate link between sanctuary law and the contours of Christian identity. From the standpoint of Christian theology, the reason for denying sanctuary protections to Jews who made insincere conversions was plain. The sanctuary protection facilitated clerical intercession. The natural conclusion of that intercession would have been the sacrament of penance and continuing pastoral oversight. But the relationship between the suppliant fugitive and the church made sense only if the suppliant were willing to submit himself to the teachings and discipline of the church. A Jew willing to submit himself to this process was a Jew no longer, but rather a Christian. The sincere convert would be fully able to claim the protections of the new faith to which he now belonged.

Other strands of early medieval sanctuary law were even less accommodating to Jews. In particular, rules regarding owners' rights over fugitive slaves tended to stress the religious identity of the owner. According to the ecclesiastical council held at Orléans in 538, "Christian slaves held in the service of Jews" could not be punished for any offense "which had been excused by the church or for which [the Christian slave's] guilt had been remitted."[81] Any Christian slave punished by a Jewish master contrary to this ruling was granted permission to flee to a church. In departure from standard sanctuary rules, priests in such cases were not required to return the slave to the Jewish master, and the Jewish master was to receive nothing, "save a price determined by the slave himself."[82] A chain of sixth-century canonical pronouncements further encouraged churchmen to facilitate the redemption of Christian slaves who fled from Jewish masters.[83] The Theodosian Code also had favored the liberation of Christian slaves from Jewish masters, but late antique Roman law had not tied the matter directly to sanctuary protection. Early canonical sources, on the other hand, did so expressly: "If Christian slaves flee to a church, *or even to any Christian*, and hold themselves out to be redeemed, unwilling to serve Jews," declared a sixth-century Arlean council, "let them be liberated from Jewish dominion and [redeemed] to the faithful" with the payment of a just price.[84]

In its sixth-century pronouncements, canon law showed significantly less regard for the proprietary rights of Jewish slave owners than was generally shown to slave owners in early medieval legislation.[85] Under the sanctuary rules received from Rome and adopted by various ecclesiastical councils, fugitive slaves were to be returned to the master, provided only that the master swear an oath to withhold physical punishments from the slave for the flight. The sanctuary rules articulated at Arles and Orléans, by contrast, not only carved out a special subset of rules governing the master–slave relation, but also set out a clear dividing line between the slave laws governing members of the body of Christ and those pertaining to Jews. These latter rules presented an open invitation for Christians to flee their Jewish masters, and made sanctuary the mechanism for liberation.

Burchard of Worms amalgamated some of these canons in his late eleventh-century *Decretum*:

> Concerning *pagani* enslaved to Jews, if they have fled to church, and they seek baptism, [or if] even they have fled to any Christian wherever: . . . let them, for a just price, be liberated from [the Jewish master's] dominion.[86]

Drawn from canon 30 of the IV Council of Arles, Burchard's presentation of the rule differed from the original text in two respects. It extended the sanctuary protection to "*pagani*," whereas the ancient canon had spoken only of Christians, and it related the flight to sanctuary to baptism. Of course, baptism would have been an essential condition for conversion to Christianity, and membership in the body of Christ was the source of the remission of sins that grounded ancient sanctuary protections. Thus, even though his presentation of the sanctuary canon differed from the original Arlean legislation, Burchard preserved two of the primary features of earlier ecclesiastical sanctuary law—its close link to the remission of the fugitive's sins and its aspect as an element of Christian legal personality.

Using sanctuary law as a marker of Christian identity was not limited to ecclesiastical sources. Charlemagne, for instance, also knew how to portray sanctuary laws as emblems of a lawful, Christian people. Charlemagne's campaigns against Saxony provide an illuminating example. The Frankish conquest of the Saxons at the end of the eighth century was the culmination of long years of conflict and violence. Gregory of Tours had recounted catastrophic losses to the Saxons in battles fought around 555.[87] Two centuries later, Charlemagne was again leading Frankish military expeditions against the Saxons.[88] In surviving monastic and Frankish royal sources, the Saxons are almost always portrayed as ungodly heathens, prone to depravity and duplicity. When the Franks had episodic success in converting Saxons to Christianity, usually on the heels of pitched battles, Carolingian propaganda stressed the fickleness of Saxon allegiance. In 777, according to Charlemagne's royal annalist, "many Saxons were baptized and according to their custom pledged to the king their whole freedom and property if they should change their minds again in that detestable manner of theirs and not keep the Christian faith and their fealty to Lord King Charles."[89] A half century later, the Carolingians had established political dominance over the Saxons. In the words of Carolingian historian Nithard, "Emperor Charles, deservedly called the Great by all peoples, converted the Saxons by much effort, as is known to everyone in Europe. He won them over from the vain adoration of idols to the true Christian religion of God."[90] It was not only Saxon idolatry that troubled the Franks. The Saxons, at least in the eyes of Carolingians chroniclers, had also shown a penchant for plundering and burning Frankish churches.[91] Violence against and within Christian churches seems to have been among the worst offenses attributed to the Saxons, though there were rumors of all kinds of depraved pagan practices.

In this light, the sanctuary laws Charlemagne gave to the Saxon region in

785 were more than a generic element of ecclesiastical law and more than a penal policy to aid in the administration of government in newly conquered Saxon lands. Sanctuary laws were a hallmark of a newly Christianized people as the opening chapters of Charlemagne's *Capitulatio de partibus Saxoniae*, issued after his successful campaign against the pagan Saxon leader Widukind, plainly show:

> 1. First . . . it is pleasing to all that churches now constructed in Saxony and consecrated to God have no less honor than the vain idols have had, but have better and more excellent honor.
> 2. If any guilty person make flight to a church, let no one presume to expel him violently from the church, but let him have peace until he can be presented at court. And on account of the honor of God and the Saints and reverence for the Church concede to him his life and all his members. However, he shall emend the wrong insofar as he is able and as he is judged. And then he shall be led to the presence of the Lord King so that the king can send him wherever his clemency pleases.
> 3. If anyone violently enter a church and while in it carry any [person or thing] away by force or fraud, or burn the church with fire, let him be put to death.[92]

The legislation that followed prohibited ritual cannibalism,[93] pagan cremation rites,[94] and "showing contempt for baptism and wishing to remain pagan."[95] Each of these offenses, like the violent invasion of a church, was to be punished with death. The brutal measures taken in subjugating the Saxon peoples elicited some disapproval from Charlemagne's own court. Alcuin, at least, thought the ham-fisted military and legislative approach to winning the hearts and souls of the Saxons was counterproductive.[96] But the place of sanctuary in Charlemagne's legislative conquest of the Saxons warrants attention here.

Charlemagne's Saxon sanctuary laws stand in the legislative tradition of the apocryphal "Ten Laws" attributed to Emperor Constantine,[97] which circulated widely in many manuscripts during the Carolingian era. The tradition that Constantine had issued sanctuary laws at the time of his conversion to Christianity explicitly linked pious sovereignty to grants of sanctuary protections. Charlemagne may be understood as following this Roman example as he expanded his own empire. On the other hand, Charlemagne's Saxon capitularies do not appear to be unqualified expressions of kingly benevolence. They were, even in their own time, harsh and somewhat unusual for their enthusiastic reliance on the death penalty, which domestic Carolingian sanctuary legislation did not ordinarily carry.

While sanctuary laws were an important symbol of Carolingian rule and imperial expansion, there was plenty of disagreement over their application to particular wrongdoers. Chapter 3 described the heated controversy at Charlemagne's royal court around 801/02 as to whether a sanctuary seeker who had not yet completed his penance merited the protections of the church.[98] What we know of the case comes from five surviving letters of Alcuin, which show that an undetermined amount of additional material relevant to this dispute is now missing.[99] Interestingly, the five letters appear never to have circulated together in the Middle Ages. Grouped together only through Dümmler's labors on behalf of the *Monumenta Germaniae Historica*, the letters portray a dispute concerning sanctuary law between Alcuin, the abbot of St. Martin of Tours, and Theodulf, the Bishop of Orléans.[100] In that dispute over whether a cleric who had been tried and convicted for some unnamed act could claim sanctuary after escaping from the custody of royal officials, Theodulf's position was that the criminous clerk should not have been allowed to enter St. Martin's basilica and should not have received the intercession of clerics there. Charlemagne also thought that since the clerk had been judged and sentenced by an imperial *missus* he should be returned from the church and placed in imperial custody.[101] In the documents that survive, neither Theodulf nor Charlemagne questioned the propriety of sanctuary for criminals who had not yet been judged and sentenced. What is clear is that the dispute was more about the nature of penance and its legal effects than about the legitimacy of sanctuary law.[102] Alcuin, echoing Augustine, thought that the protections of the church should be open to all who fled there, regardless of whether they were under judicial sentence or had not yet completed penance.

Charlemagne's Herstal capitulary of 779 had specifically stated that homicides were not to be admitted to a church and not to be excused of their crime on that account.[103] That legislation, however, left it to priests to prevent such entry, and, in the event the homicide gained the church anyway, only allowed that the fugitive should be denied food, not forcibly removed. Charlemagne's legislation for the Saxon regions, issued around the same time as his Herstal capitulary, may well have stated what he expected to happen in any case of sanctuary; that is, the fugitive was to be protected in "his life and members," but he was also to be presented to the king's agent for trial. Upon conviction, the fugitive was to be sent "where the clemency of the [lord king] pleased."[104] It is difficult to know whether these procedures were applied with any regularity, but we will later see that the connection between sanctuary and exile would be used to great effect by Angevin kings in England after the Conquest.

The sanctuary affair at Tours in 801–802 probably provoked the legislation issued by Charlemagne in 803, which stated in no uncertain terms that sanctuary seekers should be protected from forcible removal.[105] Nevertheless, once "they have confessed what they did" (here perhaps a nod to Alcuin's insistence that sanctuary seekers be allowed access to the discipline of the church), the fugitives were to be led "by the hands of good men to a public discussion" of the matter.[106] There is no mention of exile, but Rob Meens has suggested that, because the legislation was a direct response to the controversy at Tours and involved sanctuary-seeking clerics, the omission of exile may reflect the fact that a cleric would be turned over to ecclesiastical discipline.[107] In any event, the capitulary made clear that accused criminals who escaped from judgment could not be harbored by a secular lord, abbot, or bishop, even if he held a royal immunity.[108] Neither churches nor jurisdictional immunities, Charlemagne's policy asserted, could trump royal justice.

Although it is difficult to gauge whether the reforms to Frankish sanctuary law were effective, they demonstrated that it was important to the Frankish court that the newly conquered Saxons possess a body of laws that required respect for Christian churches and the fugitives within them. If legislation was a primary means by which early medieval kings communicated their *imperium,* then sanctuary laws were an important vehicle for communicating Christian *imperium*. The legislation of 803 signaled the limits of Charlemagne's tolerance when sanctuary protections and intercession diminished the status of judicial sentences passed by his *missi*, but sanctuary protections remained a crucial feature of Carolingian criminal law and an important plank in the empire's Christian legislative platform in conquered lands.

CONCLUSION

The transmission of Theodosian sanctuary rules into early medieval legislation was most direct in regard to fugitive slaves. In most cases, the provisions of the code were simply restated in abridged form. Episcopal intercession also continued to be an integral part of the sanctuary practice in early medieval Europe. Although some patristic and early canon law sources were ambiguous as to whether sanctuary justified intercession or vice versa, early medieval sanctuary laws presented sanctuary as clearly distinct from intercessory practices. Intercession and sanctuary remained intertwined, but sanctuary was not dependent upon intercession for its justification. Indeed, sanctuary was so deeply ingrained in early medieval legal traditions that it served as an important element in the legislative and military campaigns of the Carolingians and was an increasingly important aspect of pious kingship generally.

5

Sanctuary, Blood Feud, and the Strength of Anglo-Saxon Government

Thus far, Frankish sources have anchored the story of sanctuary's transmission and adoption in the early Middle Ages and demonstrated how sanctuary was insinuated into the construction of Christian identity and Frankish Christian kingship. This dependence on Frankish sources stems both from Carolingian hegemony and the fact that many of the sources for early medieval law were filtered through Frankish *scriptoria*. In the tenth and eleventh centuries, however, our source base moves westward where Anglo-Saxon legislation provides us with rich material for understanding the interplay between sanctuary, royal law, and feuding practices.

Anglo-Saxon sources, like Carolingian, provide evidence that kings were trying to bring sanctuary to heel through written legislation in the ninth century and thereafter. In the Anglo-Saxon case, royal authority tried to discipline sanctuary by integrating it withinin the laws and norms that governed the blood feud. The results were mixed. Sanctuary laws were not fully assimilated into processes of royal penal law, and sanctuary practices remained governed by an amalgamation of ecclesiastical sensibilities, feuding norms, and royal authority.

Medieval legislation made sanctuary's relation to the blood feud explicit. Yet, the corpus of sanctuary law that early medieval Europe inherited from Rome said nothing about the conduct of the feud.[1] Indeed, the relation between sanctuary and feuding practices presented a difficulty for legislators who looked to the Theodosian Code as a model. A vivid example of this difficulty appeared in the *Leges Burgundionum*, a collection of laws promulgated nominally by King Gundobad in the early sixth century, almost contemporaneously with the ecclesiastical council convened by Clovis at Arles in 511. Like the Frankish council, the Burgundian laws explicitly embraced the Roman laws regarding sanctuary found in the Theodosian Code.[2] Yet, the legal response prescribed by the Theodosian Code when homicides took refuge in a church was, from the Burgundian legislator's perspective, clearly insufficient. As the Burgundian laws explained:

> Since evidently the Roman Law has established nothing concerning the price of killings, our Lord [Sigismund?] has established that if a freeman has been slain by a freeman, and the homicide has fled to a church, he himself, who admits to the homicide, shall, with half of his goods, be placed in servitude to the heirs of the slain; the remaining half of the homicide's possessions shall be relinquished to the heirs of the slain.
>
> If, indeed, anyone's slave has been killed by a freeman, and the homicide runs to the church, it is considered that the price paid to the slave's lord in recompense will be according to the quality of the slave: that is, for a manager, a fine of one hundred shillings will be incurred; for a minister, sixty shillings; for a ploughman or swineherd, thirty shillings; for a goldsmith, one hundred; for an iron smith, fifty; for a carpenter, forty shillings.[3]

The Burgundian legislator's initial expression of perplexity is almost amusing: How could the great Roman legislator Theodosius have forgotten to set out the appropriate tariffs for homicide? One answer lay in the deep differences between early medieval feuding customs and the criminal law of Rome. The feud, along with the composition payments that would preclude or conclude it, had no place in the formal pronouncements of Roman penal law. In early medieval legal sources, on the other hand, almost all wrongdoing and punishment was understood through the lens of blood-feuding and composition payments, so that one can claim that early medieval social relations "pulsated to the rhythm of feud."[4] Unlike late imperial Roman legislation, in which sanctuary had emerged as an expression of Christian theological concerns and imperial governance, early medieval sanctuary legislation blended with blood-feuding and settlement practices and shifted away from its early Romano-Christian foundations.

Early medieval feuding practices typically restricted the places where the feud could be lawfully pursued. Among a number of locations in which violence was restricted, courts and royal halls were frequently mentioned as places where even lawful feuds should be suspended. Churches fit easily into this register. According to a Frisian law:

> A feuding man shall have peace in the church, in his home, going to church, returning home from church, going to court, and returning home from court. [The one] who has breached this peace and has killed a man, shall compound nine times thirty shillings.[5]

In declaring the church building and the road to and from it out of bounds for prosecuting the feud, the Frisian legislation shows that sanctuary law had come to occupy an intelligible position within a set of feuding practices. Its simultaneous invocation of church, home, and court is highly significant because it placed sanctuary within an early medieval legislative register that included spaces traditionally considered off limits for violence.[6]

Several early medieval laws prohibited prosecuting the blood feud at a man's homestead or at a public meeting place and prohibited violence at law courts. These laws set the parameters outside which the blood feud ceased to be an honorable pursuit and became simple brigandage and homicide. When churches were also honored as places where the pursuit of otherwise lawful violence was restrained, as in the Frisian law, the sanctuary protections bestowed by churches signaled an additional limitation on the blood feud.

Sanctuary law in ninth-century Anglo-Saxon legislation was also closely tied to the feud. King Alfred's laws, for example, clearly supposed that sanctuary claims belonged within the context of the blood feud:

> If anyone, for any wrong, seeks any minster house which owes the king's [food] rent, or any other free household entitled to immunity, he shall be guarded for the first three nights, unless he wishes to be reconciled [with his foe].[7]

Even the duration of the sanctuary protection was conditioned by the fugitive wrongdoer himself. If "he wished to be reconciled," he could attempt to come to terms with his foes. In discussing this possibility, the Anglo-Saxon text employed the verb "*thingian*" (twelfth-century Latin translations rendered the term as "*reconciliari*," to be reconciled). *Thingian* carries a strong sense of "deliberation and judgment," and would have likely denoted some form of composition payment, understood, perhaps, as a mutual exchange of gifts uniting the foes in friendship. The pursuers would give over their claims to the fugitive's life and goods, and in return, the fugitive would both confirm his own wrong by honoring the claims of his foe, and attempt to make his deed right by restoring—to the extent he was able—something of value to those he wronged.

Of course, because violating sanctuary protections would be an offense against both the king and the church, each assumed a protective stance toward the fugitive:

> If anyone assaults the fugitive and slays, binds, or wounds him, he shall make each right with the community, by *wer* and by *wite*, and he shall give one hundred twenty shillings for the church's peace, neither shall he have the forfeit property [of the fugitive].[8]

This passage from Alfred's laws referred only to protections bestowed by churches under the king's direct patronage. But Alfred's laws spoke of another protection extended to any church that had been "consecrated by a bishop."[9] This latter sanctuary protection was given a longer duration than those pertaining to churches under the king's patronage, but the blood feud remained its focal point.

> Further, we settle on each church that has been hallowed by a bishop this peace: if any feuding party runs or rides to it, for seven nights he shall not be taken out [of the church]. And whoever tries to drag him out shall be guilty of breaching the king's protection (*mund*) as well as the church's peace (*frið*), and more if he drags out more than one fugitive; provided the fugitive can live despite his hunger, or does not come out to fight for himself.[10]

This law also left considerable room for the parties to continue their fight if they wished. It might have even encouraged that outcome since the church's elder was cautioned not to "provide the fugitive any food."[11] Nothing in the legislative text suggests that a fugitive's willingness to fight was improper, merely that it was one permissible way to end the standoff between the sanctuary seeker and his pursuers.

If the sanctuary seeker might be unwilling to fight, another resolution was possible. "If he is willing to give his weapons to his foes, they may hold him 30 nights, and shall bid his kin and household [to come]."[12] This procedure invokes a traditional method for resolving the feud through settlement negotiations. In early medieval Frankish and Anglo-Saxon royal chronicles, hostage-taking was a regular means for warring kings to provide surety during peace negotiations,[13] and Alfred's legislation suggests that comparable hostage-taking practices were employed to resolve feuds. By turning himself over to his foes, the fugitive made himself a surety and (in principle) assured his own safety while his kin arranged ransom. Once the agreed-upon ransom was paid, the feud could (again, in principle) be resolved.

In fact, the resolution procedures suggested by Alfred's sanctuary legislation mirror exactly the ordinary blood-feuding rules he gave elsewhere in the same code. "If a man knows his foe is home-sitting," explained Alfred's laws on the blood feud, "he may not fight him until he bids him to make right."[14] Further: "If one has the might to beset his foe by surrounding his home, he may hold him within for seven nights, but not fight him if he wills to remain inside." Instead, "if after seven nights [the one besieged] is willing to hand over his weapons he may be kept unscathed for thirty nights and bid his kin and his friends [to come]."[15] The ransom and composition scenarios described above simply replicated those Alfred had already given in his laws regarding sanctuary.

Sanctuary was in no way a direct assault on the right of feud. To the contrary, while sanctuary laws provided some respite from armed conflict within the feud, they directed the parties to the same forms of resolution that Anglo-Saxon law held out to feuding parties. Legislation issued under Edmund and Edgar maintained the close connection between sanctuary and feud.[16] In this light, sanctuary law was aimed less at restraining violence per se and more at providing a space where warring parties might honorably come together in peace and concord.

Anglo-Saxon poetry offers interesting evidence in these matters. The narrator of *The Wife's Lament* seems to have taken refuge at the behest of her husband, who was apparently embroiled in some feud and unable to protect her. As a result, she sought shelter in an underground dwelling carved out of an oak grove,[17] perhaps the type of pagan sacred place that was the target of clerical prohibitions in Anglo-Saxon England. Archbishop Wulfstan had vigorously denounced "the superstitions practiced with many kinds of sorcery at pagan sanctuaries, elder trees, various other trees, and stones,"[18] and early eleventh-century private collection of canons from Northumbria forbade "heathen rituals" at any "sanctuary around a stone, tree, or spring."[19] Although it is difficult to draw firm conclusions from such slender evidence, it suggests another way in which sanctuary law may found resonance in Anglo-Saxon feuding practices.

Early medieval canon law collections from the European continent also demonstrate the relationship between feuding and sanctuary. Burchard harkened to the blood-feud traditions that inflected the sanctuary rules of the *Leges* in his *Decretum*:

> Similarly it is decreed in the Mâcon Synod that those who flee from their enemies, either into a church, or the atrium of a church, or the house of a bishop, or in a regular cloister house shall not be extracted unless first they receive an oath from their pursuers that they shall be secure from death, debilitation and all kinds of punishments; . . . Thus, those who have been guilty of crimes may come to agreement [with their pursuer] concerning a satisfaction. But if the one who swore the sacred oath is afterward convicted of having violated his oath, the perjurer shall be deprived of communion until he makes satisfaction.[20]

This canon is not actually from the Council of Mâcon. As Timbal remarks, Burchard's canon "would appear contrived from many pieces."[21] Unlike the Augustinian formulation of sanctuary, which stressed penance and reconciliation, the canon is intelligible within the context of feuding practices. Burchard rendered sanctuary as a protection for feuding "enemies," a role explicitly given to sanctuary in Anglo-Saxon sanctuary legislation as well as in early medieval Frankish legal traditions.[22]

At the same time, some strands of royal sanctuary legislation continued to present sanctuary as an aspect of penitential discipline. A provision of Alfred's legislation appears to have contemplated sanctuary outside the immediate context of the feud when it stated: "Further, if any man seek a church for any wrong that is not yet in the open, and there confesses in God's name, it shall be half forgiven."[23] Rather than a feud, this law supposed a wrong that had not yet come to light and a wrongdoer not in immediate danger from vengeful pursuers. It concerned, perhaps, a pre-feud moment in time and contemplated a sinner who sought to make right with God (and to receive a lesser punishment). The fugitive foe supposed in *Alf* 2 and 5 either fought or exited the church to sue for peace through the traditional forms of negotiation. But in place of the language of feud and settlement, Alfred's law here invoked the image of a contrite man who sought the church in order to repent and confess in God's name.

Sanctuary provisions specifically aimed at those who would admit to secret wrongs were not original to Anglo-Saxon legislation. Charlemagne's early Saxon legislation had a similar provision:

> If indeed for any of these [aforementioned] mortal crimes, secretly committed, anyone spontaneously flees to a priest and by giving confession wishes to perform penance, he shall be excused from death by the testimony of the priest.[24]

So while sanctuary took a new place in the practices of feuding, it retained its significance for penitent wrongdoers willing to place themselves under the pastoral discipline of the church. Such concerns can be seen in other continental legislation. The eighth-century legislation of the Bavarian Duke Odilo stated that "if any guilty person makes flight to a church, let no one dare drag him away by force after he has entered the door of the church." Then it explained the sanctuary protection in terms Alcuin or Augustine might have employed:

> No guilt is so grave that life will not be conceded on account of fear of God and reverence for the saints, since the Lord said, 'Who forgives, it shall be forgiven him; who forgives not, neither will it be forgiven him.'[25]

The concerns for priestly intercession and penance so central in early patristic writings on sanctuary law survived. Just as Alfred's sanctuary laws envisioned resolution of disputes through traditional forms of settlement, other articulations of sanctuary law relied upon the church's penitential practice.[26]

SANCTUARY LAW AND A STRONG ANGLO-SAXON STATE?

A historiographical tradition that antedated Frederick Maitland, but one solidly endorsed by him, held that Anglo-Saxon England was characterized by a politically fractured sovereign, unwilling and unable to intervene meaningfully in order to administer the realm. Three features of Anglo-Saxon law led scholars to this conclusion. First, it was widely thought that Anglo-Saxon kings had been overly willing to grant jurisdictional franchises, giving "well-endowed immunists" insulation from royal justice.[27] Second, historians looking backward from the celebrated criminal-law reforms attributed to the Angevins in England tended to assume that pre-Conquest England lacked the structures of community suretyship (like frankpledge) and public accusatorial procedures that marked the common law crown pleas in the twelfth and thirteenth centuries. Finally, the systems of composition for crime and the ever-lurking possibilities for private settlement that thread through nearly all of the *Leges* of the early medieval continent and England have been, for modern historians, a sure sign of an archaic and savage legal culture. Maitland was always on the lookout for signs of "true punishments," which he understood to be imposed by the sovereign on the wrongdoer in a manner announced through generally applicable legislation.[28] These marked, for Maitland and a generation of later historians, a certain improvement over the days of chaotic feud and episodic justice they thought epitomized Anglo-Saxon England. He rarely found them.

The orthodoxy regarding the Anglo-Saxon state has received its most sustained challenge from Patrick Wormald, who, building on the work of James Campbell, has argued that scholars have seriously "underestimated the power and aggression of the Old English State."[29] In this view, Anglo-Saxon kings, beginning with Alfred, exercised royal control over crime through law to a degree unmatched anywhere on the continent in the early Middle Ages. By Wormald's lights, even a comparison with England's Anglo-Norman successors reflects positively on the law enforcement capacity of the pre-Conquest English state.[30] Wormald argued that the key characterizations of Anglo-Saxon law and governance were mistaken. Anglo-Saxon kings were not as promiscuous or indiscrete in their grants of jurisdiction as it might have appeared looking back from the thirteenth century. Julius Goebel and Naomi Hurnard had already shown that Anglo-Saxon kings held to themselves jurisdiction over the most serious crimes. What they granted were the profits from doing justice in the lesser cases, not unfettered jurisdictional privileges.[31]

Wormald sharpened this evidence and turned it toward a powerful argument for the capacity of the Old English state to enforce royal law. Wormald also showed that even before the conquest, English law imposed forms of suretyship and local, collective responsibility for predatory acts. Legislation issued by Æthelred and replicated by Cnut made lords responsible for the acts of their men, and other Anglo-Saxon legislation ordered thegns to arrest and accuse those known to have committed wrongs.[32] Practices much like the celebrated Anglo-Norman frankpledge also appear in legislation issued by Cnut.[33] Alfred had already done something like it for the whole West Saxon realm.[34] Finally, although Maitland saw "pecuniary mulcts" doing most of the work of punishment in Anglo-Saxon England, Wormald has shown that Anglo-Saxon kings were not at all reluctant to impose (or at least call for the imposition of) repressive sanctions for wrongdoing. By Wormald's count, nearly four in five of the surviving Anglo-Saxon lawsuits involved events that fit within conventional understandings of crime.[35] And if Anglo-Saxon law was willing to compensate the kin of a murder victim, kings still imposed penalties that accrued to the royal coffers as well.[36] Moreover, archeological exploration has uncovered execution cemeteries, suggesting Anglo-Saxon kings knew how to routinize executions, at least in some circumstances.[37] Later Anglo-Saxon legislation also began a noticeable trend of attempting to isolate individual offenders from the support of their kin and lord in order bring them into a direct and unpleasant relationship with the king.[38]

Wormald's most sustained effort at rehabilitating the repressive capabilities of Anglo-Saxon kings was his 1999 tour de force *The Making of English Law*, in which he analyzed the skill of Old English kings and their ecclesiastical advisers (above all, Wulfstan) at nation building through written law in an era when the capacities of medieval monarchs is thought to be feeble at best. That book marked an intensification of Wormald's views on the place of written legislation in Anglo-Saxon governance. In his earlier work, Wormald had characterized Anglo-Saxon written law as an ideological expression of kingship but claimed that orality and customary law lay at the heart of pre-Conquest law. By the time he published *The Making of English Law*, Wormald saw Anglo-Saxon legislation as the result of a carefully crafted attempt to impose law and order from a centralized administrative position, and he placed written law much closer to the heart of Anglo-Saxon governance. The result was a deepened conviction that Old England was the strongest and most competent early medieval state.

Even skeptics acknowledge a fair amount of persuasive force in the case Wormald made, and recognize that late Anglo-Saxon kings possessed a fairly well developed ideology of royal justice. Paul Hyams objects, however, on the grounds that there is not enough evidence to show whether Anglo-Saxon kings successfully imposed the ideologies they successfully articulated. Anglo-Saxon thegns, for instance, appear not to have always jumped to royal commands, so we might rightly wonder how much slippage there was in the command and control apparatus of Anglo-Saxon kings when it came to realizing royal will in localities.[39] Hyams also forcefully argued that it is not always possible to tell what is precisely "public" about the exercise of royal jurisdiction. In the first place, he queries whether there was an appreciable difference between the "royal coercive authority" and other forms of "private competition" among landed lords.[40] Wormald would not necessarily have disagreed: "That the justice of the [Anglo-Saxon] state was the most powerful force in play is not to deny that it might be as greedy, cruel and inept as the justice of any lord."[41] It is true, as Hyams points out, that it was not always possible for Anglo-Saxon kings (nor Anglo-Norman, nor Angevin) to bring the strongest and most well armed men in the kingdom within the reach of royal justice, but this is not to deny that Anglo-Saxon kings had a fairly capacious government and that written law was one of the elements of its strength.[42] The argument concerning the strength of the Anglo-Saxon state is really over degrees. It was significantly more capable of exercising its jurisdiction than its Ottonian and Capetian contemporaries.

It is not necessary to ask here whether Wormald or his critics have the better of the argument, but it should be asked what sanctuary has to do with all this. If, as the received wisdom would have it, sanctuary laws were an antidote to feeble governance, does the existence of a relatively strong Anglo-Saxon state mean that sanctuary was less necessary than in regions of tumult and rapine? But then, how should one account for the fairly widespread recognition and endorsement of sanctuary in Anglo-Saxon law? If Anglo-Saxon kings were ahead of the game in exercising repressive jurisdiction over criminality, why did they endorse a practice that sometimes interrupted the course of royal justice?

One answer is that sanctuary legislation was not a concession of weakness but an emblem of strength.[43] That is, there is no necessary contradiction between claiming that Anglo-Saxon kings were comparatively strong and demonstrating that they recognized sanctuary rights. As Charlemagne already knew, sanctuary laws could be an important element of Christian sovereignty and a platform for imperial expansion. The Anglo-Saxon laws show that grants of sanctuary were an important element of lordship generally and that the sanctuary offered by churches was often synchronized to the sorts of protections lords could offer their men. Thus, sanctuary fit within Anglo-Saxon law because it resonated with what happened when men were pursued for their wrongs by their own enemies or by the king's men. The question, then, for sanctuary is similar to the questions scholars have asked about the blood feud: How did Anglo-Saxon law accommodate it? It did so for both the feud and sanctuary by defining the practices in terms of legal processes. Just as Hyams demonstrated that the blood feud was increasingly (though by no means completely) subject to royal legal processes in the late Anglo-Saxon period, sanctuary law, too, was increasingly shaped to reflect royal concerns with the exercise of lordly protections and ecclesiastical concerns with respect for the sanctity churches.

Tenth-century legislation of King Æthelstan shows the tendency of Anglo-Saxon sanctuary rules to place the protection that might be had in a church alongside the protections a fugitive might secure from a powerful secular lord.

> And we determined at our council held at Thundersfield: If any thief or robber sought out the king, or any church and the bishop, he had protection for nine nights.
>
> And if he now seeks out an ealdorman or abbot or thegn, he shall have respite for three nights.
>
> And if he [the pursuer] strikes the fugitive down within the allotted nights, he shall make it right by paying *mundbyrde* to the one whom the fugitive sought, or he may clear himself with a twelve-fold oath, [by swearing] that he did not know the thief was under protection (*socn*).
>
> But let the thief seek whatever protection he can seek, his life is worth no more than the nights we declared above.
>
> And he who protects the thief beyond [what we have stated] will share the thief's part, unless he is able to swear that he did not know of the wrong or theft.[44]

As Hyams has noted, this legislation is part of a trend noticeable in the tenth century to "integrate [sanctuary] into a central royal policy for the repression of serious disorder."[45] The legislation moved seamlessly from the protections a fugitive thief might find within a church building to the protections he might receive from a secular lord.

Indeed, the relation between lordship and protection is seen in the rich vocabulary Anglo-Saxon legislation possessed for sanctuary. Alfred's laws, like his treaty with the Danes, had referred to the protections one might have in a church by the term *frið*.[46] *Frið* was routinely translated into Latin by medieval scribes as "*pax*,"[47] but it bespoke more than simply "peace." *Frið* referred to the protection bestowed by a powerful man upon his friends and kin.[48] A cousin to Germanic notions of peace (*friede*), *frið* was derived from the root *freogan* ("to free," and also, "to love"), which is found also in the word *freond* (friend). It was closely related to *grið*, a word that may have had Danish origins, and also referred to a form of heightened protection, typically bestowed by royal grant.[49] For example, the treaty between Alfred and Guthrum was a *frið* constituted between the peoples.[50] The Anglo-Saxon "Edward-Guthrum," which was not an actual treaty but was rather an early Wulfstanian production, was modeled after Alfred-Guthrum and employed *grið* (where one might have expected *frið*).[51] Edward-Guthrum actually made church sanctuary a centerpiece of the peace it purported to establish, stating that church *grið* and the king's *handgrið* were both to remain permanently inviolate.[52] *Grið*, then, also bore a close relation with *mund* (lit. hand), the king's peace, the breach of which (*mundbryce*) required the payment of *mundbyrde*.[53]

The rich vocabulary of Anglo-Saxon sanctuary law also suggests that there was little practical difference between royal and ecclesiastical grants of protection. To the extent any differentiation was made in the legislation at all, it was made along gradations of dignity, not along any divide between secular and ecclesiastical authority. Those of higher dignity, whether of secular or ecclesiastical character, could offer a longer period of protection. A very similar understanding was expressed in a contemporary Anglo-Saxon collection of "peace laws":

> And this stood for all the days in England, that if a man guilty for his life sought the king, archbishop, or prince then he had *grið* for nine nights, and more [nights] if the king would protect him.

> And if he sought a bishop of a diocese, or ealdorman, or a hallowed place, then he had *grið* for seven nights, and longer if [the one to whom he fled] willed it.[54]

The close relationship between the protections that a church might offer and those that the person of a secular lord might offer to a fugitive has been discussed by David Hall.[55] What I want to stress is that the protection a fugitive criminal could find in a church or with a bishop resonated with the modes of lordly power in Anglo-Saxon legislation, such as that issued by Cnut:

> Therefore it is very right and proper that the protection given by the church of God within its walls and the protection granted by a Christian king in person should always remain inviolate; and he who violates either of them shall lose both land and life, unless the king is willing to pardon him.[56]

The penalty for breaching sanctuary protections in Anglo-Saxon legislation also often varied according to the dignity of the person or place violated, and was explicitly equated with violation of the king's *mund*.[57] According to Cnut's legislation, anyone breaching a "high church," was required to pay "the king five pounds in English law."[58] Breaches at Canterbury, however, required a payment of "five pounds to the king for *mundbryce* and three pounds to the archbishop." For other churches the penalties were lower. The breach of "medium minsters" required only one hundred twenty shillings. For churches "still smaller," but that "have a graveyard," the penalty was "sixty shillings." Lastly, for breaches of small "field churches without a graveyard" it was "thirty shillings."[59]

The collection of Anglo-Saxon "Grið Laws" also directed that different penalties applied depending on the circumstances of the sanctuary breach. "In the law at Canterbury, the king and the archbishop [of Canterbury] receive the same penalty for breaches of their protection." On the other hand:

> In the south of England it stands thus, if someone has fought in a church or the king's house, then he forfeits all that he has, it depends on the king's judgment whether or not he will keep his life.

And if anyone fights in a cloister house outside the church, he shall make it right with full compensation according to the rank of the minster.

And if anyone otherwise breaches the king's protection, he shall pay five pounds under English law; and for breaching an archbishop's or prince's protection he shall pay three pounds; and for breaching the protection of a bishop or ealdorman he shall pay two pounds.[60]

Æthelred's legislation had made homicide within a church unemendable. Yet even this type of killer might live if he was himself able to "reach sanctuary" and make full amends to God and man.[61] Cnut's legislation went a step beyond Æthelred's, ordering every "friend of God" to pursue a sanctuary breaker. Wulfstan, as with much of the most important early eleventh-century Anglo-Saxon sanctuary legislation, stood behind the legislation of both kings.

Again and again in these legal texts, sanctuary protections are articulated as extensions of personal lordly protection and the sorts of protection that a wrongdoer might seek from the king, a prince, or a powerful lord are treated as belonging to the same continuum of protections that a powerful churchman could extend to a fugitive. In short, the sanctuary protections transmitted from Roman Christendom into Anglo-Saxon England fit neatly alongside the personal protections that lordship, whether secular or ecclesiastical, afforded to wrongdoers.

As Patrick Wormald has shown, Wulfstan played a crucial role in the collection and preservation of legislation in early eleventh-century England. He served both Anglo-Saxon and Danish kings and can be credited with drafting *Grið*, which provided important material for the sanctuary provisions of Æthelred's 1014 code as well as for the *Instituta Cnuti*.[62] Wulfstan's concern that penal policy be aimed at the betterment of souls, even when it was remarkably detrimental to bodies, pervaded the laws that Cnut issued after assuming the throne. Indeed, Wulfstan succeeded in replacing execution with mutilation in Cnut's laws, explaining "thus may one punish and also preserve the soul."[63] The key point is that Wulfstan saw sanctuary laws as a laudable and essential strand of a coherent and assertive royal policy of suppressing disorders associated with the feud. Sanctuary in Anglo-Saxon legislation was not a response to weak or archaic modes of governance; it was a central feature of strong kingship and a mark of effective sovereignty. Despite Wulfstan's centrality to the transmission of Anglo-Saxon legislation, there is no reason to think the image of sanctuary presented in his texts was idiosyncratic.

CONCLUSION

There is no question that Anglo-Saxon kings and policy-shaping ecclesiastics such as Wulfstan understood sanctuary to be a crucial feature of royal law. Sanctuary expressed one of the most central forms of power an Anglo-Saxon lord could exercise, and the king was at the top of the sanctuary-granting hierarchy. At the same time, sanctuary laws denoted that churches were special places in the eyes of God and the king and that violent acts within them were not to be tolerated. In this way, while law and order could be linked to the maintenance of a "Holy Society," as Wulfstan taught both Æthelred and Cnut, sanctuary laws continued to trump concerns with apprehending and punishing wrongdoers.

Although Patrick Wormald has argued that Norman administration in England was built on solid Anglo-Saxon foundations, it is difficult to know precisely to what extent the Anglo-Saxon sanctuary experience directly shaped the later common law of sanctuary. In the century immediately following the Conquest, the interplay of feud, sanctuary, and royal power continued much as it had under the last Anglo-Saxon kings, though it may have been slightly more chaotic after 1066. But as the following chapters show, twelfth-century English kings found a way to domesticate sanctuary within the administration of royal justice to a degree unmatched anywhere in medieval Europe. The domestication of sanctuary within the medieval English common law was the result of two twelfth-century developments. In the first development, English ecclesiastics articulated an image of pious kingship that was closely tied to the establishment of sanctuary privileges and the protection of fugitive criminals (taken up in Chapter 6). In the second, late twelfth-century reforms of English royal law closely integrated sanctuary claims within the administration of felony jurisdiction and subjected sanctuary to processes determined by royal law (taken up in Chapter 7).

III

SANCTUARY IN LATE MEDIEVAL ENGLAND AND THE CANON LAW

6

Sanctuary in the Century After the Norman Conquest

Although Maitland dramatically characterized the Norman Conquest as "a catastrophe which determines the whole future history of English Law," he regarded the immediate impact of the Normans on English law as limited.[1] Maitland attributed the major reforms of English law to Henry II and his successors and did not find meaningful legal or institutional development in the first century following the Conquest.

One reason for this judgment is the nature of the legal sources that survive from the Anglo-Norman period. "There is no Norman code," as Maitland observed.[2] The collection entitled *Leges Henrici Primi* (*LHP*) carried no official authorization and has been occasionally blamed for misrepresenting both Anglo-Saxon and Anglo-Norman legal practices.[3] In any event, the *LHP* says little about sanctuary, except to note, as Anglo-Saxon legislation had, that breach of the peace of church was unemendable.[4] Yet even this statement is followed by a provision that appears to list homicide within a church (a breach of church peace) as a crime compensable by payment of the wergeld.[5] From the standpoint of legislation, little can be said with certainty about the law of sanctuary in England in the Anglo-Norman period. The Pipe Roll of 1130, like the circumstantial evidence of earlier, no-longer-extant Pipe Rolls, is clear evidence of Anglo-Norman administrative capabilities, but it does not inform us of the shape of English criminal jurisdiction or its specific relationship to sanctuary.[6] The systematic preservation of the records of crown law enforcement, which are also the documents with the richest holdings of material relevant for sanctuary law claims, was a late twelfth-century development. The wealth of sources that survive from the late twelfth century and thereafter may well distort our view of historical change in the earlier twelfth century, particularly when it comes to royal oversight of sanctuary law. Chapter 7 will argue that the administration of sanctuary law in England did undergo significant changes at the end of the twelfth century, but it is important to be mindful that those changes may have had earlier precedents that are now lost to us.

The surviving evidence relevant to sanctuary in the century that followed the Conquest tends to be found in chronicles. While the evidence is sometimes wanting, there was probably a great deal of continuity between Anglo-Saxon and Anglo-Norman England when it came to crime and the available responses to it.[7] Whether or not Wormald is right that Anglo-Norman kings actually enjoyed *less* centralized control over crime than their Anglo-Saxon counterparts,[8] legal institutions employed by the Normans in England, such as the *murdrum* fine and frankpledge, had recognizable Anglo-Saxon precedents.[9] Moreover, the feuding norms that scholars have found deeply embedded in Anglo-Saxon legal culture appear to have continued within a very similar cultural and legal framework after the Conquest and well into the thirteenth century.[10]

With regard to sanctuary laws, there is little reason to expect that the Conquest would bring meaningful change to Anglo-Saxon practices. William claimed the English throne by right of succession, not sheer conquest. The policy articulated in William's post-Conquest charters and often-repeated in twelfth-century Anglo-Norman legal collections favored confirmation of the old laws and customs of England. Presumably, this would have included Anglo-Saxon sanctuary laws as well. The "London Charter," issued by William very shortly after his coronation, provides a good example of how the Norman kings confirmed in general terms the validity of pre-Conquest laws and customs. The London Charter guaranteed hereditary property rights and promised to the citizens of London that anyone who caused them harm would have to answer to William.[11] It was similar to Anglo-Saxon grants of royal peace, and its invocation of feuding norms suggests further continuity with Anglo-Saxon legal traditions, promising that Londoners were "worthy of all those laws that were yet in the time of King Edward."[12]

There was, of course, nothing innovative about framing charters or legislation in terms of confirmation of older custom and nothing surprising in noting that sanctuary was a part of the legal inheritance taken over by the Anglo-Normans. Other attested charters issued by William contained references to Edward and his laws: a concession of land held by the Abbey of St. Peter "in the time of King Edward, my cousin;" recognition of "rights and honors held in the time of King Edward;" confirmation of "*consuetudines*" given by King Edward, and so on.[13] Invocation of Edward continued to be an important aspect of post-Conquest lawgiving in the first century of Norman rule. In the twelfth century, when Norman compilers devoted a good deal of energy to assembling collections of what were purported to be laws that William had confirmed,[14] they also fixed his legislative authority to a continuation of Anglo-Saxon legislative traditions. "I ordain and will," began the so-called *Articles of William*, "that all men have and hold the law of King Edward," though exceptions (echoing Alfred) were made for additional laws "which I have established for the usefulness of the English people."[15] The prologue to the twelfth-century *Leis Willelme* contained similar phrasing.[16]

Both the *Articles* and the *Leis Willelme* were composed after William's death, probably in the early twelfth century.[17] The invocation of Edward was very propitious for sanctuary law because another twelfth-century collection claiming to be Edward the Confessor's laws included an endorsement of sanctuary, along with specific penalties to be imposed on those who forcibly removed a fugitive from a church.[18] Interestingly, the sanctuary rules found in Edward's twelfth-century laws appear to owe some of their content to Frankish sanctuary traditions and seem to have little direct, textual relation to the sanctuary protections that Anglo-Saxon kings or Wulfstan had memorialized in Old English legislation.[19] In any event, twelfth-century legal collections demonstrate an eagerness to preserve sanctuary law and punish its breaches. Of course, regardless of what Anglo-Saxon sanctuary laws may have said about the subject, any Norman bishop acquainted with eleventh-century church canons or with Frankish law would have known that churches were supposed to offer protections to fugitive criminals. William I himself oversaw an ecclesiastical council in Normandy in 1080 which gave attention to the preservation of sanctuary law.[20] Why should matters have been any different in England?

On the other hand, it is worth exploring why sanctuary law's footing might have (but did not) become less secure after the Conquest. Even if the

Norman arrival did not immediately bring about a meaningful restructuring of English law, Anglo-Norman kings have traditionally been credited with insisting that pleas touching ecclesiastical discipline be tried only according to canon law processes. In this account, the Normans' more precise delineation between the respective jurisdictions of ecclesiastical and royal courts perceptibly secularized penal law.[21] While occasionally still relying on a combination of ecclesiastically and royally administered sanctions, the Conqueror and his successors carefully preserved their own prerogatives to impose royal sanctions for breaches of the king's peace.[22]

If there ever was a moment in which an assertive sovereign could have limited the widespread sanctuary privileges of the early medieval West, the arrival of the Normans in England would have been it. At the least, the reforms to criminal procedure and expansion of royal jurisdiction attributed to Henry II might have necessitated limiting sanctuary protections. Such would be the outcome predicted by Pierre Timbal, who followed his teacher Gabriel Le Bras in linking strong sovereignty to "restraint on the right of asylum."[23] According to this argument, we might expect to find Norman kings or their Angevin successors taking steps to restrain, not defend, Anglo-Saxon sanctuary protections. For instance, the Crown might have moved to forbid sanctuary protections to traitors, murderers, rapists, robbers, and arsonists, and instead subjected these wrongdoers exclusively to crown justice. Recall that Justinian had done something like this for homicides, rapists, and adulterers in the eastern half of the Roman Empire in the sixth century. Even Charlemagne, whose practical experiences in governance were perhaps not altogether lost on the Normans, had taken steps to assert royal authority over what sorts of wrongdoers could enjoy sanctuary, trying to exclude those who already had been convicted in court or who had not yet completed their assigned penance.

But sanctuary law in England was not limited after the Conquest. On the contrary, sanctuary protections expanded and solidified as the Crown extended the reach of royal law over criminal matters, and sanctuary law actually benefited from royal patronage after the Conquest. In fact, some scholars have identified sanctuary as evidence of continuity between Anglo-Norman and Angevin administrations.[24] The extent to which sanctuary law changed under the Angevins will be taken up in the next chapter, but despite the transformations that will be documented, it is useful to see sanctuary as a key point of continuity between Anglo-Saxon and Anglo-Norman kings and the early English common law.

A key to sanctuary law's survival in English law after the Conquest was that the recognition of sanctuary protections formed a constitutive element of English kingship. By the twelfth century a host of charters, ecclesiastical writers, and legal treatises stood for the proposition that all good kings righteously protected sanctuary-taking fugitives from violent foes. In this light, sanctuary was an important expression of royal power. Because the domestication of sanctuary law was grounded in part on the symbolic association of sanctuary with good kingship, the stories of sanctuary claims that survive in late-eleventh- and early-twelfth-century chronicles provide a glimpse at developments that reached back to Cnut and Æthelstan, but that appear to have picked up momentum in the Anglo-Norman period. Thus, after examining some instances of sanctuary in the Anglo-Norman period, the rest of this chapter will focus on the construction of sanctuary-granting kingship that English monastic houses accomplished in the twelfth century.

CHRONICLE EVIDENCE

For the century between 1066 and the reign of Henry II, evidence of sanctuary seeking appears primarily in chronicles and ecclesiastical sources. Eleventh- and twelfth-century ecclesiastics typically recounted sanctuary claims in order to establish some historical privilege relevant to sanctuary and its related jurisdictional immunities in their own day, or to decry breaches of sanctuary, or to celebrate the successful protection of a sanctuary seeker against his pursuers. Of course, what we can know about sanctuary in England from the Conquest until the last decades of the twelfth century is inflected by the particular nature and purpose of these sources. Sanctuary claims in the century after William I's arrival, as in the century before, tended to arise within the circumstances of the blood feud.[25] In this context, sanctuary still served as an important platform for resolving violent disputes under the auspices of royal and ecclesiastical authority, precisely the role sanctuary was presumed to have in Alfred's legislation.

The succession of William Rufus to the crown after the death of the Conqueror occasioned revolts by a party of barons who supported the claims to the crown of William's older brother, Robert Curthose. In late 1095, Earl Robert de Mowbray's open warfare against William Rufus was quickly put down by William's forces, and Earl Robert was forced to take sanctuary in a church.[26] According to John of Worcester: "On the sixth day of the siege

Robert was severely injured in the leg while fighting his enemies, of whom many were killed and many wounded; several of his men were also wounded and all were captured; he himself fled to the church, but was dragged out and put in prison."[27] The church belonged to the Monastery of St. Oswin, in the priory of Tynemouth. John's contemporaries would have also recognized that Robert fled to one of the churches that he had earlier wrested from the Bishop of Durham and given to the Abbot of St. Albans.

It is worth asking whether contemporaries would have framed the conflict between William I and Robert as a case of civil war, treachery against the sovereign, or as a blood feud between two powerful (and recently arrived, at that) lords with large retinues of armed men. If Robert's fight with William is framed as a blood feud, the continuity with Anglo-Saxon sanctuary and feuding practices is fairly straightforward. Robert was captured and removed from the church into which he had fled. But Robert himself appears to have come to no bodily harm beyond the arrow wound he suffered in battle. His kin were compelled to forfeit a castle to the king (according to John, Robert was to be blinded if his kin did not make this concession), suggesting the negotiation-in-the-feud provisions for sanctuary in the laws of Alfred. Symeon of Durham furnished a conclusion to the affair. In his account, the wounded Earl Robert was carried on a litter past St. Cuthbert's church in the clutches of the king's men. As he was passing by, he asked the king's barons if he might be carried into the church to pray. The barons refused, fearing perhaps that such an act might count as a sanctuary claim. According to Symeon, however, Earl Robert understood the refusal to be his just punishment for having earlier given St. Cuthbert's church to the monks of St. Albans at the expense of the monks of Durham.[28] It appears Robert lived out the remainder of his years under some form of imprisonment in a monastic house, removed from political life.[29]

It is interesting, in this light, to observe that many of the sanctuary cases recorded in Anglo-Norman sources conclude on a note of ecclesiastical or saintly vindication. According to Reginald of Durham, a conflict arose between a young servant of the Bishop of Durham and another young man. The bishop's servant was killed, and his killer fled to the church. Friends of the dead man surrounded the church (as Anglo-Saxon legislation had enjoined) and attempted to prevent anyone from bringing food to the fugitive (as Anglo-Saxon law had also ordered). The monks fed the fugitive anyway (as canon law required). Finally, Reginald reported, six of the vengeance-seeking friends entered the church and closed in on the sanctuary-seeking man as he prayed before the altar, near to the tomb of St. Cuthbert. They badly wounded the praying fugitive with their swords before some monks stopped the attack. The wounded fugitive, aided by St. Cuthbert, eventually recovered spiritually and physically, and the bishop, who was also lord of the slain man, forgave the attack and absolved his killer. By contrast the ringleader of the sanctuary breakers, indifferent to the sacrilege he had committed, was miraculously blinded by St. Cuthbert and thrown into prison where he died.[30]

Reginald's account, like Symeon's, contains important features of sanctuary claims before the Conquest. Its context is feud-like, as the fugitive was fleeing retribution by the friends of the young man he had killed. While the monks at Durham piously strove to feed and protect him, even though he had killed the bishop's man, the pursuers carried their feud into the church because they were unable to relinquish their desire for violent revenge and, perhaps more important in Reginald's mind, were unwilling to leave the matter to St. Cuthbert. The wrongdoer, on the other hand, was eventually reconciled with the two parties he had offended: the bishop, who was lord of the slain man, and St. Cuthbert. Although neither the monks nor the secular authorities were able to prevent the violation of sanctuary, the wronged saint miraculously intervened to set things right. In sum, the story conveys a widely held expectation that sanctuary claims should be honored, but it leaves the enforcement of sanctuary and the sanctuary violator's comeuppance to the jurisdiction of the saint.[31]

Other sanctuary stories from the period share some of the same features. Around 1155, a certain adolescent was condemned to death for theft. As the boy was taken to the execution site, "he had recourse to the common refuge, that is, St. Wilifrid and other patrons of this church." In this case, however, the boy took refuge "with his heart though not with his body" since he was bound and unable to flee to the church itself. The refuge his heart took appears to have satisfied St. Wilifrid. As the executioner lifted his sword, the boy cried out "Help me now, Wilifrid, for if you refuse to do it now, quite soon you won't be able to." The executioner found the boy's observant plea so hilarious he was overcome with laughter before he could land the fatal blow. The comic relief was timely. "During the delay, two young men turned up on very fast horses." Friends of the condemned boy, they paid a surety for him so that he went free.[32]

Not every twelfth-century sanctuary case was left to the intervention of saints. In the summer of 1150, Gilbert Foliot, Bishop of Hereford, was asked by King Stephen to "do canonical justice" to Gilbert de Lacy, who claimed that some of his own men had been wrongfully captured by the Earl of Hereford's men while they were in sanctuary. After hearing the case, Foliot entered a judgment against the Earl of Hereford, who then appealed the judgment to the Archbishop of Canterbury. In a letter encouraging Gilbert de Lacy to let the appeals process run its course, Foliot cast the case entirely as a matter of canon law process. The merits of the case were not even discussed beyond Foliot's acknowledgment that he had adjudged the earl's men guilty of violating the sanctuary privilege. Even King Stephen seemed to think the case belonged in the church courts, although in the 1150s his own political position was so weakened he probably could not have interposed himself effectively into a dispute between his barons. What Gilbert Foliot's letter adds to our view of sanctuary in the century after the Conquest is evidence that at least one English king entrusted adjudication of sanctuary violations to an ecclesiastical court. By the end of the twelfth century, such cases would belong within the scope of crown pleas.

The Anglo-Norman evidence, episodic as it is, shows less royal involvement in sanctuary than one would expect in light of Anglo-Saxon legislation. Some of the stories, like that of St. Wilifrid and the thieving youth, show that expressions of contrition were thought to be an appropriate precondition of sanctuary (as Carolingian and Anglo-Saxon sources suggested as well). Others depict sanctuary at work under circumstances that can easily be framed as feud-like, in which one party to a conflict found a refuge from which to negotiate some sort of terms. Sanctuary thus continued to play its role at the conjunction of feud, penance, and divine intervention. The middle of the twelfth century appears to be a transformative period in the history of sanctuary. The practice was no longer as intimately tied to feud resolution, but had not yet been fully absorbed into the processes of royal law and abjuration.[33]

ECCLESIASTICAL CONSTRUCTIONS OF THE SANCTUARY-GRANTING KING

The twelfth century gave rise to two distinct movements that were pivotal for the common law's later domestication of sanctuary. In the first half of the twelfth century, English churchmen began a fairly concerted effort to educate English kings on the virtues of granting fugitives protection within sanctuaries, and complimented and elaborated the relationship between sanctuary law and pious kingship that had been presented in Anglo-Saxon law. Subsequently, in the late twelfth century, Angevin reforms to penal law marked the domestication of sanctuary within royal legal process. Angevin law reforms relevant to sanctuary will be discussed in the next chapter. Discussion of the monastic efforts to emphasize the place of sanctuary protections within the scope of royal patronage are examined first.

Like Constantine, Clovis, and Charlemagne before him, William the Conqueror belonged to a tradition of sanctuary-granting sovereigns. The following words were attributed to William in charters produced at Battle Abbey in the twelfth century:

> I William, by God's grace, King of the English, make known to those to come as well as for those present, to archbishops, bishops, abbots, counts, barons, and all the faithful, French and English: Whereas when I had come to England and just outside Hastings where I pressed with [my] army against my enemies, who unjustly attempted to wrest my kingdom from me; in readiness for battle, at that time armed, in the presence of my barons and soldiers, with the favor of all, to bolster their hearts, I made a vow then to construct a church to the honor of God for [our] common salvation; if, by God's grace, we would be able to obtain victory. As we have attained, accomplishing the vow to God, in honor of the Sacred Trinity and the Blessed Martin confessor of Christ, I have constructed a church for the salvation of my soul, and of King Edward my predecessor, and of my wife Queen Matilda and of my successors in the realm: for the salvation of all, with whose labor and aid I obtained the realm; and of those especially who lie fallen in that battle. And since in this place where the church is constructed, God aided me to victory in battle, in memory of the victory, I will to name this same place Battle. Therefore . . . *if any thief or homicide, or anyone other accused person flee from fear of death to this church, let him in no way be hurt, but he should be released wholly free.*[34]

The image of William presented in the charter is carefully crafted. Flush with victory and pious gratitude, mindful of his oath, he founded an abbey and made sure to announce the sanctuary protections that it would provide for homicides and robbers. The charter itself is spurious, forged by monks at Battle Abbey in the early twelfth century, but the relationship between kingship and sanctuary that it imagines is telling nonetheless.[35]

The forged charter was intended to provide documentation for the rights and immunities Battle Abbey claimed to have received from William. The vow William was said to have sworn is a characteristic part of the charters forged at Battle in the twelfth century. Eleanor Searle has shown that accounts of William's vow before the battle owe a great deal to the *Roman de Rou* that was then quite popular in courtly society and also known to have been available in the abbey's library in the twelfth century.[36] According to her research, William's vow first appeared in a Battle Abbey charter of 1154 or 1155, more than a half century after William's death. Still, the vow may have had some historical basis. David Bates has identified two documents, dated perhaps as early as 1070, in which William expressed to Lanfranc that he had "granted and confirmed" Battle Abbey, "which I founded on account of a vow by which God gave victory to me."[37] In either case, whether the vow was completely fabricated or had some authentic basis in William's actions, it was only in twelfth-century documents that both the vow and the founding of the abbey came to be explicitly linked with grants of sanctuary for crimes.

The *Chronicle of Battle Abbey*, probably completed around 1180, shows how sanctuary protections continued to be presented as an element of the Abbey's royal patronage. After recounting William's vow and victory, the battle chronicler described the construction of Battle Abbey and the jurisdictional prerogatives William granted it. The abbey

> might have its court for all pleas, and a royal liberty, and the custom of managing its own affairs and its own business within all its estates; and its judgments enforced by itself; and that it shall be free and quit forever from all subjection to and exaction of bishops. . . . And if any thief or homicide or any other accused one, fleeing in fear of death, should flee to this church, he may be in no way harmed but he should be released wholly free.[38]

Although the author of the chronicle quoted from a forged charter (1166–67) that was surely in the possession of the abbey at the time he wrote, he was careful not to claim that William had actually issued a charter granting the privileges listed, perhaps distancing himself, Searle suggests, from documents he knew were produced during his own time at the abbey.[39] The dubious assertion that William himself had declared the sanctuary privileges claimed by Battle Abbey was dressed up with important hallmarks of medieval kingship: military success, benevolent gifts, and patronage on behalf of the church.

Twelfth-century legal collections consistently credited William with promulgating laws that protected criminals who fled to churches. The so-called *Leis Willelme* affirmed sanctuary in its very first chapter, immediately following the prologue:

> This is to preserve the peace [which touches] the holy church. Concerning some misdeed that a man has done, if he is able to come to a holy church, he shall have peace of his life and his limbs.[40]

The *Leis Willelme* itself did not purport to be an "official" law code issued by William.[41] Much as the *Instituta Cnuti* did for Cnut in the twelfth century, the forgeries at Battle and the contents of the *Leis* reflect what their compilers knew, expected, or hoped the laws of William to have been like,[42] and they emphasize sanctuary among the acts that gave William his kingly attributes.

The early-twelfth-century *Laws of Edward the Confessor* also contained provisions for sanctuary.[43] Their fifth chapter provided that only a bishop or his ministers could remove one who was guilty or accused of a crime who had fled for that reason to a church.[44] The sanctuary articles in the *Laws of Edward*, consistent with contemporary canon laws, extended the protection to houses of priests and to ecclesiastical courts.[45] At the same time, the laws commanded thieves who fled to sanctuary to return what they had stolen or to make restitution from out of their own goods,[46] and they provided that those we might today call recidivists, those who took frequent recourse to sanctuary, were to "foreswear the province and never return."[47] If such a repeat offender did return from exile, the laws declared: "Let no one presume to receive him" except by consent of the king.[48] Finally, the *Laws* specified that violations of sanctuary were to be judged by the bishop. As we saw above, Gilbert Foliot adjudicated at least one such case as Bishop of Hereford. After late-twelfth-century Angevin reforms to English law, however, such matters were typically handled in royal courts.[49]

Edward's laws reserved the possibility of royally imposed penalties (outlawry, for instance) on sanctuary violators.[50] The possibility that the king might make a sanctuary seeker abjure the "province" had been implied in Carolingian laws but had not been tied, as it was here, to recidivist thieves. On the other hand, very-late-twelfth- and thirteenth-century plea rolls indicate that common law practice had by then required every sanctuary seeker, not just those who claimed the protection "frequently," to abjure the realm. The discretionary abjuration process implied in the *Laws of Edward Confessor* possibly reflected an early move in that direction. It has been observed that the sanctuary provisions in Edward's laws bore more similarity to the canons of Frankish church councils than to Anglo-Saxon sanctuary laws, but the important point conveyed by the text to the twelfth-century reader was that Edward stood firmly in favor of sanctuary.[51] In fact, although the *Laws of Edward* sometimes betrayed considerable ignorance of Anglo-Saxon law in the time of Edward, portions of them have been considered to "derive from [twelfth-century] experience."[52]

Important sanctuary traditions were also formed at monastic houses in the north of England in the twelfth century, particularly by Symeon of Durham in his *Historia Dunelmensis Ecclesiae* composed in the early years of the twelfth century (c. 1104–1108). Symeon recounted how at the end of the ninth century Saint Cuthbert (d. 687) asked the Viking King Guthred to acknowledge some liberties on behalf of the church, building on an earlier anonymous presentation of St. Cuthbert's tomb as an important sanctuary site.[53] By the 1070s, a Durham chronicler had described hefty fines, consistent with those found in Anglo-Saxon legislation, imposed for dragging fugitives from that sanctuary.[54] Indeed, Æthelstan's army may have paid just such a fine for breaching St. Cuthbert's sanctuary in 934.[55] Twelfth-century sources, however, provide the most details. According to Symeon of Durham, at the end of the ninth century St. Cuthbert had intervened to ask King Guthred for "all the land between the Wear and Tyne," because he wanted his "church to be a place of refuge for all refugees, so that whoever for any cause might flee to my body shall have peace for thirty-seven days."[56] Guthred granted the request and Symeon tells us that King Alfred later confirmed the grant.[57] Politically astute, Symeon knew the value of tying ecclesiastical privileges to historical figures, preferably pious saints and kings.[58] It is probably not a coincidence that Symeon's account of a sanctuary between the Tyne and Wear followed immediately after his account of a dream in which St. Cuthbert endorsed Guthred for the throne.[59]

The story of Cuthbert's request is also interesting because it gives a specific number of days to the duration of the sanctuary protection. Alfred's laws had done so as well, though their seven-night allowance was considerably less generous than the thirty-seven days St. Cuthbert had requested from Guthred. Wulfstan had been conscious that sanctuary customs in the north of England differed from those in the south. The difference may be explained by local practice. Still, Symeon's version comes remarkable close to the forty-day rule that would crystallize in the late-twelfth- and early-thirteenth-century royal law governing sanctuary, and gives a tantalizing hint about the obscure origins of the forty-day rule later imposed at common law.

Ecclesiastical houses were not the only sources of stories about sanctuary-granting kings. According to Geoffrey of Monmouth, Dunwallo Molmutius, whom Geoffrey placed in pre-Christian Cornwall in the days after Brutus, had built a new Troy on the Thames. In Geoffrey's account, which was completed around 1136, Dunwallo expanded his father's kingdom in Cornwall and subdued the whole kingdom, returning it "to its ancient state," and establishing the "Molmutine laws," of which "St. Gildas wrote." To St. Gildas's description of Dunwallo's governance, however, Geoffrey added that Dunwallo had decreed that that "the temples of the gods should have the privilege of giving sanctuary and protection to any fugitive or criminal that should flee to them from his enemy." Likewise, highways and "husbandman's ploughs" were to have the same privileges.[60] Knowing that good kings granted sanctuary privileges, Geoffrey wrote that because of laws such as these, in Dunwallo's day "cruelties committed by robbers were prevented, and everybody passed safe, without any violence offered him." Geoffrey's insistence that the pre-Christian Dunwallo legislated in favor of sanctuary protections provides interesting corroboration for the frequency with which monastic houses sought to link English kings to sanctuary law in the twelfth century.

Sanctuary was an important part of Anglo-Saxon legislation and a noticeable feature of the laws and customs Anglo-Norman kings repeatedly confirmed after the Conquest. But twelfth-century monks took no chances. Good kings, they continually reminded, urged the kingdom to respect sanctuary rights. Through these ecclesiastical efforts, kingship and sanctuary enjoyed a certain mutual support. When clerics such as Symeon and the monks at Battle Abbey, or legal compilers like the author of the *Leis Willelme* invoked (or invented) sanctuary laws granted by the old kings, they were clearly leveraging history and tradition so that contemporary kings would feel moved to continue honoring them. At the same time, promulgating sanctuary laws and punishing breaches of sanctuary were acts that contributed to the glory and honor of a king. History writers and law-code compilers in the twelfth century taught English kings that giving homicides and thieves a place to claim sanctuary was a pious and noble act, an expression of a particular form of kingly power that proved to be incredibly persistent. The construction of sanctuary-respecting kings was sufficiently powerful that Henry I told Pope Calixtus II in 1119 that frequent sanctuary breaches in Normandy were a primary motivation for his 1106 invasion of France. He apparently thought he could justify his actions to the pope by reference to his desire to protect churches and sanctuary rights.[61] That Henry thought of such a justification for his invasion at all suggests how important sanctuary protections were for understandings of good kingship in the twelfth century.

There were, of course, voices of resistance. Some of King Stephen's men complained in the middle of the twelfth century that some bishops at Salisbury, Ely, and Lincoln were fortifying their churches to the advantage of sanctuary seekers. "Bishops," they said, "should be evangelists of peace, not builders of houses that might be a refuge to doers of evil deeds."[62] The complaints of Stephen's men may provide a helpful corrective to a view of sanctuary law as an unquestioned virtue in twelfth-century England. Still, the sources show that twelfth-century English churchmen and legal compilers had effectively taught English kings just how fond of sanctuary their predecessors had been and just what pious kingship required.[63]

CHARTERED LIBERTIES AND SANCTUARY

Nevertheless, the baronial complaint about fortified sanctuaries coincides with a tendency detectable in the twelfth century for some of the great ecclesiastical immunities to offer a form of sanctuary that went beyond the traditional protections fugitives might hope for by fleeing to an ordinary church. R. H. Forster understood these more extensive sanctuary sites as uniquely English.[64] The development of jurisdictional immunities for ecclesiastical houses, however, can be traced to earlier continental practices, and suggest important continuity between English and continental legal practices. As Barbara Rosenwein has shown, however, jurisdictional immunities on the Continent remained relatively distinct from sanctuary protections for criminals in the Carolingian and Capetian eras.[65] In England, on the other hand, sanctuary protections seemed to have become conflated with broader claims of jurisdictional immunities in the twelfth century. For example, late medieval English charters pertaining to Westminster included sanctuary for crimes amidst other royally granted ecclesiastical immunities:

> King Edward himself, being present in the aforesaid church with Edward his son and the . . . worshipful archbishop Saint Dunston and other bishops and barons and his counsel, following the example of his predecessors . . . added to and strengthened all the charters and privileges of the same place. . . . That any men that are fugitive for what sin or trespass that ever it be, fleeing to the church of Saint Peter, . . . be he foot man or horse man of king's court or of the city or of any town of what condition that ever he be of; for what man trespass or cause against us or our successor kings of England or against any man of holy church we will that he be there safe, free, and quiet and that he have both life and limb.[66]

These late medieval claims were commonly grounded on the names of Anglo-Saxon kings. Æthelstan, remarked Forster wryly, "was always a favorite peg to hang a legend on."[67] In some cases, simple renown was enough to elevate a particular church to the status of a chartered sanctuary. A legend that Joseph of Arimathea had once visited made the church at Glastonbury an especially revered sanctuary.[68]

On rare occasions, sanctuary rights were even granted to secular authorities.[69] Secular liberties were not in any strict sense sanctuaries. Crimes committed within them were, in principle, to be punished by the lord of the liberty. But in practice it is clear that some lands that were exempt from royal justice operated as if they were ecclesiastical liberties in which sanctuary might be claimed. Hence, many fugitives fled there, where the king's writ did not run, living beyond the reach of royal law. Together, these "chartered sanctuaries of England formed a class by themselves."[70] Isobel Thornley thought that secular liberties, where they were able, adopted a "false ecclesiastical colour" so that the distinction between secular and ecclesiastical liberties became conflated.[71]

Scholars have generally treated chartered liberties in a separate class from sanctuary law. There are good grounds to do so. In addition to their apparent development in the twelfth century, chartered sanctuaries usually had a defined territorial reach that was significantly more expansive than anything permitted to ordinary churches. For example, at Durham, four stone crosses set a mile from the church in each direction marked the territory within which a fugitive could claim sanctuary. Fines for seizing a fugitive within Durham's boundary markers were set along a graduated scale, increasing with proximity to the church itself. In ordinary sanctuaries, protection could only be claimed at or within the church itself, or within ecclesiastical buildings attached to the church.

The length of time one could remain in a chartered sanctuary also differed from the common law procedures that were settled in the late twelfth century. Within the procedures that obtained in the late-twelfth- and early-thirteenth-century common law (treated in Chapter 7), fugitives to a church were ordinarily allotted forty days within which to abjure the realm or submit to the king's peace. At many chartered sanctuaries, however, the traditional forty-day rule was not followed. At Durham, according to a tradition Symeon of Durham presumed began with St. Cuthbert, fugitives received thirty-seven days of respite, at Beverley thirty. When the allotted time had elapsed, the fugitive was required to abjure. By the fourteenth century, some liberties offered permanent protection from royal law (see Chapter 7), and appear to have prompted many of the attacks on sanctuary law that gained momentum in the fifteenth and sixteenth century in England.

CONCLUSION

English ecclesiastics devoted considerable attention to stressing the relationship between the Crown and grants of sanctuary for crime in the twelfth century. Their efforts led to the emergence in various parts of England of jurisdictional immunities that might operate as sanctuaries for fugitive felons. Chartered liberties continued even after Angevin reforms brought sanctuary to heel within the administration of royal law in the late eleventh and early twelfth centuries, and belong in a separate category from the protections available in any consecrated church. Chartered liberties were not peculiar to England, though English monks may have been somewhat better at anchoring their claims to historical kings and preserving their claims in writing. Continental chartered liberties emerged in the Carolingian era and figured in litigation before the papal curia in the fourteenth and fifteenth centuries, though it appears that only in England did such sanctuaries develop into permanent protections from royal law. Moreover, chartered liberties would be at the center of controversies that led to the eventual abolition of sanctuary in the sixteenth century (Chapter 8). But before examining the role of chartered liberties in the jurisprudential attacks on sanctuary in the sixteenth century, it is necessary to look first at how the English crown domesticated sanctuary within the administration of common-law felonies in late-twelfth-century England.

7

Sanctuary and Angevin Law Reforms

Sometime shortly before 1241 in Berkshire, Richard le Vacher and John Dobyn came to the home of Matilda la Daye and killed her. Afterwards, they fled to the Church of St. Laurence in Reading. There, they claimed sanctuary, acknowledged their felony before the king's two coroners, and, in exchange for safe passage and immunity from prosecution, swore that they would abjure the realm of England and never return. John and Richard appear to have left the church separately, for as John traveled out of Reading, Matilda's two daughters pursued him raising the hue and cry so that John was soon captured by villagers and taken to nearby Charlton. After being tried by the bailiff and men from Charlton and the surrounding hundreds, John was hanged.[1]

When the eyre came to Berkshire in 1241, twelve jurors from the hundred of Charlton informed the royal justices of these events. The first matter the justices inquired about was why a man who had claimed sanctuary and abjured the realm before two of the king's coroners was captured, tried for felony by a hundred court, and hanged. The jurors attempted to explain the events by claiming that John had only "abjured the fee of the abbot" of the Church of St. Laurence, not the realm of England, implying thereby that the abjuring felon was not protected once he left the abbot's jurisdiction. It appears that the eyre court was suspicious of this explanation, because the plea roll contains an interlinear addition in which the scribe remarked that this account was "according to what is testified by the jurors." The coroners who administered the abjuration oaths offered a different account, claiming that John had "abjured the realm of England," and was therefore illegally seized and executed. Because the jurors had misrepresented the facts of John's abjuration in their testimony, they were amerced, as were the bailiffs and hundreds that had illicitly hanged John. Richard le Vacher avoided the summary justice that John had received. While he was apparently also captured after abjuring from the church, he was still alive and in custody when the eyre arrived. He was brought before the eyre justices where he elected to stand trial and was acquitted of the felony and allowed to go free.[2]

The case demonstrates the extent to which sanctuary had been incorporated within the administration of royal law in thirteenth-century England. Although sanctuary protections had been an important feature of English law since before Alfred, it appears that it was only in the latter half of the twelfth century that English royal law regularized the processes that governed sanctuary and abjuration and incorporated them into the routine administration of royal criminal jurisdiction. Whereas Anglo-Saxon sanctuary legislation had been directed primarily at feuding foes and the churchmen who interceded between them, by the late twelfth century the central figure in the process of administering sanctuary was the coroner, a royal official. The coroner was responsible to hear the sanctuary seeker acknowledge his felony and to keep a record of each sanctuary claim so that the name of the sanctuary seeker and his crime could be enrolled in the plea rolls at next eyre visitation. Moreover, the coroner was charged with receiving the abjuration oath of sanctuary seekers and overseeing their abjuration of the realm. While abjuration had pre-Conquest roots, its direct linkage with sanctuary, whereby all sanctuary seekers were required to abjure the realm or stand trial, was a late-twelfth-century development. These late-twelfth-century developments—the centrality of the coroner, the oversight of abjuration through the eyre, a relatively firm window of forty days within which abjuration had to be performed, and royal concern with sanctuary breaches—mark sanctuary's domestication within the English common law.

As this chapter will show, the domestication of sanctuary belongs to the larger "shift in control" by which Henry II and his successors expanded the reach of royal jurisdiction and granted English subjects much wider access to the king's justice. The watershed is traditionally thought to be the decade between 1166 and 1176, when Henry issued the Assizes at Clarendon and Northampton. The Assizes undoubtedly confirmed much that had already been going on, but they also marked the "definitive introduction into England of public prosecution of crime."[3] It is important not to overstate Henry's innovations. His reforms relied on some institutions, such as judicial visitations in the counties and accusing juries, which had been employed episodically before 1166, but his reforms regularized and strengthened the ability of Englishmen to air and conclude their disputes in front of royal justices, using procedures determined by royal law.[4] The stated goal of the Assizes was conservative: to bring things back to how they were before the disorder and violence of Stephen's reign.[5] But the outcome of the Assizes was to put royal law in a position to claim more of a monopoly on dispute settlement and legitimate violence than English kings had known before.

The Assizes of Clarendon in 1166 and Northampton in 1176 can be understood as decisive skirmishes in the attempt to subject private feuding behavior to the processes of royal law.[6] Realization of a royal monopoly on legitimate violence and coercive force was still some way off, but Henry appears to have set out with this goal firmly in mind as he steadily extended the reach of the king's peace over acts of private violence. The money he put into building jails is one measure of his intention.[7]

Given the energy and resources that Henry II dedicated to regularizing and reforming English law enforcement, it is worth examining the impact of these developments on the practice of sanctuary in English law. Rather than becoming unnecessary or counterproductive in the midst of these efforts to centralize and unify jurisdiction over crimes, sanctuary law was made an integral part of the common law. As a consequence, sanctuary law was unmoored from the penitential discourses of the patristics and given a place in royal law that was compatible with, but not dependent upon, the logic of feud resolution.

The import of sanctuary law's domestication is somewhat muted, however, if one takes the view that, like outlawry and jurisdictional immunities, sanctuary protections are indicia of a feeble and inefficient legal regime.[8] Medieval English law enforcement, despite whatever regularity Henry II might have brought to it, has not generally received positive assessments from historians. Maitland judged it to be "exceedingly inefficient," with "few out of many criminals coming to their appointed ends."[9] Exclaimed Milsom, "The miserable history of criminal law in England can be shortly told. Nothing worthwhile was created."[10] Plucknett, too, asked why an age that showed "what could be done by a vigorous and very skillful government" when it came to formulating rules governing land transfer and ownership could not achieve anything comparable in the area of criminal law.[11] The implicit assumption that medieval criminal law should be judged by its effectiveness in apprehending, punishing, and deterring wrongdoers (and potential wrongdoers) has guided a substantial portion of scholarship on medieval criminal law since at least the age of Beccaria.[12] Also embedded in these scholarly accounts is the assumption that practices that interfered with the operation of royal justice and muted the exemplary potential of punishment imposed by sovereign authority signified a deficiency in the law. Because sanctuary was perceived as one of the jurisdictional prerogatives that interfered with the proper reach of penal law, sanctuary's inclusion within the early common law seems to confirm judgments that the response of medieval English law to criminality was inept.

Two recent strands of medieval legal scholarship suggest that these judgments may be misplaced. Paul Hyams, pursuing hints made by Maitland, has suggested that the "questions of land title," which occupied so much of the development of early English law, "are more intimately related to law and order than is generally supposed."[13] Behind questions of "title and tenure" was the "potential for violence."[14] In this light, the gulf that earlier scholars thought separated the weak law-enforcement capacities of English government from its relatively strong capacity to provide workable rules for land ownership is not so wide. As Hyams notes, not only were reforms to real property law part of a larger "law and order" campaign initiated by Henry II, but many apparent criminal law processes also were initiated in a competition for real property. Hyams argues for reconciling the rules governing land tenure with the historical shift from "feud to felony" in the English common law.

Additionally, Henry Summerson's important observations about "law and order maintenance" in thirteenth-century England reframed Maitland's indictment of medieval English criminal law enforcement by questioning whether it should be judged by the percentage of felons who were subjected to arrest, conviction, and afflictive punishments.[15] Instead, Summerson observes that thirteenth-century English law was comparatively efficient at identifying wrongdoers, publishing their identity to crown officers and local communities, and excluding identified felons from the lawful members of their communities. By showing that early English common law aimed in many instances not at punishing offenders but instead at excluding them physically and legally from the "law-worthy," Summerson's thesis suggests why sanctuary, without any apparent resistance or controversy, was not only accommodated in twelfth- and thirteenth-century English law, but even helped further the law enforcement goals of the Angevin crown.

THE COMMON LAW'S DOMESTICATION OF SANCTUARY

Because sanctuary not only survived but also thrived within the common law, it is necessary to set it within the larger context of legal reforms that defined the common law's criminal jurisdiction in the late twelfth century. Henry II signaled the direction of some of his concerns in the Constitutions of Clarendon, a sixteen-clause document promulgated in January 1164 that purported to record the customs of the realm in matters touching the prerogatives of the church and the crown. Four of the constitutions attempted to demarcate spiritual and secular jurisdiction in disputes over benefices, property held in free alms, and criminal jurisdiction over clergy.[16] Six more addressed the limits of royal and papal authority.[17] Yet, as G. O. Sayles notes, for all of the high politics addressed in the constitutions, it was "into the question, not of papal supremacy but of 'criminous clerks,' that all the current disagreements between Church and State were telescoped."[18] Becket apparently approved initial drafts of the constitutions, and Pope Alexander III was at least willing to discuss their provisions, but once Henry published the constitutions in written form, Becket's opposition famously crystallized.

The crown insisted that its courts should have jurisdiction over all accusations of serious crime, whether the accused was clergy or lay. In the event an accused felon was convicted in royal court and pled clergy, he would be delivered to the appropriate episcopal court for trial with the proviso that a royal officer remain on hand to observe the trial. If the accused cleric was convicted under episcopal jurisdiction, the crown asserted the right to retake the now-deposed cleric and punish him as a layman. By the time the constitutions were published, Becket firmly objected to each provision regarding criminous clerks: the initial process in royal court, the presence of a crown officer in the episcopal court, and the prospect of corporal or capital punishment of deposed clerics. Any ground for compromise eroded at the moment of Becket's murder, and recognition of the Church's jurisdictional priority over clergy was an element of Henry's soul-saving settlement with the church.

The failed attempt to assert royal jurisdiction over criminous clerks was only one aspect of Henry's reforms to criminal law. Two years later, he issued the Assize of Clarendon, requiring twelve lawful men from every hundred and four men from every vill to appear before his justices and sheriffs and report which of their neighbors had been accused of killing someone, of stealing something, or of harboring those that had. Requiring leading men from the villages and hundreds to report to royal officials the tales neighbors told on one another was not an Angevin invention. William Rufus and Henry I had done so periodically. But Henry regularized the process into the presentment jury and used it to forge a network of institutional links among frankpledges, vills, local crown officials, and itinerant justices. Many of these institutions had antecedents that reached back before the Conquest, but Henry asserted control over them and brought them more fully within the purview of royal officials who were answerable to the crown.

Henry further required that those accused of felony who managed to clear themselves by compurgation or ordeal, yet "have a very bad reputation," abjure the realm within eight days. Abjuration was explicitly presented as a form of outlawry: "Let them [those who abjure] be outlaws, and if they return [from abjuration] let them be taken as outlaws."[19] Like many other features of the Assize of Clarendon, abjuration had pre-Conquest analogues, but it appears to have been more closely associated with sanctuary after the 1160s. The sanctuary provisions in the *Laws of Edward the Confessor* had held that felons making frequent flights to a church should abjure the realm, but they did not require all sanctuary seekers to abjure. Henry's reforms appear to have made abjuration a favored penal outcome in the common law, ranking alongside outlawry and probably ahead of execution as the most likely consequence of a felony conviction, and it was probably at this time that the common law practice of requiring all sanctuary seekers to take abjuration oaths began. While there is no source that allows us to pinpoint the moment when all sanctuary seekers who confessed to a felony were required to forswear the realm of England, the abjuration clause of the Clarendon Assize is suggestive. Henry de Bracton (c. 1250), as good a treatise source as we have, claimed that the rule requiring sanctuary men to abjure within forty days was a product of Henry II's reforms.[20] It is difficult to be more specific. The introduction of coroners in 1194 marks the point at which that office began overseeing the abjuration of sanctuary seekers, but there is evidence that they took this task over from sheriffs and their serjeants, who may have been overseeing the abjuration of sanctuary seekers in isolated cases as early as the 1160s.[21] The insertion of coroners within the sanctuary process may have been an extension of policies introduced by Henry II aimed at reducing the power of sheriffs in the administration of criminal law.

In 1170, Henry promulgated the Inquest of Sheriffs, a considerable undertaking that divided the realm into administrative districts and made sheriffs and other local officials answerable to the crown for predatory and illicit conduct. One result, which apparently surprised contemporaries, was the removal of many sheriffs from office. Henry's inquest also helped to prevent the office of sheriff from becoming a hereditary claim of local magnates. In place of the deposed sheriffs, Henry placed men who he hoped could provide a sustainable link between centralizing royal interests and local administration. Then, at Northampton in 1176, "a fresh set of instructions were given to the itinerant justices; the Assize of Clarendon was to be enforced, but in a yet more severe form."[22] Arson and forgery were added to the list of acts that violated the king's expanding peace, and "to increase the severity of the law," convicted felons were still made to abjure the realm, but only after having had a hand and a foot removed.[23] In contrast, sanctuary seekers, perhaps the most common group of abjurers, were not subject to amputation.

The Assizes of Clarendon and Northampton indicate the seriousness with which Henry set about invigorating law enforcement in his realm. Many of the hallmarks of public prosecution: grand juries, the conceptual separation of law and fact,[24] and crown control over private settlements,[25] find their genesis in this period.[26] Following the failed attempt in 1164 to claim royal jurisdiction over criminous clerks, both Assizes targeted certain forms of jurisdictional prerogatives. Holders of immunities could not invoke their liberties in order to refuse to hand over someone named by the presentment jury.[27] In what was probably understood as a related move, Henry reiterated that castles built without license during the anarchy of Stephen's reign were to be razed.[28] Yet, nowhere in the Assizes was there an indication of suspicion or hostility toward the sanctuary protections offered by ordinary church buildings or the chartered monasteries.

Even as Henry moved against clerical privilege and jurisdictional immunities, he left sanctuary intact because sanctuary protections were not in tension with the fundamental aims of royal law. Maitland was right that English law rarely saw a felon to his "appointed ends" on a gallows, a chopping block, or the ground beneath a high cliff. Apprehension of fleeing felons in medieval England depended almost entirely on the vigilance, speed, and strength of village folk who dutifully answered the hue and cry. Those who were not caught red-handed, but were suspected of crimes, were to be presented at the next eyre. But they had to be successfully held in jail until the justices arrived again. Escapes were frequent, in which case a sentence of outlawry would be declared. Those who actually stood trial were frequently acquitted, often by the same juries that presented them.[29] In the event of a conviction or outlawry, royal pardons were available (again with a surprising frequency) to those who could afford them or who had friends who could.[30] The poor and friendless could still turn "approver" and save their necks by defeating those they accused in judicial duels.[31] And, of course, anyone who was able to reach a church could claim sanctuary and abjure the realm. It was a strange system indeed if it is judged by the metrics of conviction rates and its capacity to impose exemplary punishments with consistency.

Sanctuary in particular seems to have suited the goals of crown and local officials. Fugitives in sanctuary were required to identify themselves and acknowledge the felony for which they had fled. Because men from surrounding villages were required to guard against escape from the church, the sanctuary seeker and his crime were likely to become known in the locale, if they were not already. This information was duly recorded by the coroner and corroborated when royal justices arrived for the sitting of the eyre. After the felony was acknowledged and the abjuration oath given, the sanctuary seeker was assigned a port from which to leave the realm and the system of watches and frankpledges along the way helped prevent abjuring felons from rethinking their decision to emigrate. Common law sanctuary processes proved to be good at identifying felons, eliciting their confessions, making them known to men in the environs of the church to which they had fled, and excluding them from the community and realm.

Although the documentary records of Henry's reforms at Clarendon and Northampton say nothing explicit about sanctuary, thirteenth-century treatises paint a detailed picture of the process of sanctuary and abjuration.

Britton, for example, offers an oath that combined the confession of felony with the promise to abjure the realm:

> Hear this, coroner and other good people, that I, for such act that I did feloniously or assented to do, will go out of the realm of England . . . and never will I return unless by consent of the king or his heirs, so help me God and the Saints.[32]

The sanctuary seeker was required to select a seaport from which to depart (though occasionally the plea rolls show coroners or others assigning the port).[33] According to *Britton*, abjurers then were required to don the garb of a penitent exile or crusader and travel "with a wooden cross in their hands, unshod, ungirt, head uncovered and in their tunic only."[34] Abjurers were to keep to the main highways until they reached the port and sailed away from England, never to return without royal permission.[35] The author of *Fleta* (who otherwise paraphrases Bracton on sanctuary) adds that the abjuring felon should carry himself somberly, as if on his way "to be hanged on the gallows . . . and when he come to the sea, if he find no passage, he must plunge in up to the neck and, having [cried out loudly], he must remain on the shore until he find passage."[36]

The accounts in *Britton* and Bracton also accord with the picture of sanctuary and abjuration given in royal legislation that purported to regulate the practice in Wales in the late thirteenth century:

> Moreover when a Thief, or Manslayer, or other Malefactor shall fly to the Church, the Coroner, as soon as he shall be certified thereof, shall direct the bailiff of our Lord the King to cause to come before him at a certain day the good and lawful Men of the neighborhood; and in their presence, after Recognition made of the Felony, shall cause the abjuration to be made in this manner; That the Felon shall be brought out unto the Church Door, and a Sea Port shall be assigned him by the Coroner, and then he shall abjure the Realm; and, according as the Port assigned shall be far or near, the term shall be set for his going out of the Realm aforesaid: So that in journeying towards that Port, bearing in his Hand a Cross, he shall not in any manner turn out of the King's Highway, that is to say, neither upon the right hand nor upon the left, but shall always hold to the same until he shall depart the Realm.[37]

The thirteenth-century common law sources show that the administration of sanctuary was entrusted to royal officials and subject to royal processes. While the availability of sanctuary certainly presents an important point of continuity between Anglo-Norman and Angevin legal practices,[38] the late twelfth century was also an important moment of transformation. Sanctuary's penitential aspects were replaced with royal process. The common law required the sanctuary seeker to confess his crime to the coroner. The sources appear indifferent as to whether sanctuary seekers also confessed to a priest or performed penance. Likewise, as the thirteenth-century royal sources increasingly submerged feuding practices beneath the veneer of common law pleas, sanctuary transformed from a platform of feud resolution into means for ensuring the abjuration of felons.

Common law sanctuary rules also show that although the crown began exercising more direct control over the process of sanctuary and criminal law, the common law reforms were not necessarily concerned with deploying criminal law in a manner that suppressed crime. The absence of an explicit discourse of deterrence in the common law of sanctuary stands in contrast to jurisprudential trends that were emerging in canon law in the course of the thirteenth century, and attention to contemporaneous developments in the canon law of sanctuary serve to highlight important features of English sanctuary practice.

DETERRENCE AND SANCTUARY IN THE THIRTEENTH-CENTURY CANON LAW

In contrast to developments within the English common law, twelfth-century canon lawyers appeared less concerned about integrating sanctuary into the larger processes of the criminal law. In the thirteenth-century, however, canon lawyers turned increasing attention to sanctuary law, interrogating its place not only within the administration of criminal law, but its specific relationship to punishment. This attention to the relationship between punishment and sanctuary interjected a discourse of deterrence into questions of sanctuary that did not take root in the English common law in the thirteenth century.

Causa 17. q. 4. c. 9 of Gratian's *Decretum* had stated the basic rule of sanctuary: "No one should dare to drag out a guilty one who has fled to a church: neither should the fugitive be given over to punishment or death."

The thirteenth-century gloss to this passage asks "whether, afterward, the fugitive is able to be accused of his crime?"[39] That is, did the fugitive's flight to sanctuary end the matter of penal prosecution altogether, or only temporarily? Some canonists, including Laurentius Hispanus (d. 1248), argued that a fugitive to sanctuary should later be subject to *accusatio*, an ancient form of private prosecution recognized in canon law, or even handed over to secular justice.[40] The ordinary gloss went on to explain why some canon lawyers argued for this position:

> If no one is able [to bring an accusation] crimes would remain unpunished: but this ought not be. For in this manner the privilege of the Church would be an occasion for much delinquency. On account of this some say that [the sanctuary seeker] is able to be accused by anyone, lest in this way [sanctuary] permit impunity.[41]

After raising this objection, however, the ordinary gloss rejected it. The subsequent prosecution of a sanctuary seeker would "render as a nullity the privilege of churches," and this would be both "unjust" and "heretical."[42] What profit is there, if "the Church gains the fugitive's life and he is afterward decapitated?"[43] Confirming the ancient protections that attached to sanctuary seekers, the gloss declared that the fugitive should "in no way lose his life or his members," then offered two alternatives. Either the fugitive should "make pecuniary satisfaction,"[44] or if he was destitute he should be put into servitude to those he wronged or to whom he owed debts.[45]

The thirteenth-century gloss to the *Decretum* reveals that the prospect that sanctuary seekers could achieve impunity for their crimes had become a gripping problem for canon lawyers. Although the gloss rejected the position taken by Laurentius that sanctuary seekers ought to be prosecuted and punished lest sanctuary result in impunity for crimes, it conceded the force of the argument. The answer provided by the gloss—that this would be a heretical nullification of the church's privilege—merely asserted that the church's privilege trumped any other interests at stake.

A remarkable breach had opened between the thinking of the canonists and the ancient patristic traditions. Augustine had asserted that one who fled to the penitential discipline of the church "did not permit his wrongdoing to remain unpunished."[46] Rather, by "punishing themselves" through penance, supplicants assured that their punishment was more complete than that offered at court.[47] By contrast, nowhere did the thirteenth-century gloss suggest that sanctuary opened the way to a more profound form of punishment, nor did medieval canonists pick up this ancient line of thought. Instead, the gloss seemed to grant that sanctuary was a restraint on punishment, for canon law permitted only restitution and servitude where secular law might otherwise demand blood. The argument that sanctuary invited wrongdoers to further delinquency was not challenged; it was merely countered with an overriding concern—the integrity of the church's privileges. Having lost its identity in the canon law as a way in which wrong might be undone or amended, punishment had been tacitly placed in the service of preventing wrong.

Scholars studying secular criminal courts in the Italian city-states and in Angevin Marseille have shown that the "primary goal of government" even into the fourteenth century was "to reconcile criminal and victim rather than to punish the offender," suggesting that the intellectual currents evident in thirteenth-century canon law had not been integrated into government practices in European penal practices.[48] The domestication of sanctuary in the English common law was likewise not grounded in a commitment to deterrence, and as a consequence sanctuary and punishment did not come into direct conceptual conflict within the common law.

DOMESTICATED SANCTUARY: A VIEW FROM THE PLEA ROLLS

Sanctuary meshed quite well within the overall framework of English law enforcement, despite its incompatibility with deterrent-oriented doctrines that the canonists had been developing. The common law domesticated sanctuary by integrating it within the procedures of felony jurisdiction. By domestication, I mean only that the sanctuary protections that had long existed in England were brought within the scope of royal law in such a way that the feud-resolving and penitential aspects of sanctuary were muted and the prerogative of royal officials to oversee sanctuary claims and abjuration was decisively established. English kingship had long endorsed sanctuary and sought to regulate it, but by the late twelfth century, sanctuary had been incorporated into the routine administration of criminal jurisdiction. As we saw before, the administration of criminal justice in twelfth-and thirteenth-century England was not much concerned with deterring crime, and objections that sanctuary might undermine the deterrent force of law received little attention within the common law. Rather, sanctuary allowed medieval English law to publicize and exclude a large number of felons, while maintaining effective royal jurisdiction over a wide range of disputes. At the same time, sanctuary remained the emblem of pious, benevolent kingship that English ecclesiastics had articulated in the first half of the twelfth century.

Examining the sanctuary claims in the records of thirteenth-century royal justice suggests that such claims were entirely commonplace. Men and women of all stations and trades, nameless wanderers, and (though considerably less often) clerics took sanctuary for all sorts of felonies. At any given eyre visitation, scores of suspected or accused homicides, thieves, and other malefactors were entered in the rolls as having "fled to the church, acknowledged the felony, and abjured the realm." For example:

> Two malefactors fled to the church at Halliwell. It is not known where they were from, nor are their names noted. At the church they acknowledged thefts and abjured the realm.[49]

Or, "William and Radbert, under suspicion of wrongdoing, fled to the church, acknowledged thefts, and abjured the realm. They were strangers."[50] Or again: "Two men and two women stole bread in the village of Ballingsbury, fled to the church, acknowledged the theft, and abjured the realm."[51]

Sanctuary might be a family affair, as husbands and wives sometimes took sanctuary and abjured the realm together.[52] On the other hand, a woman named Edith is reported to have fled to a church, confessed to killing her husband, and abjured alone;[53] the man who had assisted her in the killing, Gernasius, fled as well, but not to a church, so he was outlawed.[54] Infrequently, women abjured alone;[55] more often, they did so with company.[56] When "Greta who was the wife of Walter Russel put herself in the church" and abjured, "the jurors testified that Angus of London, Alicia his consort, William Potter, and Henry of Winton" abjured as well.[57] It may be that coroners consolidated abjurers when they arrived at a church to take acknowledgment of felony, assigning a single port to all the sanctuary seekers that had arrived at a church since the last batch had been dispatched. Fathers and sons sometimes fled to sanctuary together,[58] as did brothers,[59] and occasionally entire bands of marauders.[60]

The common law required sanctuary seekers to forfeit their goods when they abjured. Because the amount of chattels they possessed was recorded in the rolls, we can get a sense of how much property they owned. Most owned very little, and the rolls often recorded that the sanctuary seeker "had no chattels." Others had some money that was forfeited to the crown. Possibly they gave their goods and money to others before claiming sanctuary in order to avoid forfeiture. Sometimes they simply forfeited whatever they had stolen. Although the *Laws of Edward the Confessor* had suggested that sanctuary-seeking thieves had to restore the goods they had stolen, from the thirteenth century onward the common law considered all of the goods in a fugitive's possession forfeit to the crown. An entry from the Cornish eyre of 1302 reported that the rightful owner of some stolen oxen pursued the rustler until he took sanctuary. When the coroner arrived to oversee the thief's abjuration, he returned the oxen to their owner "because he had followed up and tried to take the thief." The justices took a different view and fined the coroner for his "folly" in not turning the stolen goods over to the crown.[61]

Sanctuary and Clerical Privilege

Clerics seldom claimed sanctuary,[62] and abjured the realm even less frequently.[63] In principle, though not always in practice, criminous clerks were to be taken into the discipline of the Church rather than exiled. Among the examples of clerics who claimed sanctuary were some who abjured from Westminster. When they later returned to England, they were simply handed over to the bishop, but a layman who returned from an abjuration had to produce a charter proving the king's pardon, or face outlawry.[64] In another instance, Alex, a vicar in Oxfordshire, killed Adam de Bryton and fled to the church,[65] where he remained for five months (well in excess of the traditional forty-day limit) before leaving the church "and returning himself to the king's peace."[66] Because of his clerical status, Alex was delivered to the Bishop of Lincoln who vouched that Alex was undergoing ecclesiastical discipline.

Indeed, the question of clerical abjuration appears to have been something of an ongoing controversy. In 1286, the Bishop of Lincoln complained to the king that a larcenous chaplain "was prepared to abjure the realm, to the prejudice of the liberty of the church."[67] The bishop "besought the king to cause the chaplain to be delivered to him as diocesan, to be treated in accordance with the liberty of the church without making abjuration."[68] The king held the matter for discussion with his council.[69]

Other clerics, however, abjured without objections from their bishops. A clerk named John de Wylverton, "wanting to shoot arrows at a certain target . . . shot Anne, the daughter of Henry, with an arrow under her left breast [while she was] standing in the house of Henry her father."[70] Anne "died two days later and John quickly afterward put himself in the church of St. Thomas, acknowledged having killed Anne, and abjured the realm of England."[71] This time, no objections from the church were registered. Similarly, when a chaplain named Roger stole some cloth from the church of the Holy Trinity, the Bishop of Salisbury appeared and told the justices in eyre that the cloth was taken without authority, and Roger was made to abjure, possibly at the bishop's insistence.[72] Continuing controversies over clerical abjuration prompted Edward II to issue legislation on the matter in chapter 15 of the *Articuli Clerici*:

> A Clerk fleeing to the Church for Felony, to obtain the Privilege of the Church, if he affirm himself to be a Clerk, he shall not be compelled to abjure the Realm; but yielding himself to the Law of the Realm, shall enjoy the Privilege of the Church, according to the laudable Custom of the Realm heretofore used.[73]

There is little reason to believe that the *Articuli Clerici* completely settled the matter. As a practical matter, it suggests that episcopal discretion, rather than that of the coroner or king's bailiff, would thereafter be decisive when the question of clerical abjuration arose.

Getting to Sanctuary

Sanctuary entries in the rolls often obscure the details of flights to a sanctuary. The phrase most often favored in the rolls, "*fugit ad ecclesiam*," might describe a casual stroll to the church to confess a deed long past,[74] or it might describe a desperate flight from armed and angry pursuers. When details of how fugitives actually got to the church are included in the rolls, however, they reveal some remarkable routes. With astonishing frequency, sanctuary seekers arrived immediately from the prison where they were being held for trial. At Kent in 1228:

> Hugh le Orp killed Richard Fallon with a hatchet and was captured. He was delivered to Hugh le Windesoy, then sheriff. Afterwards, he

broke gaol and fled to the church of St. Augustine, acknowledged the death, and abjured the realm.[75]

Royal justices imposed fines on officials and communities for jailbreaks with a frequency that suggests that escape from custody was not terribly difficult or uncommon. For instance, Walter Steward, "quickly captured, fettered, and put in the custody of the prior of the hospital of St. John of Jerusalem at Clerkenwell" after he struck and killed a man in a brawl, escaped from the hospital and simply put himself (*posuit se*) "in the church of St. John of Jerusalem at Clerkenwell."[76] John, son of Thomas, in Kent was able to escape from prison in Canterbury, and later from custody in Stowington before finally taking flight to a church and abjuring.[77]

Because the crown fined jailers for escapes, sanctuary seekers might well encounter people intent on keeping them from reaching sanctuary. Captured among a band of thieves (a band that included his mother), Richard Garlich "fled toward the church."[78] Along the way, "Richard was opposed by a William. Richard slew William with a knife, then immediately placed himself in the church, acknowledged that he had killed William, and abjured the realm before the coroner."[79] Although little is known about this William, others made something of an office out of preventing sanctuary seekers from reaching the church. In Stafford towards the end of the thirteenth century, a clerk named William Tyssington appears in the rolls on more than one occasion, capturing felons who had escaped from jail and tried to take sanctuary in the Church of the Blessed Mary at Tuttebury. When one particular thief escaped from prison by night, William Tyssington, "perceiving this escape, approached the church in order to impede the thief from entering the church."[80] The "janitor of the prison, William Porter," hastened to the church "for the same cause"[81] and stood sentry in the dark waiting for the fugitive. As Tyssington arrived, Porter, "seeing him coming towards the church, believed him to be the escaped thief and quickly struck him with a sword under his left ear." Tyssington, "assaulted, gravely wounded, and believing the janitor to be the escaped thief . . . quickly struck him back with a hatchet in the head" and killed him.[82] The escaped thief apparently was not captured. One sanctuary seeker, who found that the clerics within had barred the church door, turned to fight his pursuers, even managing to kill one, but was himself killed at the threshold of the church.[83] Escapee Copinus de Bruge complained that "he was intercepted when part of his body had been within the boundary of the church."[84] Although his pursuers said "that Copinus was totally outside the boundaries of the church when he was taken,"[85] the royal officials simply "concede[d] by special grace that Copinus be restored to the church, afterwards [to do] according to the law and customs of the English realm."[86] Even as late as the middle of the fourteenth century, some friars in York complained in a petition to the king that some men "have often wickedly made ambushes against felons fleeing for sanctuary" and set "watches by day and night within the churchyard."[87] But Yorkshire was not the only English county where fleeing felons faced serious risk. Elyas, a chaplain imprisoned at Staffordshire to await trial for murder, "killed the jailer's attendant, escaped from the prison, and fled toward the church."[88] Clerical status did not help Elyas in this case. "The jailer and others from Staffordshire, pursued him and cut off his head" before he could reach the church.[89] Still, these are exceptional instances. Evidence from the rolls suggests that astonishing numbers of felons were able to escape from custody and gain the church without great difficulties.

Reginald Underwood's flight to sanctuary was a bit more unusual. He "was captured red-handed with twenty shillings stolen from Richard de Lyndon" and was led before the royal justices, where he "put himself on the country" (i.e., consented to a jury trial).[90] He was judged guilty "and was hanged."[91] Afterwards, several of Reginald's friends "came to take his body down . . . intending to carry the body to the guest-house of the convent church in preparation for burial."[92] When they arrived at the convent house with the body, "Reginald drew breath, and revived."[93] Finding himself conveniently within a building that possessed the sanctuary privilege, Reginald "acknowledged that he had stolen the twenty shillings and abjured the realm before the coroner." The pen of a twelfth-century monastic writer might have been turned Reginald's case to the glory of some saint. But the plea rolls were administrative records and the justices were not inclined to credit Reginald's revival to divine intervention, so the coroner who allowed Reginald to abjure after he revived was fined.[94]

In a more mundane instance, "Alan de Bloyon, rector of the church of Ludwon, killed Michael the Steward . . . and quickly put himself in his own house at Ludwon, *which is a sanctuary*."[95] Alan lived in a house attached to the church that, by canonical rules, also counted as a sanctuary.[96] Even if he had been captured, Alan might have pled clergy, but by "fleeing to the church," he avoided capture and pleading his clergy altogether. For those who were not fortunate enough to live in a house that qualified as a sanctuary, it helped to know someone with special access to a church. In Norfolk, an outlawed felon named Nigel sought aid at the house of the prior, Richard. Richard not only received Nigel, which was itself a serious offense on account of Nigel's outlawry, but he also "gave Nigel the key to the church" just as the bailiffs were coming to seize him. Nigel "quickly placed himself in the church, and there acknowledged a theft, and abjured the realm before the coroner."[97]

Restrictions on Claiming Sanctuary

Medieval English common law knew few restrictions on the sanctuary privilege, in contrast to both contemporary canon law and Roman law. A thirteenth-century decretal of Innocent III specifically excluded from sanctuary "thieves, those who destroy fields by night, and highway robbers,"[98] categories of criminals that Roman law excluded as well. Although some medieval common law treatises held that "thieves, robbers, murderers, and night prowlers" ought not to have sanctuary, a clear reference to Roman-canon rules, the common law knew no such restriction to the right.[99] Murderers, thieves, robbers, and marauders of all sorts regularly claimed sanctuary at common law, as did rapists, a category of criminal that canon law excluded from the protection of sanctuary but English law did not.[100] Moreover, canon law also denied sanctuary to those guilty of sacrilege, but in practice English law did not. When some roving thieves came to Hertfordshire around 1255 "and stole bread and some ornaments from the Church," an act clearly within the canonical definition of sacrilege, they were permitted sanctuary.[101] Likewise, Henry de Stanford, captured at Berkshire in possession of some stolen church ornaments, was able after escaping from custody to take sanctuary.[102] English common law did, however, require that the sanctuary seeker had committed an actual felony, a rule that could create curious incentives. As the author of *Fleta* explained:

> There are, however, certain timid men who seek the protection of the Church, although they have not committed a felony. In this event they will be well advised to acknowledge that they have slain someone whom they will be able to produce afterwards alive and well, so that they may be in a position to sue for the king's grace should they require it.[103]

Roman canon law excluded some types of criminals from sanctuary, while the common law only excluded non-felons.

Canon Law in the Common Law of Sanctuary

Although the English common law did not enforce the same restrictions found in the Roman-canonical tradition, canon law did influence sanctuary law in England. While murderers and thieves were not excluded from sanctuary, not every church to which felons fled turned out to offer protection. Canon law only recognized sanctuary claims made in churches that had been consecrated, or in which a mass had been performed.[104] One group of felons learned this the hard way. After Roger of Churlington, Richard le Bole, Thomas of Churlington, and Hugo Messer "feloniously broke into the houses of Hugo Wild and John Messer," they carried off some of their goods. The hue and cry was raised and a group of villagers set out after the four burglars, who were able to reach a small field church before their pursuers surrounded them. The four "held themselves in the aforesaid church and fired arrows at their pursuers and committed other wrongs until their pursuers came upon them with force and arms and decapitated them."[105] Because the men had fled to a chapel that "was not consecrated," their capture and execution was not considered a breach of sanctuary.[106] The entry in the plea roll does not hint that canon law was explicitly invoked to determine the case, but the rule employed had canon-law antecedents.

In another instance, however, the royal justices consulted canon-law rules directly. At London in 1321, the king's justices sitting in eyre consulted with the Bishop of London when they were unsure whether sanctuary ought to be granted to a woman who killed a priest in a church and then remained in the church claiming sanctuary.[107] The bishop replied that she should not have sanctuary, sending along a copy of a papal bull stating the rule.[108] The justices read "the tenor" of the bull aloud, and the woman was denied sanctuary. Refusing to follow the justices' advice to admit the crime and plead mercy, she put her fate in the jury's hands and was hanged.

A Latin text appended to the end of a Yearbook from the thirtieth year of Edward I's reign also sheds light on the common law's adoption of the canon law rule mandating that sanctuary claims were only valid when made within a consecrated church. A man on trial for theft addressed the court saying, "Lord, I was in a church and I was dragged out. I ask for the benefit of the right [of sanctuary] that I may be sent back whence I was forcefully extracted." But the justice responded, "We say that this church was never consecrated by a bishop." When the prisoner asserted that it was, the jury was asked and answered that "the church never was consecrated by the bishop." Asked again how he would like to plead, the prisoner responded that he wished to stand trial. The justice perceived what the prisoner evidently did not: The same jurors who decided the church was not consecrated, and therefore of no protection to the prisoner, were probably not disposed favorably toward the prisoner. The justice appeared to like the prisoner more than the jury, for he addressed the prisoner again, saying, "Prisoner, we believe that their verdict will work against you. You are healthy and strong. It is better for you to acknowledge the truth and become an approver (give testimony against another) before you are convicted by the jury. After you are convicted, you lose your voice."[109] The man then gave testimony against his companion, but because the companion was acquitted by the jury, the young man was hanged anyway.[110]

It is noteworthy in this case that the jury was left to decide whether the church was consecrated. When a question arose about the status of a prisoner who pled clergy (in order to be removed from the royal jurisdiction), the bishop was typically consulted to decide the case. Presumably, a bishop would know whether a church had been consecrated and could tell the court. It was not always a straightforward question, since under canon law a church that had not yet been consecrated by a bishop could still be considered consecrated for purpose of sanctuary if a mass had been said within the building. Under the common law, however, the jury apparently was able to determine the sacred status of a church building.

Clearly, royal justices did not consult canon law in every case in which they might have. In 1329 at Northampton, "a contention arose in the cemetery of the church at Brampton between William Hanred, on the one side, and Magister Richard, parson of the church."[111] In the graveside dispute, "William struck the parson with a knife in the belly so that he died the morning of the next day."[112] Under the canon law, killing someone in a cemetery was considered the same as killing someone in a church. It nullified a sanctuary claim. Nevertheless, when William escaped from the prison in which he was being held for his trial, he fled immediately to a church, where he appears to have been received in the sanctuary. According to the roll, after "putting himself in the church at Stoke," however, William did not abjure, but "returned himself to the peace of the lord king." He was then delivered to stand trial, convicted, and hanged. The roll does not shed light on why William returned to the king's peace, so we do not know whether he hoped for acquittal, was unwilling to go into exile,[113] or perhaps was ultimately denied sanctuary. In any event, the roll did not explicitly say that William could not have sanctuary because he shed blood (of a parson, no less) on sacred ground, whereas in London a few years earlier the justices had relied directly on a papal bull to say just that.

"Unclaiming" Sanctuary

We saw above that the author of *Fleta* thought only felons could have sanctuary, recommending that "timid men" who wanted refuge in a church without having committed a felony should lie and say they had killed someone. But some did claim the protections of the church before they actually fell within reach of crown penal law. When Richard Jordan in Middlesex "was captured for burgling . . . some barley and taken to Newgate prison," his wife, "perceiving that Richard had been led to prison, placed herself in the church from fear that she would be captured."[114] There, she waited for forty-six days "guarded from without by men of the vill," "until a certain Agnes Gaymer came to her," and informed her "her husband had been acquitted." Agnes exited the church, placed herself in "the custody of the village," stood trial for the stolen barley, and was likewise acquitted.[115] Agnes not only was able to take refuge without acknowledging any felony, but she was also able to stay within the church six days longer than the common law allowed until her husband's legal fate became clear. Had things gone badly for her husband at trial, Agnes would have been well positioned to abjure the realm safely.

Agnes appears to have been exceptionally fortunate. Other cases suggest that once a refugee claimed sanctuary, it became difficult simply to exit the church and return home. To claim sanctuary was to initiate a set of legal procedures that could not always be easily discontinued. A 1298 entry in the *Coram Regem* rolls shows a man captured and brought to crown justice for leaving a church within which he had taken refuge. He tried to explain that he was not under indictment and had not committed a felony but had fled to the church in fear of his enemies and thought that he could freely leave the church once they had gone. He was mistaken, and the royal pardon he later secured, explicitly listing wrongful exit of the church among the trespasses for which he was forgiven, shows the extent to which royal law exercised control over sanctuary.[116] Another man, after wounding his foe in a fight, fled to the church in the expectation that the wounded man would die.[117] Discovering that his enemy had recovered, he exited the church. Still, the common law considered this an escape from sanctuary and the man was required to secure a pardon "for his escape from the said church and any consequent outlawry."

Because practices were not always consistent, in rare cases a sanctuary seeker was able to leave the church without either putting himself to trial or needing to seek the king's pardon. At Sussex in 1235, "a certain boy from Tyrningham wounded his friend by accident while wrestling."[118] Fearing his friend would die from the injuries, the boy "fled to the church, and held himself in the church."[119] As it turned out, his friend "was not badly wounded," and the sheriff (and subsequently, the justices) permitted the boy free exit from sanctuary.[120] Others were able to exit sanctuary without abjuring if they were able to make peace with the king from within sanctuary. In 1236, Henry III ordered his justiciar in Ireland to insure that "John Travers is able to exit the church and return to his land."[121] Captured "in war against the king," John had "redeemed himself and made satisfaction to the king," but Richard de Burgo continued to "distress John" and would not let him leave the church. Consequently, the king wrote to grant John free exit from the church and to suggest ominously that further word of "this repeated quarrel should not reach us."[122] This was a special dispensation. Ordinarily, a fugitive could only leave the church by abjuring the realm or by handing himself over for trial.

Once claimed, sanctuary was difficult to revoke. Sometimes fugitives to the church were forced to abjure the realm even when they should not have been. "Walter Miller of Codham fled to the church at Codham and abjured the realm." Thereupon, "Adam de Greneford, sergeant of the hundred and Burgh of Codham, acknowledged that he was present where Walter abjured and caused him to abjure even though Walter did not acknowledge any theft or anything other thing for which he ought to abjure the realm."[123] The sergeant was amerced for this wrongful abjuration. In a similar manner, a coroner at Berkshire in 1241 was called to answer "for making William de le Grave abjure the realm for such a small theft; namely, some corn worth only six pence."[124]

Sanctuary and Pardon

Sanctuary also provided time to arrange legal affairs or seek royal pardon. Juliana Helwenham, who put herself in the Church of the Mount Carmel

Friars, acknowledged that she had received her husband home after he had abjured England for committing a homicide.[125] The eyre record indicated that Juliana abjured England, but she was able to prove "that the lord king pardoned her and her abjuration,"[126] and she was acknowledged to belong within the king's "firm peace."[127] Securing a pardon from sanctuary was not uncommon. When "Nicholas de Secheford was riding upon his horse from one place to another with his infant daughter," she "accidentally suffocated and quickly expired in route." Nicholas "fled to the church," and made "supplication that the lord king deal with him mercifully."[128] After Henry Paris petitioned the crown for mercy while in sanctuary at St. Martin's in London, an entry in the Close Roll ordered the "mayor and sheriffs of London . . . to permit him to exit [the church] and come to the king's peace" because the king had pardoned him.[129]

Guarding Sanctuary Seekers Within the Church

It was the task of the village where the church was located to ensure that a sanctuary seeker did not exit the church and abscond before the coroner came to oversee his abjuration. Laws concerning the local community's obligations to guard against escape from sanctuary can be traced to Anglo-Saxon legislation. By the thirteenth century, the crown regularly imposed fines on villages that permitted a felon to escape from sanctuary before the coroner arrived. Still, a fair number of felons did just that, often with help. In 1311, a crown commission of oyer and terminer investigated a coroner's claim that "as he approach[ed] the church to receive [a felon's] abjuration according to custom, divers persons obstructed [him] in the discharge of his office, forcibly broke into the church . . ., compelled [the felon] to go forth from it, and beat the men appointed to guard him in the church."[130] Earlier, in Buckinghamshire in 1272, "John Baldwin and his brother Nicholas" killed a man over some sheep, then "fled to the church at Herselaw."[131] There, "they delayed five days [until] certain strangers, by night, and by force and arms, led them away" before the brothers had properly abjured in front of the coroner. As a result, the strangers were outlawed, and the village of Herselaw was amerced for their escape. In Norfolk, "Simon, the son of Thomas Gwythorp, fled to the church and acknowledged himself to be a thief, but afterwards escaped from the church." It was testified "that Simon . . . gave [to those guarding him, including at least one cleric] ten pounds for their aid and counsel in helping him to escape from the church."[132]

The assistance that some sanctuary seekers received in escaping suggests that the task of guarding against escape was not always a welcome one. It could be violent and it could be expensive. In the mid-fourteenth century, men from Huntingdon complained that they were guarding a felon in sanctuary "at heavy cost and not without depression of their estate."[133] Some villages, however, embraced the duty to guard a church against the escape of fugitives with enthusiasm prompting complaints from clerics.

Among articles submitted by clerics to Edward II was the following complaint:

> Whilst [fugitives] be in the Church, [they] are kept . . . by armed men [and] . . . so straightly, that they cannot depart from the Hallowed Ground to empty their Belly, and cannot be suffered to have Necessaries brought to them for their Living.[134]

The king responded:

> When [fugitives] be in the Church, their Keepers ought not abide in the Churchyard, except Necessity or Peril of Escape do require so. And so long as they be in the Church, [they shall not be compelled to flee away, but they shall have] Necessaries for their living, and may go forth to empty their Belly.[135]

Nevertheless, when one sanctuary seeker, seized as he was leaving the boundaries of the church where he had claimed sanctuary, claimed that he was only going to use the privy, it was decided that he should have used a place closer to the church, and he was denied sanctuary.[136]

Sanctuary and Abjuration

While it is not clear what earlier English practice entailed, by the end of the twelfth century a sanctuary seeker who refused to stand trial or was unable to secure a pardon was required to abjure the realm.[137] The plea rolls show that some felons were reluctant to abjure, and that administrative efforts were expended making sure that they did. In 1232, Henry III issued a writ commanding that two of his "coroners be sent to Horncastle to see a certain thief who holds himself in the church of Horncastle and who has confessed himself to be a thief and malefactor . . . [and make] him abjure according to the custom of the land and according to the liberties conceded to the bishop."[138] Likewise, the rolls of the itinerant justices recorded that when "Walter Bret . . . held himself in the church" without abjuring, the coroner had "*milites* sent in to him" to apprise him of his choices and assist him in his decision.[139] Finally, "he abjured the realm, electing Dover" as his port of departure. Had Walter refused to abjure, it seems from the sending of the soldiers that the crown would have allowed him (despite Bracton's hesitancy about laymen removing fugitives from a church) to be seized and jailed.

The advice preserved by happenstance in a fourteenth-century cartulary suggests the same. In a letter to an unnamed lady, who may herself have been lingering within sanctuary, Johannes Wollys explained: "*My Lady . . . yf the felon wyl not have a coroner he* [the coroner] *may take hym out of sentuary and bring him to the kyngys gaol by the law.*"[140] As Wollys, who may have been a coroner, explained: "*for the law of Ynglonde requiryth none odyr thyng but that the chyrche shal safe a[ll] those from deth and not to kepe a felon or a mortherer* [more than] *XL days.*"[141] At the end of such time, the "*coroner sholde execute hys offyce acordyng to hys dewte*" and see to the fugitive's abjuration or imprisonment.

The duties that Johannes Wollys described were assigned to coroners in the 1190s, but were not exclusively performed by coroners until the middle of the thirteenth century. In the late-twelfth- and early-thirteenth-century plea rolls, in fact, abjurations are often recorded without any mention of who oversaw the abjuration, though we know that sheriffs and their serjeants administered abjurations before 1194.[142] By the 1230s, however, abjurations are increasingly recorded as "*coram coronatoribus,*" that is, before the coroners.

In the thirteenth century, not only did coroners begin playing a more consistent part in the administration of abjurations, they were sometimes subjected to fines for improperly handling abjurations. For instance, in 1247 at Northamptonshire, " . . . Henry de Faund, the coroner, was not present "*in propria persona sua*" at the abjuration of a felon, sending instead "Walter de Faldingwurth and Gilbert Proportum, his servants, and Simon Crotte, then bailiff" to hear the felon acknowledge his wrong and abjure the realm.[143] Doing so was out of order, and the bailiff, who appeared to have taken the lead in improperly "making the felon to abjure," was amerced for it.[144] Similarly, in 1248 at Gloucester, when a felon "abjured the realm without the coroner and before the bailiff," the bailiff was amerced.[145] The respective power and responsibility of coroners vis-à-vis bailiffs seems to have been an ongoing source of controversy. Three decades later, in 1279, the justices had to explain that bailiffs "have no power to perform the office of coroner."[146] The bailiff in that case was fined, and his abjurations were annulled, making outlaws of those whom he had abjured.[147]

The coroner also was responsible to assure that fugitives who abjured left by the proper port. In some instances the abjurer "elected a port" himself;[148] in others the coroner assigned a port to him. Hunnisett claims that coroners might give relatively benign felons close ports while sending particularly undesirable felons to far away ports. But the rolls show that the coroner did not have complete discretion in assigning a port. At Staffordshire, a coroner was amerced "because he gave the felon port at Berwick-upon-Tweed when he should have assigned a nearer port."[149]

Roger of Burton, the king's coroner, gave Juliana de Kington some "vestments and shoes" as she abjured alone from Staffordshire in 1293, but was fined for it by royal justices.[150] Recall Bracton's directive that the abjurer was to travel unshod. It is not clear how the coroner's misdeed in this came to light, but it suggests that some sanctuary seekers were able to negotiate some of the terms of their abjuration. Indeed, there must have been an economy of abjuration that does not appear in the rolls. C. A. F. Meekings shrewdly suggested that aspects of the finances of abjuration remain hidden from view. "Abjuration must have cost something," he speculated, before noting that summoning a coroner probably involved expenses for room, board, stabling, and gifts for the services involved with recording an abjuration.[151] Abjuring felons, of course, had to forfeit their chattels to the crown, but this accounting was kept by the coroner and there may have been some slippage.

Removing Fugitives from Sanctuary

Not every sanctuary seeker abjured the realm. Some were extracted by crown officers. According to a 1278 entry in the Rolls of Parliament, Ivo Texton made delay in the sanctuary of the St. Berean church for "half year and more," even marrying a woman and living with her in the sanctuary. The sheriff, after lengthy efforts, was finally able to capture Ivo and had him held by men of the four nearest frankpledges. The petition does not mention Ivo's suspected crime, as it was primarily intended to complain that the sheriff's actions violated the charter of liberties held by the church where Ivo had married and lived.[152]

Others were able to remain in sanctuary almost indefinitely without provoking crown officers. At Shireburn, a "mute, named Richard, held himself in the church of Kerswell for eight and one half years for the death of John Baldwin."[153] Prompted by some unknown petition, the crown merely "conceded to the abbot of Shireburn" the authority "to lead Richard from the church and keep him during his lifetime in [the abbot's] house in Shireburn." According to the roll entry, the abbot was to be responsible for providing Richard with necessities and to safeguard that Richard did not leave the house without permission.[154]

Breaches of Sanctuary

A noteworthy instance of sanctuary breach, occurring in the late twelfth century, comes to us in narrative, rather than legal sources, and provides details not ordinarily found in the plea rolls. William Fitz Osbert, known as William Longbeard, led a tax riot in London in 1196. Longbeard, who was credited with a modest education but unusual eloquence, was consistently described as a rabble-rouser, though Matthew Paris and Roger of Hoveden both offer a slightly sympathetic accounts, suggesting that oppressive taxation in London was unjust to the poor. William Newburgh credited Longbeard with 52,000 followers and a large cache of iron tools to be used for breaking into houses and fortifications. Longbeard was apparently politically astute as well because he successfully played his opposition to London's nobility as loyalty to the crown.[155] Summoned by the magnates of the realm to answer for stirring up London's poor, Longbeard arrived at the appointed hour surrounded by a mass of poor people who tried to protect him from being captured. When armed men were sent into the crowd to seize Longbeard, a melee ensued. Longbeard reportedly killed one of the men sent to capture him before taking sanctuary in the Church of St. Mary le Bow. Most of Longbeard's throng dispersed at this point, and the church was surrounded by the men of Hubert Walker, who was both the king's justiciar and the Archbishop of Canterbury.

Hubert Walker apparently commanded his men to smoke Longbeard out of the sanctuary.[156] Although Ralph de Diceto suggested that Longbeard himself set fire in the church,[157] Gervase of Canterbury simply reported that a "fire was started" after stressing that Longbeard was offered and refused an ecclesiastical trial and safeguard of his "life and limbs" if he came out of the church.[158] Whatever its source, the fire drove Longbeard into the open where he was captured. At trial he was convicted and his death sentence was carried out at Tyburn after Longbeard was dragged along the streets of London behind a horse.

Roger of Hoveden's account stated that churchmen took severe umbrage at the fact that the Archbishop of Canterbury ordered his men to burn a fugitive out of the church, remarking that relations between the monks at Canterbury and Hubert Walker were badly strained for some time afterward. In contrast, William of Newburgh's account implied that the extraction of Longbeard was not a violation of sanctuary law. According to Newburgh, Longbeard gave a gallows confession in which he admitted having implored the help of Satan and having had sexual intercourse with his concubine within the church, thus "polluting the church with his semen."[159] Newburgh was trying to show the foolishness of venerating Longbeard after his death (a nascent martyr cult was brutally and effectively suppressed by the crown). Polluting a church with semen and committing sacrilege by making an oath to the devil just happening to be two acts very high on the list of things that could deconsecrate a church and nullify its sanctuary protections. Longbeard, in Newburgh's account, could have scarcely done a better job had he consulted a checklist of things he might do to insure that the sanctuary he was in would lose the protections he sought. Newburgh, and other chroniclers such as Gervase of Canterbury, gave justifications for Longbeard's extraction and execution, but they did so within the canonical language of the desecration of a church.

Longbeard's case was exceptional in a number of respects. He was not, in so far as the sources reflect, offered an opportunity to abjure the realm. The archbishop best positioned to object to Longbeard's extraction also happened to be the king's justiciar who probably ordered the church to be set afire. Other than the strained relations between Hubert Walker and the monks at Canterbury, no other consequences for the violation seem to have followed. Rather, Longbeard's late-twelfth-century sanctuary claim appears to straddle the transformation of sanctuary as it moved out of its Anglo-Saxon and Norman feud context and into the context of the common law of felony. In the century that followed, sanctuary claims, as well as breaches of sanctuary, were handled under the routinized forms of the common law of sanctuary.

Despite Longbeard's fate, the thirteenth-century plea rolls suggest that the common law was responsive when sanctuary rights were breached and fugitives dragged out. For instance, after Henry Stanford escaped to sanctuary from the prison where he was awaiting trial, "the next morning Henry Lorim, William Petipas, Roger Farham and Henry Patchet came and forcefully dragged Henry from the church and threw him in prison . . . where he was detained for six months until he died."[160] At an inquest into the violation of sanctuary and the death of Henry the four men were found guilty by a jury and were put in prison.[161] Likewise, "Arthur and Thomas, sons of John, and Robert de la Port extracted by force and arms a woman from the church of All Saints," and "they threw her in prison where two days later she perished."[162] Those men, too, were held responsible for their actions. An elaborate breach of sanctuary orchestrated in 1284 prompted the king to issue a commission of oyer and terminer to the mayor of London and some other men concerning "the Satellites of Satan . . . who by night entered the church of St. Mary le bow, London, and violently seized Laurence Duket, . . . and after various torments hanged him with a rope in the said church."[163]

If the extracted fugitive was still alive, petition could be made for restoration to sanctuary. An exemplar of a writ for such restoration preserved in a register at Oxford dates from around 1318:

> The king to his beloved and faithful C. and D., his justices assigned to deliver the gaol at T., greeting. The venerable father R., bishop of Carlisle, has informed us by his letters patent that, whereas A., lately taken and detained in our prison at T. for a crime of theft alleged against him, had escaped from the said prison and fled to the church of the said vill to obtain the immunity of the said church, certain malefactors, unmindful of their salvation, going to the said church violently dragged said A. from the cemetery of the said church, or from the aforesaid church, and carried him off to Carlisle and delivered him to our then sheriff of the aforesaid county to be committed to prison, in which he is still detained to the manifest prejudice of the ecclesiastical liberty. And since we are unwilling that ecclesiastical liberty should in any way be infringed by us or by our ministers we command you that, if you establish the facts to be as alleged, you shall cause the said A. to be taken back to the same place from which he was dragged out . . . to remain there in the same condition as at the time of the aforesaid dragging forth, according to ecclesiastical liberty.[164]

A typical sanctuary restoration writ in the king's *Calendar of Close Rolls* read thus:

> To the sheriff of London. Order to cause Andrew de Sutton to be taken from prison and brought to the church of All Hallows, Haywharf, London, without delay, to stay where according to the ecclesiastical liberty, as S. bishop of London has shown the king that although Andrew had taken sanctuary at the church, and had entered the porch and held the ring of the door in his hand, and stayed there for some time, yet certain sons of iniquity drew him, who then called himself John de Catton, violently from the porch and led him to prison.[165]

When a sanctuary seeker was extracted and killed, symbolic restoration to the sanctuary might be required. In 1301, a man was dragged from sanctuary in Bury St. Edmund by the parents of the man he slew, taken before the bailiff, and hanged. Because it was impossible to restore the actual fugitive to sanctuary, the bailiff was ordered to give "sign of the restitution of the said Liberty" by placing an effigy "in the form of a man with the name and place of the aforesaid felon" displayed.[166]

At other times, apparent breaches of sanctuary did not prompt royal action. In an unusual case in Norfolk, a sheriff took a group of men out of sanctuary but was not held accountable for a breach of sanctuary. As the roll describes:

> Hubert, the vicar of the church at Westbarsham came with a gathering of strangers to the house of Roger the Chaplain of Barsham and by force and arms ejected him from his house. Roger went out and raised the hue and the aforesaid Hubert and the others . . . fled to the church. Afterwards, Hamo Passelawe, then sheriff, of the county came and seized them from the church and led them to the castle of Herewiti and there put them in prison. Then, the sheriff sent them away after securing pledges [to ensure the wrongdoers would appear before the justices].[167]

The sheriff removed the men from sanctuary, but he did not harm them physically. Instead, he took them to the castle prison, where it was probably much easier to guard them than in the church, made them give pledges for their appearance before royal justice, and let them go. Assuming the good vicar had enlisted clerics (the roll speaks only of "*ignoti extranei*") in his attack on Roger the Chaplain, the sheriff only anticipated the outcome of the case, for clerics would ultimately be delivered from royal justice to the church if they pled clergy. No one appears to have complained of the sheriff's actions, and he was not fined for them. In another of the rare removals that were not treated as breaches of sanctuary, a man who had enlisted in an army that was to be sent against the Scots but took sanctuary instead was made to exit and perform his military duties.[168]

After Abjuration

Sanctuary seekers who took an abjuration oath were guaranteed safe passage to their designated port, but they still might face significant dangers when they left the church to abjure the realm. By law, the abjuring felon was bound to leave immediately and stay to the main roads. If he lingered or strayed, he could be killed with impunity. Occasionally, even felons keeping to the main roads were molested, sometimes in private vendettas. Remaining close to the main highways while abjuring could be very important. After a certain Hugh from Lincoln fled to the church and abjured the realm, he was "captured off the highway and led to Northamptonshire." When the eyre arrived, "it was testified that Hugh had not exited far off the highway," and so the justices allowed him to continue his abjuration, implying that if he had been captured further from the highway his fate would have been different.[169] Not all felons captured during abjuration were afforded trials in order to sort out the legality of their capture. "After Walter Guyt exited from the church," abjuring for the murder of a cleric named William, six men "followed him until Stirling and there captured him . . . and amputated his head."[170] The six men were fined for their actions.[171] Likewise, six men ran afoul of the king's justices in Norfolk after they seized Margaret Whiting, an abjuring thief, and "cut off her head."[172] A third case, though unique in some respects, involved transportation of sanctuary seekers across the English Channel. In 1355, two men accused of piracy took sanctuary in a church on the Isle of Guernsey in the English Channel, abjured to France, and somewhat imprudently boarded a boat departing from Guernsey to Normandy. The felons, who should have thought twice before taking passage from an island whose inhabitants they had previously pirated, were taken only part of the way to France before they were made to exit the boat. Later, the Earl of Arundel was able to get pardons for some of the crewmembers who forced the pirates overboard.[173]

William Taylor of Whappelod was considerably more fortunate. After he killed Henry Harald "he fled to the church of St. Peter, Ely, where he acknowledged the felony before William Petrich, the king's coroner there, and abjured the realm." Along the way,

> the king, meeting [William] with the cross in his hands as he was on his journey to the sea to cross it according to the form of his abjuration, moved by pity, admitted him into his grace and pardoned him the abjuration and the suit of king's peace for the death as well as any consequent outlawry.[174]

Such gracious pardon, granted even to murderers, continued to be an emblem of medieval kingship. Even the men of Guernsey, despite their treatment of the abjuring pirates, benefited from royal grace. In 1354, they secured a royal pardon on behalf of a felon who had abjured England, traveled as far as Guernsey, and lived there in good repute.[175]

The Special Case of Hubert de Burgh

Although the plea rolls show that sanctuary claims had been subjected to the administrative processes of royal law since the late twelfth century, there are instances of sanctuary that suggest that sanctuary protections might sometimes operate outside the processes dictated by the common law. When Hubert de Burgh, the earl of Kent, one time justiciar for Henry III, and husband to the daughter of the king of Scotland fell out of royal favor in 1232, he sought refuge a church. Hubert's fall from power was spectacular. He had been named justiciar of England in 1215 at Runnymede, where, as one of King John's leading servants, he had encouraged the signing of Magna Charta. Hubert held the office of justiciar from the regency of Henry III until his precipitous fall in 1232. During that time Hubert had also played a crucial role in defending Dover against French invasion during the civil war. In a sense, Henry III owed his kingdom to Hubert. At one point, it could be said that Hubert "lacked nothing of royal power save the dignity of the royal diadem."[176] But the first decade of Henry III's regency was rife with conflict among the leading factions of the kingdom, much of it held over from fissures formed in the days of John. By 1227 Hubert's position at court had weakened, to the benefit of one of Hubert's oldest rivals, Peter de Roches. Hubert's relationship with Henry III took a devastating turn when Hubert was implicated in inciting riots in London against Italians holding English benefices granted by the pope.[177] Henry III sided with the interests of the papacy, and Hubert was divested of several of his castles and pursued by the king's soldiers. Hubert first took sanctuary in the priory at Merton.[178] But Hubert was forced from the priory when it appeared the mayor of London would obey an order from the king and seize Hubert. Hubert fled from the priory and took sanctuary again elsewhere. The king was eager to keep Hubert contained within the church, mandating to the "sheriff of Essex . . . [to] diligently guard Hubert so that he cannot exit the chapel in which he holds himself without being quickly captured and led immediately to the Tower of London." But Hubert seemed always able to make an escape, sometimes with help.[179] At one point, Hubert even delivered himself over to the king, taking the king up on his offer that if Hubert "*gratis et spontea* wished to exit the chapel in which he holds himself, then he would have safe custody . . . to the Tower of London."[180] But Hubert later escaped again to sanctuary. At another point, when Hubert was actually seized, he successful petitioned to be restored to the church.[181] By this time, others in Hubert's household, including his wife, had taken sanctuary as well. To the sheriffs in Norfolk and Suffolk Henry commanded "if Margaret, the wife of Hubert de Burgh, Earl of Kent, exits the liberty of St. Edmund, quickly capture her and lead her to the constable of the same Tower."

Sanctuary law seemed to play a significant role throughout the conflict. While Hubert was hiding within the church, the King went to great lengths to insure that he was not able to receive counsel from his allies. To the sheriff of Essex he wrote:

> [Do] not permit anyone, either religious men or any other, without the special mandate of the king, to have access to Hubert, neither to speak with him nor to carry any letter or mandate to him. Neither permit his men, who by license of the king prepare his food and serve him, to go in to him at any time or bring him his food, [unless] . . . they first swear that they bring no message or mandate to him or receive any other message from him. [Then] his food can be brought in the chapel to him. Also, . . . break and smash the small seals that he keeps still with him [which he apparently used in his communications with others.]

The king also restricted Hubert's diet, forbidding him more than "a half-penny loaf and a magnum of beer" each day. Later, while Hubert was still in sanctuary, the King allowed "Luke, the bishop of Dublin, to have access to Hubert in order to speak with him."[182] But at another time Henry forbade anyone "to bring or sell to Hubert any food or victuals." This later mandate is interesting because it conflicted with the canonical principle "that whoever impedes food to be administered to fugitives [in] the immunity of the church shall be excluded, by ecclesiastical censure, according to the judgment of the ordinaries."[183]

In the end, the king and Hubert settled at least some of their differences. Hubert avoided perishing in London Tower and Henry granted Hubert partial remission, "receiv[ing] him into his grace, and returning to Hubert [some of the] honors" which had been stripped from him.[184] That Hubert was able to communicate successfully with allies and arrange his affairs from the churches he took refuge in is demonstrated by the King's eagerness to control those with whom Hubert spoke in the church, those to whom Hubert communicated by letter, and what he ate. But Henry never directly attacked a church where Hubert sought protection. Henry had the church set under close guard, and more than once he exhorted the guards to be even more vigilant. Henry showed himself content to let Hubert remain safe so long as he was within the confines of sanctuary. There also seems never to have been any consideration that Hubert would abjure the realm in the manner common felons did. Perhaps it was unthinkable that an earl would be subject to such a thing, or merely impracticable. Hubert took to the church for wrongs done against his king, and from within the church he was able to come to terms with his foe. Indeed, there are hints in this case of the older modes of sanctuary and feud-resolution supposed in Anglo-Saxon sanctuary law, but the case is exceptional both for the status of the parties involved and for the manner in which the common law procedures for sanctuary were bypassed.

THE SPECIAL PROBLEMS OF CHARTERED SANCTUARIES

There was another aspect of sanctuary in medieval England that escaped the procedural rigor of the common law, and over time created more instability within English sanctuary than any other aspect of the practice. As we saw in the previous chapters, some English ecclesiastical houses, like their continental counterparts, possessed jurisdictional immunities secured by royal charters. In the thirteenth century, sanctuary seekers who fled to a chartered liberty appeared to be subject to the same rules that governed flight to ordinary churches. For example, in 1231, a cleric named John took sanctuary in the church of the liberty of St. Peter in York, but still "abjured the realm, electing for his port Dover, within 40 days."[185] Even though chartered liberties could prevent the entry of royal officials, thirteenth-century evidence suggests that fugitives reaching chartered sanctuaries were not yet assured permanent protection. In 1293 at Westminster, a man named Robert Carpenter "was staying in the liberty of the abbot of Westminster."[186] When it was discovered that Robert "had been indicted before the justices in the last eyre for the death of a man from Hereford," the sheriff of Middlesex tried to capture Robert. Because Robert was within the liberty, the sheriff could not do so. But this did not mean Robert was altogether beyond the reach of law. Instead, the abbot of Westminster had his own bailiffs seize Robert within the liberty. Robert subsequently "escaped, fled to St. Mary at Westminster, acknowledged that he had killed the man from Hereford, and abjured the realm." Despite Robert's escape, the case shows that Westminster was not allowing its chartered sanctuary to serve as a permanent respite for felons.

Other evidence, however, suggests that some thirteenth-century chartered liberties were offering more permanent protection to their fugitives. For instance, when Margaret de Elleghton did not appear before royal justices at York in 1231 to prosecute her appeal of rape against John, Hugh's son, the jurors explained that Margaret and John "were now married and living in the liberty of the Bishop of Durham," and therefore beyond the reach of royal law.[187] Still, the plea roll evidence shows that in the early thirteenth century royal justices were exercising close oversight in regard to chartered liberties, respecting them, but requiring that they prove the legitimacy of their claims. At Hexham in 1256, the itinerant justices complained that no one could tell who was responsible for the escape of a certain murderer because he fled to "the liberty" and "the bailiffs of the same liberty permit neither coroners nor sheriffs to enter the liberty," but they could not act against the immunity holders.[188] At Tynemouth in 1279, however, the prior could not show that he held a right to receive sanctuary seekers. In the eyes of the justices, he had simply been receiving fugitives, not offering legitimate sanctuary, and for this he was made to answer to the royal justices.[189]

Eyre records surviving from Cornwall in 1284 suggest there was some confusion in the western counties concerning the relationship between sanctuary and chartered liberties. For example, "Robert Peytenyn put himself in the church of St. Petroc in Aldestowe (now Padstowe) and before the coroner acknowledged himself to have committed many thefts and abjured the realm." But Robert did not leave the realm, for it was "testified by the twelve that Robert . . . and some others who had committed felonies in parts of Devonshire and Cornwall put themselves in the liberty of St. Petroc and held themselves there as if they were in a church." The assize roll does not say how long this went on, but eventually the coroner came into the liberty and made all "those men not living [directly] within the church," abjure the realm. In the end, the king's justices found that almost everyone had behaved wrongly, moving to judgment against the "prior holding the manor with the aforesaid liberty" as well as the coroner. The text does not specify, but it seems that the liberty holder was at fault for allowing Robert and the others to live within the liberty "as if in a church" when they should have abjured, and the coroner was at fault for infringing on the liberty and taking abjuration oaths from the felons there.[190]

In 1302, the liberty at Cornwall was better able to establish the legitimacy of its status as a sanctuary for felons. Among the privileges claimed by the liberty before the itinerant justices that year was the following: "If any thief was captured in the aforesaid sanctuary he should be led to the broken stone cross and there liberated."[191] Nonetheless, abjuration was required of sanctuary seekers as if they had fled to any other church. In 1302, "Thomas Stratton, from fear and in order that he not be captured, put himself in the liberty of St. Petroc of Padstowe, which is a sanctuary, and there acknowledged himself to be a thief, and abjured the realm before the coroner."[192] There was still at this point, at least in the liberty in Cornwall, no hint that someone might put himself permanently beyond the reach of authority by reaching a chartered sanctuary.

York provides some additional evidence for these developments. *Quo Warranto* proceedings held there around 1330 forced the cathedral of York and its dependent minsters to vouch for the liberties and customs exercised there. Among the documents produced by the Church of St. Peter in York was a letter purporting to record ancient liberties that had been challenged in 1106 by the sheriff of York, a man named Osbert. The letter explained that Osbert had tried to deprive the cathedral of the privileges it had held since Æthelstan's day. The church of St. Peter prevailed against Osbert and Henry I is said to have issued a charter confirming the old privileges, as determined by the wisest men of York, granted by the ancient kings. The inquest of 1106 probably happened as the 1330's letter stated, but contents of Henry I's confirmation charter are lost. It may have contained many of the same provisions confirmed for Yorkminster in 1253 by Henry III.[193] Henry III's charter confirmed the punishments to be imposed for capturing a criminal within liberty and specified the harshest penalties for those who dared take a man from out of the *frithstool* by the altar. But the 1330s letter produced for the *Quo Warranto* proceedings at St. Peter's contains considerably more detailed sanctuary privileges than anything in Henry I's extant charter. While the basis of St. Peter's sanctuary privileges was probably historically grounded, the detail produced in the 1330s is probably the result of overenthusiasm on the part of the church. After the penalties for breaching sanctuary were recited, additional information not found in York's comparable 1253 charter was included:

> If a homicide or thief or criminal or outlaw takes refuge in the church of St. Peter to protect his life and limbs, he shall enjoy peace there for the duration of thirty days. If within that period they cannot reconcile the man with those whom he has wronged, the clerics can bring him within those thirty days to any place the malefactor chooses, up to thirty miles away, with some emblem of the peace of the church and with relics, and if anyone breaks the peace against them in the aforesaid space he shall be guilty of a breach of the peace of the church.[194]

At this point the church of St. Peter seems to be describing a modified form of the sanctuary rules enforced in royal courts. The duration of the protection was shorter, thirty days, and the "abjuration" was limited to a thirty-mile area.[195] But the following portion from the same letter shows how such chartered liberties could also become permanent:

> If, however, somebody living amongst evil people wants to break away from their company and comes to the church of St. Peter preferring to live there in peace rather than stay with criminals, he can according to the customs of the church be in peace there as long as he likes.[196]

The remainder of the passage delineates the conditions under which such permanent refugees could leave the liberty temporarily to conduct outside business. The letter also claimed that churches in Durham, Hexham, Ripon, and Beverley possessed the same privileges. We see here perhaps the emergence of the permanent sanctuaries that would vex the king and parliament until the sixteenth century (see Chapter 8).

The chartered liberties represent an interesting exception to the otherwise close oversight that sanctuary received from royal justices in the common law.[197] Fifteenth-century common law records show that sanctuary seekers were still required to confess their felony to a coroner and abjure the realm within forty days. Yet, the permanent protection offered by the chartered liberties was a destabilizing force, prompting complaints, petitions, and legislative reforms that would transform English sanctuary law and prepare the ground for sanctuary's abolition.

Outside the chartered liberties, sanctuary continued to operate under the common law rules that had been in place since the late twelfth century. Until the sixteenth century, sanctuary seekers continued to be required to acknowledge their felonies to the coroner, and they continued to abjure the realm within forty days.[198] While the system may not have been much of a deterrent, save the fairly serious impositions caused by flight or abjuration, it seems to have been a fairly effective system for identifying felons and ensuring their exclusion from the realm. It also brought sanctuary claims within the administrative gaze of the crown.

The relationship between sanctuary and abjuration established by the common law seems to have been exceptional. In other parts of Europe, where the evidence is much less complete, sanctuary was also an important part of the criminal law, but seems to have been more closely related to temporary exile practices. As Dan Smail has shown for late-medieval Marseille, and Kathryn Reyerson for thirteenth-century Montpellier, sanctuary protections were well known and frequently invoked.[199] Marseille was an Angevin holding in the late Middle Ages, but its legal system was an amalgam of Roman law and local legislation that had been subjected to reforms by Charles I. Thirteenth-century Montpellier was a complicated combination of competing jurisdictional claims, as part of the city was subject to the king of Majorca, another to the king of Aragon, and episcopal jurisdiction competed with both. Nonetheless, both Marseille and Montpellier recognized sanctuary for crimes, and records suggest frequent recourse to sanctuary by criminals in both cities.

Unlike English sanctuary law, however, sanctuary in these continental cities appears to have been closely related to exile and reconciliation practices overseen by criminal courts. In urban Marseille, sanctuary seems to have provided a temporary safe space from which fugitives would escape into the countryside and negotiate peace with enemies and the city's justices.[200] Reyerson made similar findings in medieval Montpellier.[201] The situation is reminiscent of the English case, where fugitives sometimes used the time afforded by sanctuary to obtain royal pardons. Although it is difficult to know how many English abjurers slipped undetected back into England, it appears that the porous boundaries between city and countryside made it easier for sanctuary takers in continental cities to reintegrate themselves into their neighborhoods within a few months, in some cases years, of their sanctuary claims and flight. It is more difficult to know what circumstances were in the Italian city-states. Late-medieval Italian jurists certainly knew the practice, but some of them assumed a strong power on the part of secular authorities to extract and punish fugitives.[202] What actual practices were in Italy is hard to know, but William Jordan has suggested that the situation may have resembled medieval cities like Marseille, where fugitives took flight to the countryside in order to negotiate with their pursuers or to arrange matters with city magistrates while avoiding corporal sanctions.[203]

CONCLUSION

In the medieval common law, sanctuary meshed well with the primary administrative aims of the English crown and local communities. Wrongdoers were identified, felonies were confessed, and felons were excluded from the realm. Local communities sometimes complained that guarding fugitives was onerous and costly duty, and the church sometimes complained that laymen were overzealous in fulfilling their duties to guard fugitives, but sanctuary was a well-established feature of medieval English governance. It also accorded an important place for the church in the administration of discipline in England. After the common law's domestication of sanctuary, the practice was no longer connected in any direct way to the penitential discipline and care of souls that patristic writers had defended, but it still maintained an important place in the administration of felonies under English royal law. Evidence from the continent suggests that sanctuary was less centralized there, but that sanctuary claims operated within similar parameters, facilitating negotiations between feuding parties and allowing for the eventual reintegration of criminals into their neighborhoods.

Complaints against sanctuary law began mounting in the fourteenth century and appear with increasing regularity in the fifteenth century. Because the tenor of these complaints matched a growing line of criticism found already in late medieval canon law, it will be useful to examine sanctuary in the canon law before returning to the events that culminated in Henry VIII's attack on sanctuary law in England and corresponding attacks on sanctuary on the continent.

8

The Role of Canon Law in the Destruction of Sanctuary

The manner in which canonists defended sanctuary for crimes in the late medieval period signaled a remarkable change. Increasingly, they emphasized that sanctuary was a jurisdictional immunity of the Church, a territorial privilege against intrusions by temporal justice and an extension of the Church's dignity, power, and liberty. Unlike early medieval sources, late medieval canon law texts rarely discussed penance and reconciliation as cornerstones of sanctuary law. Rather, these texts grounded sanctuary law squarely on the Church's claims to impose, at least at certain times and places, its own law, unfettered by secular claims. Had matters stopped there, we might say that sanctuary law was transposed onto new intellectual foundations, that ancient understandings of sanctuary gave way to attempts to make more explicit the legal authority that grounded sanctuary. But matters did not stop there.

Late medieval canon lawyers also articulated new conceptual foundations for criminal law. In doing so, they eventually undermined the intelligibility of sanctuary itself. Canon lawyers, like civilian jurists, began in the thirteenth century to voice a new conviction that punishment, if properly administered, might prevent future wrongdoing and secure public interests. Although there was nothing particularly new about this idea, the concerted effort of the canon lawyers to justify criminal procedure and punishment in terms of the social utility of preventing crime worked an intellectual transformation within canon law. The implications of this new conception of punishment were fateful for sanctuary, for, as medieval canon lawyers began to point out with increasing frequency, sanctuary seemed to offer impunity to wrongdoers. Twelfth-century English kings had been taught by churchmen that liberal respect for sanctuary was an element of good kingship, but by the fifteenth century, even the papal curia was cautioning English kings against showing overmuch deference to sanctuary when it came to pursuing criminals and was restricting the classes of criminals who could claim sanctuary.

Unlike the English common law, jurists within the tradition of the learned laws paid considerably more attention to the question of who could make a valid claim to sanctuary. The common law of sanctuary was open to every sort of felony, and was only closed to debtors in the fourteenth century, even as it remained available to murderers, thieves, and other felons. Although civilians and canonists agreed that "those who are in churches cannot be extracted against their will"[1] and that those who forcefully extracted fugitives from churches could be punished by secular authorities,[2] they sometimes disagreed about what kind of criminals could claim sanctuary and how fugitives who did not warrant the privilege could be extracted from a church. Faithful to the rules inherited from classical Roman law, Roman lawyers favored the exclusion of homicides, *virginum raptores*, and highway robbers, and insisted that fugitive *servi* be returned to their owners as soon as a guarantee for their physical safety was given. Canon law was perceived to be more liberal in this regard, since under some conditions it admitted homicides and *raptores* into the protection of the church. The real difficulties, as these two groups of jurists saw it, lay in determining who had the authority to extract a fugitive who did not qualify for sanctuary. This question, as we will see below, was important for how both canonists and civilians articulated the conceptual foundations of sanctuary law in the late medieval period. While this chapter focuses on the development of the canon law jurisprudence of sanctuary law, it will be necessary to tack back and forth between the opinions of the civilians and the canonists on several key points in order to demonstrate the conditions of thought that accompanied the eventual demise of sanctuary law.

The sources of classical canon law only occasionally hint at the disposition of actual cases. By the twelfth century, the discordant mass of papal decrees, pronouncements by ecclesiastical councils, and writings of the Church Fathers presented a problem for canonists trying to understand the law of the Church, and considerable efforts were expended in the twelfth century and afterward to bring these canons into a workable order.

Because the history of the inception of canonical jurisprudence has been well told, we can focus our attention on what late medieval canon law had to say about sanctuary for crimes. Compared to the English plea roll material examined in the previous chapter, the canon law of sanctuary has received closer scholarly examination, though very little of this scholarship has appeared in English. Richard Helmholz has examined the development of medieval sanctuary law as part of a larger project to illustrate how civilians and canonists sought to reconcile difficult doctrines within their respective traditions,[3] but my aims here differ. I want to show how the debates over the fate of sanctuary law in the Roman canon tradition eventually influenced the fate of sanctuary in the English common law as well.

Nowhere would sanctuary's place seem more assured than in medieval canon law. Sanctuary was, after all, granted to those who fled to the protection of a church. Yet, intellectual preparation for the abolition of sanctuary emerged relatively early within canon law sources. More precisely, it emerged within understandings of the relationship between sovereignty, sanctuary, and punishment first articulated within canon law. This is not to say that the late medieval Church launched a direct attack on sanctuary law itself or actively sought its abolition. To the contrary, canon lawyers vociferously defended sanctuary law, in some cases as late as the eighteenth century.[4] But increasing reliance on deterrent-oriented understandings of punishment created a tension between sanctuary law and the emergent jurisprudential commitments of the canon law.

Traditionally, historians have attributed to Roman lawyers, not canonists, the first assault on sanctuary law on the European continent.[5] But the intellectual groundwork for the abolition of sanctuary was laid out within the canon law itself.[6] So when civilian jurists began criticizing, often with enthusiasm, the harmful effects of sanctuary law, they were following a path that had been marked out by canon lawyers.

SANCTUARY IN THE CLASSICAL CANON LAW

Although Gratian's *Decretum* was a schoolbook, not a window on twelfth-century legal practice, it provides insights into the place of sanctuary within the classical canon law, and it provided the starting point for later canonical accounts of sanctuary. Remarkably, the earliest recension of the *Decretum* hardly mentioned sanctuary at all.[7] At just the time that twelfth-century Anglo-Norman scribes were busy finding sanctuary protections in the laws of England's ancient kings, a massive collection of canon law was produced that barely noticed the matter.

Causa 36, q. 1, c. 3 contains the only mention of sanctuary in the first recension of the *Decretum* and it appeared among a group of canons that were not primarily concerned with sanctuary or ecclesiastical immunities. Rather, sanctuary appeared first in the *Decretum* within a discussion that distinguished the crime of rape from actions that were better classified under canon law as forced marriage, adultery, or fornication. While noting that the death penalty applied in cases where a girl was violently taken from her father's home and violated, the *Decretum* offered a dictum explaining that men who committed this deed would receive impunity if they fled with the girl to a church.[8] Gratian then included an adapted text from a Frankish council explaining that *raptors* who fled to the church with the women they seized received sanctuary protection (contrary to medieval Roman law). The Orléans canon had also been included in the *Decretum* of Ivo (3.108), the *Panormia* of Ivo (2.72), the *Tripartita*, and the *Decretum* of Burchard. According to Gratian's *Decretum*:

> If a *raptor* flees to church with her whom he has seized, and it is evident he has done violence to her, quickly free her from his power. The *raptor* shall be conceded impunity from death or punishment, but he shall be subjected to servitude, or if he has means he shall redeem himself [with a composition payment to the girl's father]. If the girl who was seized has a father, and she consented to the seizure, let her be excused and returned to the father's power. And let the *raptor* make satisfaction and put the father in a superior condition.[9]

The canon was ancient, dating back to the Arlean council convened by Clovis in 511. In its original context, the deed contemplated by the canon was not necessarily one of sheer sexual violence, but also of forced marriage (or at least marriage against the will of the girl's father).[10] The protections the *raptor* received once within a church, and the emendation he was expected to perform, were perfectly consistent with sanctuary as it appeared in early-medieval sources.

Every other sanctuary canon in Gratian's *Decretum* can be attributed to the later recension of the text. All but one was put into *Causa* 17 of the *Decretum.* The lone canon to appear elsewhere, included in *Distinctio* 87, combined canons 5 and 6 from the Council of Orange:

> Concerning those who flee to church: they should not be dragged out, but defended by intercession and out of reverence for the sacred place.[11]

Gratian's *Decretum* dispersed sanctuary rules into various rubrics as they became relevant, but did not treat sanctuary in a self-contained title.[12]

The remaining thirteen sanctuary canons in the *Decretum* all appeared in *Causa* 17. It is not readily apparent what prompted the compiler of the later recension to pay so much more attention to sanctuary law than his predecessor, or why he inserted sanctuary canons in the place he did. The questions posed in *Causa* 17 concerned a set of legal issues that arose when a *presbiter* renounced certain benefices and later wanted to recover them.[13] For example, it was imagined that a *presbiter* fell ill. Anticipating impending death, he announced that he wished to be only a monk and renounced all his churches and benefices. But then he later recovered his health and wished to recover his churches and benefices as well.[14] What rules governed what was to be done in such cases?

At first glance, it may not be obvious how rules regarding the renunciation or recovery of ecclesiastical benefices related to sanctuary law. The principles governing what could be taken from a church or monastery, or whether benefices could be given away without the church's permission, hinged on a determination of what belonged to God and what belonged to man. And wrongfully taking something that belonged to God was a sacrilege. As the *Decretum* explained, sacrilege is "taking away something sacred from the sacred, or something sacred from the non-sacred, or something non-sacred from the sacred."[15] An important legal distinction lurked here. For example, "whoever steals money from his neighbor works iniquity, but whoever steals money or things from a church commits sacrilege."[16] Moreover, "all robbers of churches and those who alienate [ecclesiastical] resources are anathema, damned, and judged sacrilegious."[17] Violent acts committed within churches were considered in a similar light. This, then, was the link to sanctuary. "If anyone fights or commits homicide within the atrium (including courtyard) of a church, he must make amends at the altar of the violated church."[18]

Interspersed amongst these definitions of sacrilege and the sanctions attached to it, the *Decretum* offered the rule of sanctuary in its classic form. Thus:

> Let no one dare drag forth a guilty one who has fled to a church, neither give him over to punishment or death, that the honor of churches may be preserved; but let rectors strive to obtain the fugitive's peace, life and members. However, let [the fugitive] make lawful composition for that which he did iniquitously.[19]

A significant portion of the remaining sanctuary canons in the *Decretum* concerned the sanctions due to those who violated sanctuary privileges. A fifth-century papal letter was included that directed that anyone who "violates churches is judged unworthy to enter them."[20] This was an expression of the canonical principle that those who dishonored sacred places could not have the protections bestowed by the church. Elsewhere, this principle was expressed thus: Whoever dared to drag a fugitive from a church "should be segregated from the place he did not give honor, until he has performed a worthy penance."[21] Those who violated churches and dragged forth refugees from within them were characterized as "contumacious and prideful, neither fearing God nor revering sacred churches."[22] According to an epistle that a later editor of the *Decretum* attributed to Pope John VIII but that was formed from several separate sources, such violators were to make amends for their wrong. Significantly, the amends were required for "the injury to the immunity" and might include secular punishments.[23] The *Decretum* thus maintained the link between sanctuary and immunity that had also been made in the collections of Ivo and Burchard and that would become the common opinion in the century to come.[24] Sanctuary, like immunities, was increasingly conceived as grounded solely in the church's jurisdictional prerogative.

Like classical Roman law, the *Decretum* also contained canons that restricted the reach of sanctuary protections. In fact, many of the restrictions appeared to be borrowed from Roman law. For instance, the *Decretum* included a letter of Pope Nicholas II (d. 1061), which proclaimed:

> Whoever attempts to breach their confines, either to drag away a man's person or his goods, shall be excommunicated until he makes amends and returns what he has taken, *unless [the fugitive] is a public thief.*[25]

The exclusion from sanctuary of "public thieves"—that is, thieves widely known to be such—was a policy that could be traced to Justinian. Moreover, Timbal pointed out that legislation removing public thieves from the ambit of ecclesiastical tuition had been foreshadowed before the *Decretum* in the Peace of God movement. For example, according to eleventh-century constitutions issued by the episcopate of Barcelona, "bandits and thieves" who fled to sanctuary but later proved "unwilling to justly abide by the precepts of the bishop or of the canons of this bishopric" were deemed "without the defense" of the church.[26] The sanctuary rule announced by Pope Nicholas II differed in not distinguishing between public thieves who submitted to the discipline of a bishop and those who did not.[27] Other passages of the *Decretum*, however, seemed to contradict this position. For instance, elsewhere, but not in the context of sanctuary, the *Decretum* stated: "It does not seem unjust . . . that those who are implicated in public thefts are defended [by the church]."[28] The only qualification appeared to be that clerical intercession for wrongdoers was not to be done "indiscreetly" or "recklessly" lest "the repute of the Church be sullied."[29] Whatever intercession may have been understood to require, the canon law of sanctuary specifically excluded public thieves and those who laid waste to fields, activities one might associate with warfare and border conflict more than everyday crime.

Canonists generally perceived the Roman law to exclude more types of criminals from sanctuary than canon law. As the ordinary gloss to the *Decretum* noted:

> These alone [public thieves and "nocturnal destroyers of fields"] are excluded [from sanctuary] by the canon law. The Roman laws exclude many persons: homicides, adulterers, and those who rape virgins. But in the canons those who rape virgins are protected in a church.[30]

Roman lawyers did indeed argue for a wider set of exclusions. Some thought that the severity of the punishment that would have been imposed on the criminal had he not fled to a church should determine whether he received sanctuary. In this view, offenses that warranted capital punishment did not qualify for sanctuary.[31] Others distinguished according to the particular character of the crime itself. For example, some thought that a homicide who acted on account of a pre-existing enmity could not have sanctuary, while someone who killed without premeditation might.[32] The unifying principle most Roman jurists settled on was that those who committed crimes *ex deliberatione* or *per insidias* were excluded from sanctuary.[33] Some civilians simply said that those committing "atrocious crimes" could not have sanctuary.[34] The categories of *ex deliberatione* and *atrox delictum* appeared, to the civilian jurists, to lead to less arbitrary results than the canon law seemed to allow. As Pierre de Belleperche (d. 1308) saw it, the canon law allowed a *raptor virginis* to have sanctuary even though this was a crime committed *ex deliberatione*. But at the same time, some canonists held that only homicides committed in the heat of the moment (*propter calorem*) should be admitted to sanctuary while homicides who acted *ex deliberatione* should be excluded from sanctuary. Belleperche thought the position of the civilians was more consistent. But even the canonists could not always agree on whether homicides could have sanctuary.[35] Canon lawyers also tended to exclude from sanctuary protections anyone who committed a crime within one church and then fled to a different church. Roman lawyers did not distinguish this sort of criminal. But for canonists, the reason to do so was clear. "Because there is only one Church in the whole world," an injury committed against one of them was committed against all.[36]

OUTSIDE THE COMMON LAW: SANCTUARY LAW AND THE PAPAL CURIA

The rules of sanctuary contained in the *Decretum,* along with the rules incorporated from Roman law, formed the basis for the application of sanctuary in ecclesiastical jurisdictions on the continent. We saw already that the English common law also occasionally applied canon law to determine particular issues that arose, but this was done at the initiative of royal justices, not (insofar as the records allow us to see) at the insistence of episcopal or papal jurisdiction. On the continent, in places where sanctuary was not adopted as fully into royal administration of crime, many sanctuary cases were decided by ecclesiastical courts, or were appealed to the papal curia. In 1332 Pope John XXII asked the seneschal of Provence to help bring to justice a royal official who had violently extracted a fugitive from a church. That official, who had not "feared to publicly break the liberty churches," was to be punished under "both laws."[37] Even Roman lawyers agreed that a breach of sanctuary was to be punished as the crime of *crimen lese majestatis*.[38]

While the church sometimes invoked excommunication against those who violated sanctuaries, it was also willing to absolve such crimes on occasions. A woman named Bela in the diocese of Tournai pretended to befriend a cleric who had taken sanctuary within a church for his hand in the murder of her brother in 1335. Bela apparently convinced the cleric it was safe to exit the church, then had him captured, handed over to secular authorities, and hanged. The whole affair rested on some fairly sordid facts. Bela's brother had been a servant to a "certain noblewoman" and had "known her many times carnally." When the affair soured, the noblewoman, with the help of the cleric, killed Bela's brother "with swords while he slept in bed." Bela was excommunicated because canon law treated trickery as violence when it came to extracting fugitives, but later she was absolved for her role in violating sanctuary.[39]

While the evidence is not nearly as complete or early as that available for English sanctuary, papal letters permit us to draw some inferences about the papacy's application of sanctuary law in continental Europe in the late thirteenth and early fourteenth century. In 1317, Pope John XXII forcefully explained that heretics could not have the protection of sanctuary. In the face of the heresy inquisitions that took place in France in the early fourteenth century, it appeared to the papal curia that "not a few depraved heretics, whether convicted, suspected, or accused, had fled to churches, not for the remedy of salvation, but to escape the hands of the inquisitors." Recent converts from Judaism had apparently also sought to evade the inquisitors by fleeing to churches. The pope mandated that the inquisition proceed against the fugitives "even if they have fled to a church or religious place."[40] The papal letter implies, of course, that royal and church officials were reluctant to initiate legal processes against fugitive heretics. In 1328, a full decade later, John wrote to King Philip of France complaining again that "apostates and heretics" were "fleeing to churches so that through the immunity of churches they might be defended in their apostasy and heresy." The pope asked the king's help in removing these fugitives, and expressly permitted that the fugitives could be "dragged out, even by the secular arm."[41]

In addition, the papacy embraced a policy of excluding debtors from sanctuary. It does not appear this policy met with much success. In 1363, when Urban V commanded the prelates and clerics in Montpelier not to admit fugitive debtors, lest they use the church's immunity to defraud creditors. He reminded them that Pope Alexander IV had ordered the same thing over one hundred years earlier.[42] Pope John XXII had also reminded them of the prohibition in 1318, apparently to no avail.[43]

The papal curia seems also to have allowed sanctuary for homicides, despite the Roman law's express prohibition. In June of 1310, William, the lord of Bocheto (modern: Bucquoy), came to the papal court in Avignon and explained that his son John had been killed by a cleric and a layman, both of whom had fled to the Church of St. Anianus in Orléans and remained there, "presuming" that they might have the "immunity of the church." Pope John ordered that both men answer for their crime, but also commanded that they only be punished "according to canonical sanctions."[44] Accordingly, neither man was subjected to corporal or capital punishment for the homicide.

Canonists and civilians disagreed over whether ecclesiastical or secular power had the right to restrict sanctuary. Alciatus, though late evidence, summed up the civilian position neatly in the early sixteenth century: "But it was simply on account of reverence that the legislator [i.e., Roman emperor] prohibited that his subjects drag anyone from a church. Such a prohibition he can revoke whenever he wishes."[45] Canonists, however, had long held that their immunities, including sanctuary, were grounded in divine law and could not be revoked by secular powers. Pope Clement VI in 1344 had written a chiding letter to the king of Majorca, expressing his wonder that the king could think that he might extract criminals from a church without committing sacrilege. As Clement pointed out, even if the fugitives were preserved "in life and limb," their extraction was a "breach of the liberty and immunity of the Church" which had existed there "from ancient times."[46] Innocent VI had similarly defended a liberty in Bourges against encroachments by the king's men in 1353. The monastery there, explained Innocent, "has held and holds a liberty or franchise" so that "all malefactors" who flee there can "evade the punishment of their wrong." Although Innocent reminded the French King John that such a liberty was established by "the apostolic and blessed memory of your predecessors," he ultimately based the validity of the liberty on the fact that it was older than any human memory.[47] The papacy occasionally had allowed the secular arm to remove fugitives from a church in the exceptional case of heretics, but the Church jealously guarded control of the sanctuary privilege in the fourteenth century. The privilege, according to canonists, was not given "in favor of the fugitives," who were often the "worst sort," but on account of "reverence for the holy place."[48] The crucial question seemed to be whether the secular power could revoke grants made out of such reverence. In the view developed by late-medieval canonists, the validity of sanctuary laws inhered in the power that granted them, not in the meaning of the act of sheltering or disciplining a criminal who sought sanctuary.

The particular jurisprudential problems raised by jurisdictional immunities were felt in England as well. By the fifteenth century, a general perception that sanctuary seekers were attempting to remain in chartered liberties permanently was part of a powerful line of criticism against all forms of sanctuary in England and on the European continent. The juristic critique of sanctuary, which grew out of such complaints about chartered liberties, gained traction in the fifteenth and sixteenth centuries. Already, as we saw earlier, thirteenth-century canon lawyers had set up an ultimately irresolvable tension between the principle that "crimes ought not remain unpunished" and the apparent impunity sanctuary offered. As a result, the emerging jurisprudential movement would impact all forms of sanctuary, not just the chartered immunities.

THE NASCENT CRIMINAL LAW THEORY OF THE CANONISTS

Chapter 7 showed that some canonists were troubled by the impunity that sanctuary offered to criminals, arguing,

> If no one is able [to bring an accusation] crimes would remain unpunished: but this ought not be. For in this manner the privilege of the Church would be an occasion for much delinquency. On account of this some say that [the sanctuary-seeker] is able to be accused by anyone, lest in this way [sanctuary] permit impunity.[49]

While most thirteenth-century canonists maintained that a sanctuary seeker could not be subjected to a criminal prosecution after fleeing to a church, they never challenged the underlying assertion of their critique that sanctuary offered impunity. Where they might have drawn on patristic texts to present sanctuary as an integral feature of penitential discipline, canonists instead asserted that sanctuary was a prerogative of the church that must be respected even though it allowed some criminals to escape punishment. The result was a theoretical tension that medieval canon law was never able to resolve, for the canonists were simultaneously developing doctrines of deterrence that would eventually clash with the underlying logic of sanctuary.

As Richard Fraher has shown, a coherent jurisprudence of deterrence in the canon law began to emerge in the pontificate of Innocent III. One source of this new deterrent-oriented approach to penal law was a maxim employed to great effect by Innocent III: "It is in the public interest that no crimes remain unpunished." In 1203 Innocent III wrote to the Bishop of London, William of Ste. Mère-Eglise.[50] The letter, now known as the decretal *Ut fame*, was issued in response to an inquiry from the Bishop William concerning permissible treatment of miscreant clerics. In it, Innocent III pronounced that Church officials, as well as laymen with ecclesiastical mandate, could forcibly arrest and incarcerate delinquent clerics. It is the reasoning Innocent III gave for his pronouncement that is of interest here. As Innocent explained, Church officials "should correct the excesses of their subjects. *It is in the public interest that crimes do not remain unpunished.*"[51]

Like so many other canonical maxims, this phrase had roots in classical Roman law. Justinian's Codex had admonished: "It is in the public interest that punishments are not remitted too easily, lest perchance some hasten to [further] wrongdoings."[52] Similar notions appear in the *Digest.*[53] For instance, punishment is said to serve the public because "it is an example to others" by which they are deterred from wrong.[54] Fraher's research suggests that Innocent III did not have to reach back to these ancient sources. Innocent may have lifted the maxim from a contemporary French canonist,[55] who, argues Fraher, may well have taken it from a twelfth-century civilianist.[56]

The maxim circulated widely very quickly. In 1210, Tancred explained his decision to discuss crime and criminal procedure first in his *tractatus* by remarking: "since it is in the public interest that crimes do not remain unpunished."[57] By mid-century, the maxim appeared in the ordinary gloss to Gratian's *Decretum*. Teutonicus, who produced the gloss to the *Decretum*, employed the maxim in other texts as well.[58] So did Hostiensis, who occasionally replaced the words "*publicae interest*" (public interest) with "*interest cuiuslibet*" (the interest of everyone).[59] At the end of the thirteenth century, William Durantis included the maxim in his *Speculum iudiciale*. Durantis not only clothed the maxim in its canon and Roman law citations, but also added biblical authority: "since it is useful to the republic that no crimes remain unpunished . . . according to which 'you shall not suffer wrongdoers to live' (Exodus 22:18)."[60] In stereotypical fashion, a rhetorical indulgence of ancient Roman law had been revived by medieval jurists, cast as a juridical principle, and made to flourish throughout the textual tradition.[61]

Civilian jurists soon adopted the maxim as well. Albertus Gandinus, a late-thirteenth-century Italian jurist, thought it "advantageous to the republic that no wrongdoing remain unpunished."[62] Consequently, judges had a special duty to impose exemplary punishment, as "it would be a bad example for a homicide not to be punished."[63] Other civilians followed Gandinus. In the fourteenth century, Luca de Penna remarked that punishment was "related to the utility of the republic"[64] and "*pro commodo rei publicae.*"[65] Thus, by the fourteenth century, the maxim was profoundly entrenched throughout Roman-canonical tradition. After the Reformation, however, not every jurist continued to cite Innocent's *Ut fame* for the maxim. Nicholas Mylerus, a seventeenth-century German jurist who often decried "abuses of papal law," asserted that there was a public interest that "*ne crimina manerent impunita,*" but he cited Tacitus, not the pope.[66]

The maxim figured prominently in the late-medieval Roman-canonical tradition in two distinct ways, the first of which linked it to the proposition that punishment should prevent future wrongdoing. This was not a necessary conclusion. As a group, the classical Roman sources had been ambiguous on this point. Some had spoken of the necessity of punishing wrong so that "others would be deterred by the example."[67] But others expressed a different necessity in making sure wrongs were not unpunished, stating simply that "it is proper and expeditious that the wrongs of the noxious be known."[68] When Ulpian stated the maxim he seemed concerned only that the wrong itself be vindicated; he did not speak of an exemplary benefit of punishment.[69] We might imagine that patristic writers such as Augustine would have agreed, but their agreement would have stemmed from a concern that the sinner expiate his sin and reconcile with God. It would not have been grounded in a conviction that others could or would be deterred, or that public authority had much of a stake in the matter. On the other hand, when Innocent resuscitated the maxim in the decretal *Ut fame,* he linked it directly to a preventive concept of punishment. The reason wrongs ought not to remain unpunished, Innocent had explained, was that "through impunity . . . the wicked become still more wicked."[70] Civilians were somewhat more likely to be explicit about this. The public benefit drawn from punishing wrong was that "others would be deterred by example."[71] In fact, some fifteenth-century jurists radicalized the position by stating: "No one prudent punishes because there *has been* sin. They punish so that there *will not be* sin."[72]

Besides bolstering the proposition that punishment should be preventative, the maxim that crime ought not to remain unpunished played a second role as part of a conceptual transformation in medieval canon law. As Richard Fraher has shown, medieval jurists systematically employed the maxim when they set about replacing ancient penal traditions with new institutions.[73] For instance, Hostiensis, justifying abandonment of the ancient rule that witnesses could not be compelled to testify in criminal cases, wrote that even "infamous criminals," long excluded by ancient proprieties from testifying in court, were now to be heard because of the public interest in punishing crime.[74] Likewise, medieval jurists taught that *ex officio* inquisitorial procedures should supersede private, discretionary forms of prosecution lest the unwillingness of a victim to prosecute allow some crimes to go unpunished.[75] Again, de Penne pushed the reasoning furthest, stating that "all wrong is public" and all criminal prosecutions and punishments were matters of public interest.[76] Whatever elements of self-help and private concord had remained from the older traditions were being dismantled and replaced by a transformed understanding of wrong and punishment.

Perhaps the greatest coup accomplished in the name of this new understanding was the dismantling of sanctuary law. At first, it seemed sanctuary might resist. The ordinary gloss to Gratian's *Decretum* juxtaposed sanctuary with the principle that crimes ought not to remain unpunished but asserted that infringement on the church's privilege was heretical. Nonetheless, the prospect of impunity for wrong nagged, and the gloss hinted that fugitive wrongdoers might still be enslaved.[77]

The tension was neatly evident when the king of Scotland wrote to Innocent III, asking, "What should be done in regard to those who, perpetrating wrongs, flee to church so that, on account of reverence for the sacred place, they might succeed in evading due punishment?"[78] Innocent's answer first harkened to ancient principles, "according to the sacred canons and the civil law . . . it must be distinguished whether the fugitive is a freeman or a *servus*."[79] Regarding *servi*, Innocent followed the rules that had survived from the Theodosian Code: "If a slave has fled to church, after his master has given an oath of impunity before the churchmen, let the slave be compelled to return to the service of his master, even unwillingly."[80] As to freemen, Innocent also began with the ancient principle: "If free, no matter how grave a wrong he has committed, he is not to be violently dragged from the church, nor should he be condemned to death or punishment; but rectors of churches ought to strive to save the fugitive's life and members."[81] Then, partially following the *Decretum,* Innocent added: "Above this, however, what he has done iniquitously should be punished in some other legitimate way." The text of the *Decretum* had actually said that, once the fugitive's life and members were secure, "he should *make composition* for what he did iniquitously." Innocent replaced composition with punishment. But the truly remarkable change Innocent worked came next, when Innocent added: "That is, unless the fugitive was a public thief or destroyer of fields by night, who often had insidiously and aggressively beset public highways."[82] At first glance, Innocent appeared to gloss Pope Nicholas II's exclusion of public thieves from sanctuary by giving the term "*publicus latro*" a wider definition.[83] He went further, however, explaining that "for wrongdoing of this magnitude, which both impedes public utility and noxiously molests everyone, the fugitive can be extracted" so that he does not succeed in gaining impunity."[84]

Pope Gregory IX added yet another principle of exclusion. "Some," wrote Gregory, "hoping to obtain impunity for their excesses by defense of the church, are not afraid to commit homicides or mutilations within churches themselves or their cemeteries."[85] These same criminals, Gregory explained, "would not have committed their excesses except that they believed they would be defended by the church to which they fled."[86]

This was the direction the papacy continued to move in the fourteenth century. Noting that the dangers that emerged in an age where the "rod failed to correct," Pope Clement V ordered a bishop to remove a criminal from sanctuary in 1310. That the criminal had been complicit in a homicide may have sufficed under Roman law to remove him from the privilege, but Clement never invoked a rule excluding homicides from sanctuary and the papal court seems not to have applied a consistent policy in such cases. Instead, Clement stated that even though the sanctuary to which the killer fled was approved "from ancient times," he was unwilling that crimes "*remaneant impunita.*"[87] A decade later, Pope John XXII absolved Oddo, the duke of Burgundy, for seizing a criminous cleric from an ecclesiastical immunity at Cluny. The duke had humbly explained that he had acted, not from "contempt of the Church, but from zeal for justice" and made sure to catalogue the cleric's considerable misdeeds.[88] It was now, in the fourteenth century, possible to justify breaching sanctuary, and to oppose sanctuary laws in general, by claiming a laudable "zeal for justice."

CRITICISM OF SANCTUARY IN LATE-MEDIEVAL ENGLAND

Criticism of sanctuary consonant with the canonical critique appeared in English sources by the end of the fourteenth century. A series of councils held at Westminster between 1387 and 1389 entertained strenuous challenges to the liberties claimed by the clerics there. The whole debate was prompted by a notorious breach of sanctuary described by Thomas Walsingham, a monk and chronicler of St. Albans.[89] While on campaign against the Spanish, Robert Hawley, along with his companion, Thomas Shakell, had taken a wealthy and valuable hostage, the son of the count of Denia. When, upon their return to England, they refused to turn their hostage over to the duke of Lancaster, Robert and Thomas were thrown in the Tower of London.[90] According to Walsingham, the men escaped from the tower and headed for the sanctuary of St. Peter's Church at Westminster. Thomas Shakell was captured in flight, and was thus "deprive[ed] of the liberty of the Church."[91] Robert, however, managed to reach the sanctuary of St. Peter where he remained for a time. Despite being unarmed, Robert was attacked by the king's men during mass. They chased Robert around the sanctuary twice and threatened the monks who tried to protect him before braining Robert and dragging his corpse out of the church.

The council that resulted from the sanctuary breach was a significant affair. Even Wycliffe took part. Walsingham, a strong defender of sanctuary (except for debtors who he thought "had a fine time feasting and making merry" in sanctuary), considered the whole affair, and especially the harm that came to Robert while in sanctuary, a sign of his age's depravity and "justice vanished."[92] In the debates of 1387, sanctuary's defenders carried the day, and the only consequence of the whole affair was legislation excluding debtors from sanctuary protections, which even defenders of sanctuary protections like Walsingham had favored.[93] In fact, it was canon lawyers themselves who argued at the parliament in 1387 that the king had no power to grant sanctuary to debtors.[94] The canon lawyers had solid authority for their position. The papal curia at Avignon had denied sanctuary to debtors as early as the 1250s.[95] But as a result of the council of 1387, the English crown did not restrict sanctuary, and the common law continued to recognize sanctuary and abjure sanctuary seekers.

In 1394, the issue of sanctuary came before Parliament again. The commons of Essex complained that both the abbot of St. John's at Colchester and the abbot of Abingdon at Culham were sheltering fugitive debtors, but no resolution was reached.[96] In 1399, 1414, and 1421, statutes were passed that subjected fugitives who exited chartered liberties to royal justice.[97] Nevertheless, complaints made by Buckingham (and expressed later through the pen of Thomas More) suggest that the problems with chartered sanctuaries targeted by this legislation re-emerged in the 1480s and in the 1540s,[98] in the wake of sensational, usually political, cases of sanctuary.[99]

When Thomas More authored Buckingham's arguments against sanctuary, he tracked with some proximity the arguments in a late-fourteenth-century manuscript entitled *Objectiones et argumenta contra et pro privilegiis sanctuarii*, which may have been related to the Hawley-Shakell affair in 1387. Copied in the late fifteenth century, probably by William Evesham, it was used in debates that erupted under Edward IV and Henry VII[100] concerning who had the power to grant and revoke sanctuary protections. It also concerned what sorts of criminals were eligible for sanctuary. These debates were not peculiar to England, as canonists and civilians had been rehearsing them for some time.

In 1465 a complaint was lodged by the Commons to Edward IV that "persons of diverse estates, resident both in the city of London and in its suburbs, as also from other parts of the kingdom . . . flee with their masters' goods to the college of St. Martin le Grand in London with the intent of living there."[101] Almost two decades later, and again to Edward IV, the Commons complained anew of the permanent character acquired by the chartered sanctuaries so that felons in them:

> daily depart and go out of the said sanctuaries doing treasons and robberies and felonies . . . despoiling [people] of their goods . . . [And then] they resort again to the said sanctuaries . . . there living by the goods . . . [and by this] many of your people [are] undone.[102]

Although Edward rejected the bill, the characterization of sanctuary as a cause for criminality, and the concomitant claim that reducing the scope of sanctuary would deter crime, stuck.

A petition made to Parliament in 1483 furthered the critique, which had begun in canon law, that sanctuary seekers "be not sorry of their outrageous treasons, felonies, and other offences." Instead, "by occasion of the said sanctuaries they . . . commit great or greater treasons, felonies, and other offences [than] ever they did before time.[103] Not only were sanctuary seekers perceived to lack sorrow for their crimes, the existence of sanctuaries appeared to encourage ever more audacious crimes. The petition linked this lack of sorrow to an insufficient "dread for the sovereign's laws."[104] The rhetoric of the petition was rife with anxieties about the capacity of the penal law to prevent lawbreaking and firm convictions that sanctuary laws only hindered good order. As such late-fifteenth-century complaints against sanctuary grew more vociferous, chartered sanctuaries, such as Westminster, became the foil for sanctuary's opponents.[105] But restricting these perceived abuses was not simply a matter of royal fiat. Because liberties once granted to the church could prove difficult to take back, the last half of the fifteenth century featured several abortive attempts to undo the chartered liberties and the sanctuary privileges they offered.[106]

No longer understood as an appropriate response to serious crime, sanctuary had come to be seen as a potential nuisance. Some wrongs were perceived to pose such a threat to public interests that their perpetrators could not be protected by sanctuary. Rather than a way in which wrongdoers might make satisfaction for their wrongs, sanctuary was simply a way to "evade punishment."[107] Worse yet, because some wrongdoers committed wrongs only in anticipation of sanctuary, sanctuary was recast as an invitation to commit crime. Canon law could now routinely express a tension between sanctuary and the new conception of punishment. As Pope Eugenius IV wrote to the Bishop of Lincoln in 1442, by virtue of sanctuary, wrongdoers "escape the punishment of their evil deeds and the satisfaction of their debts" and effect "the supplanting of justice," providing a "detestable example to others."[108] Many "live [in sanctuary] for a long time, even with dishonest women," to the "scandal and corruption of the religious other honest men who dwell therein."[109]

CONCLUSION

With a frontal attack, Henry VIII accomplished what his predecessors had half begun, restricting sanctuary privileges almost completely. Given Henry VIII's break with the papacy, the classic view was that the fate of English sanctuary law was entirely determined by a struggle between royal prerogative and ecclesiastical privilege.[110] Henry did remove "willful murder, rape, burglary, robbery in the highway or any house" as well as arson from the sanctuary privilege.[111] As a result, churches could only serve as sanctuaries for lesser offenses, while the most serious felonies, which had made up the majority of sanctuary cases in the earlier centuries, were excluded from the privilege. By 1540, Henry had designated eight towns in England as permanent sanctuaries, though there were limits on how many fugitives could reside in a sanctuary town at one time. These alternative sanctuaries were intended, in part, to curtail abjuration because Henry feared that abjuring Englishmen were teaching archery and other martial skills to the French. Meanwhile, a significant effort by royal justices steadily narrowed the scope of the sanctuary privilege.[112] Canonists and civilians, however, carried out precisely the same move as Henry's justices, and Queen Mary's attempt to restore Catholicism did not include any attempt to revive sanctuary.

As Isobel Thornley noted, "sanctuary was a very tough privilege which survived more than one legal abolition."[113] It is clear that sanctuary men were part of an abbot's procession in 1556,[114] so apparently the practice continued in some form through the sixteenth century. Under James I there were several attempts to draft legislation that abolished the privilege entirely, and the legislation passed in 1623 seems to have accomplished this aim.[115] At that point in seventeenth-century England, the promiscuous availability of sanctuary for murder and theft was all but gone.

Given that Henry VIII's sanctuary legislation is roughly contemporaneous with his break from the Roman Catholic Church, it is tempting to read the demise of sanctuary in England as a strand of confessional conflict. Yet, sanctuary was also undergoing important restrictions at this time in Catholic countries as well.[116] In France, large-scale restrictions on sanctuary were issued in 1539, 1547, and 1555. The frequency of legislation prohibiting sanctuary is in part a testament to the endurance of the practice in regions of France, but also a result of the decentralized legislative power in sixteenth-century France.[117] In 1597, a papal bull from Gregory XIV all but abolished sanctuary within the canon law, but the groundwork had already been laid in the previous centuries.[118] Indeed, the canon law was an important source for arguments against sanctuary in fifteenth-century England, for a great deal of the restrictions on sanctuary that Tudor kings attempted had already been urged by the papacy itself.[119]

In a 1519 session of Star Chamber, Henry VIII said:

> I argue that St. Edward, King Edgar and the other Kings and Holy Popes who made the Sanctuary never intended that the sanctuary should serve for willful murder and larceny outside the sanctuary, done in the hope of re-entering . . . Therefore I will have reformed the abuses which have encroached and have the matter reduced to the true intent of the original makers.[120]

E. W. Ives characterized these words as "the king attempting to bluster his way" through arguments against ecclesiastical privilege.[121] Isobel Thornley found them evidence of Henry's "fine disregard for legal arguments and proofs."[122] In fact, Henry was closely paraphrasing canon law. The *Liber Extra* had spoken explicitly of those who committed crime "*sub spe immunitatis.*"[123] Moreover, in explicitly asking Henry's predecessors to curb the abuses caused by sanctuary, the papacy had referred to it as a "royal privilege, confirmed by papal authority."[124] A mid-fifteenth-century papal letter described "former kings of England and the other faithful, who by papal authority and the authority of the said kings founded" sanctuaries over-zealously.[125] According to that letter, because the king was "the patron of a number of the said places," the church expected that the king would "modify . . . the privileges, immunities, exemptions and liberties" and "ordain whatever else may be necessary for the remedying of the said abuses."[126] In his *Doctor and Student*, St. German argued firmly that power over sanctuaries belonged to lay authority.[127] In sum, when the English crown moved against sanctuary, it was following the church's wishes and using the canonists' map.

The restrictions on sanctuary advocated by civilian jurists can be viewed in the same light. Just as English kings had based their prerogatives over sanctuary on historical grants of foundation charters, Roman law jurists searched the ancient texts and found sanctuary was instituted by emperors. As one civilian argued: "It is not true that the emperor was unable to revoke such a law."[128] Rather, the "legislator, simply on account of reverence, prohibited his subjects from dragging anyone out of a church,"[129] but "what the legislator can prohibit, he can revoke."[130] Civilians also moved to narrow access to sanctuary. Although Belleperche thought all "atrocious crimes" should be disqualified from sanctuary, in the end, civilian jurists excluded a list of crimes that looked much like the list produced by the sixteenth-century church. According to Timbal, the civilians moved "with admirable logic, but with tendencies very dangerous to the institution" of sanctuary.[131] In fact, the logic had been articulated by Innocent III and thirteenth-century glossators, whether later canonists recognized it or not. The civilians may have pushed the notion to its furthest conclusions, but their thinking was of a piece with that of the canonists and was evident in the English abolition of sanctuary law as well.

In the late-medieval canon law, "the number of exceptions to sanctuary accrued without cease."[132] By the mid-fifteenth century, the jurists Rebuffus and Covarruvias could add many cases that were excepted from sanctuary to those few that had been articulated in the ancient laws: public thieves, nocturnal marauders, sacrilegious persons, armed fugitives, those who commit crimes within churches, Jews, heretics, ravishers of maidens, traitors, blasphemers, homicides, exiles, those who kill clerics, prison escapees, assassins, highway robbers, and anyone convicted before a judge.[133] This list approximated the one eventually promulgated by Pope Gregory XIV in 1591, a bull that conceded to lay authorities the power to extract anyone falling under the exceptions.[134] In some parts of Europe, the concession in Gregory's bull was only an acceptance of practical realities. The sixteenth-century Italian jurist Guilo Claro, noting that canon law forbade that sanctuary seekers should suffer sanguinary punishments, wrote, "This is certainly not observed among us." Instead, "Those who flee to a church after some crime either hand themselves over to the prelate, or otherwise leave the church spontaneously, or are forcibly extracted and punished."[135] Episcopal permission was required, and extractions were to take place in the presence of ecclesiastical officers. In fact, Gregory's concessions, and more, had been claimed by French and English kings more than half a century earlier.[136]

Even though secular powers across Europe had begun to abolish sanctuary as early as the fifteenth century, Gregory's bull formed the basis for the sanctuary law of the church thereafter. The *Codex Juris Canonici* of 1917 offered a distilled, but recognizable version of the rule:

> A Church enjoys the right of sanctuary. . . . Wrongdoers who have fled to church should not be dragged out without the consent of the ordinary or rector. An exception is allowed only in extreme necessity.[137]

In the most recent edition, the rule does not even appear.[138] But in truth, this was only the quiet disappearance of a law whose claim had fallen silent long before. Once sanctuary was universally understood as an impediment to punishment and an invitation to further wrongdoing, the interest of authority in certain and exemplary punishment swept the field and the venerable privilege was no more.

Notes

INTRODUCTION

1. See, e.g., Simon Pegge, "A Sketch of the History of Asylum, or Sanctuary," *Archaeologia* (London: Society of Antiquities of London, 1787), 8:1–44; Norman M. Trenholme, *The Right of Sanctuary in England: A Study in Institutional History* (Columbia: University of Missouri Press, 1903); Isobel D. Thornley, "The Destruction of Sanctuary," in *Tudor Studies Presented to A. F. Pollard*, ed. R. W. Seton-Watson (London: University of London Board of Studies in History, 1924); J. H. Baker, *The Reports of Sir John Spelman* (London: Selden Society, 1977–78), 2:334–45.

2. F. W. Maitland and Francis Montague, *A Sketch of English Legal History* (London: G. P. Putnam and Sons, 1915), 71.

3. Pegge, "A Sketch of the History of Asylum, or Sanctuary," 2.

4. Norman Trenholme, *The Right of Sanctuary in England* (Columbia: University of Missouri Press, 1903), 96.

5. Cesare Beccaria, *On Crimes and Punishments*, ed. Richard Bellamy, trans. Richard Davies (Cambridge University Press, 1986), 92.

6. Ibid.

7. Baker, *The Reports of Sir John Spelman*, 2:334.

8. Pegge, "A Sketch of the History of Asylum, or Sanctuary," 2.

9. Henry Hallam, *A View of the State of Europe During the Middle Ages* (London: J. Murray, 1818), 2:449.

10. Thomas John d'Mazzinghi, *Sanctuaries* (Stafford: Halden and Son, 1887), 101.

11. Maitland and Montague, *A Sketch of English Legal History*, 70.

12. Trenholme, *The Right of Sanctuary in England*, 98.

13. Ibid., 1.

14. Hallam, *A View of the State of Europe During the Middle Ages*, 2:449, quoted also in Mazzinghi, *Sanctuaries*, 114; Thornley, "The Destruction of Sanctuary."

15. Arthur Penrhyn Stanley, *Memorials of Westminster* (London: J. Murray, 1861), 414.

16. Mazzinghi, *Sanctuaries*, 102.

17. Gabriel Le Bras, "Asile," in *Dictionnaire d'histoire et de géographie ecclésiastiques*, ed. Alfred Baudrillart (Paris: Institut Catholique de Paris de L'Académie Française, 1930), col. 1035–1047.

18. Timbal, *Le droit d'asile*, 454.

19. Ibid., 453.

20. Charles H. Riggs Jr., *Criminal Asylum in Anglo-Saxon Law* (Gainesville: University of Florida Press, 1963), 60. This monograph is the only published portion of Riggs's Ph.D. dissertation, "A History of Criminal Asylum in England from Ine to James I: A Study of the Medieval Institution of Temporary Asylum with Special Emphasis on the Custom of *Abjuratio Regni* from 1202 to 1279" (Columbia University, 1962). Riggs's account of postconquest sanctuary, particularly his use of the plea rolls, should be consulted with caution.

21. Ibid.

22. Ibid. Timbal suggests this as well (*Le droit d'asile*, 343).

23. Gervase Rosser, "Sanctuary and Social Negotiation in Medieval England," in *The Cloister and the World: Essay in Honour of Barbara Harvey*, ed. John Blair and Brian Golding (Oxford: Clarendon Press, 1996), 61.

24. Ibid., 75. Only at the dawn of the early modern period, then, when sanctuary had outlived its usefulness as a concession to local communities, was the stage set for the abolition of sanctuary in what E. W. Ives has described as the "assertion of central authority . . . against the tradition of delegated local authority and high-handed provincial autonomy." See his "Crime, Sanctuary, and Royal Authority under Henry VIII: The Exemplary Sufferings of the Savage Family," in *On the Laws and Customs of England: Essays in Honor of Samuel E. Thorne*, ed. Morris S. Arnold, Thomas A. Green, Sally A. Scully, and Stephen D. White (Chapel Hill: University of North Carolina Press, 1981), 320.

25. William Chester Jordan, "A Fresh Look at Medieval Sanctuary," in *Law and the Illicit in Medieval Europe*, ed. Ruth Mazo Karras, Joel Kaye, and E. Ann Matter (Philadelphia: University of Pennsylvania, 2008), 17–20. I am grateful to William Jordan for sharing a draft of his essay prior to its publication.

26. Richard Helmholz, *The Ius Commune in England: Four Studies* (Oxford: Oxford University Press, 2001), 22. I am very appreciative to Richard Helmholz

for sharing a draft of this essay with me before it was published. See also his *Oxford History of the Laws of England: Volume I, The Canon Law and Ecclesiastical Jurisdiction from 597 to the 1640s* (Oxford: Oxford University Press, 2004), 35–6, 497–98, in which some of his arguments from 2001 are recapitulated.

27. Trisha Olson, "Sanctuary and Penitential Rebirth in the Central Middle Ages," in *Boundaries of the Law: Geography, Gender and Jurisdiction in Medieval and Early Modern Europe*, ed. Anthony Musson (London: Ashgate, 2005), 38–52; "Of the Worshipful Warrior: Sanctuary and Punishment in the Middle Ages," *St. Thomas Law Review* 16 (2004): 473–549.

1. AUTHORITY, INTERCESSION, AND PENANCE

1. Servii Grammatici qui feruntur in Vergilii carmina commentarii, vol. 1, *Aenidos Librorum I–V Commentarii*, ed. Georgius Thilo and Hermannus Hagen (Hildesheim: George Olms, 1961), 326–27. The relevant comments are to Book 2, line 761 of the *Aeneid*: "*unde nullus posit ad supplicium extrahi.*" The clause "*ad supplicium*" was added by Peter Daniel, a seventeenth-century editor of an important Servius manuscript tradition. The Servius commentary text can also be found in *Virgil Aeneis II, mit Servius*, ed. Ernst Diehl (Bonn: Marcus & Weber Verlag, 1911), 126; and *Servianorum in Vergilii Carmina Commentariorum editionis Harvardianae*, ed. Edward Rand et al. (Lancaster, Penn.: American Philological Society, 1946), 2:499–500.

2. *Servii Grammatici*, 326–27: "*hoc autem non est in omnibus templis, nisi quibis consecrationis lege concessum est . . . primo autem apud Athenienses statutum est ab Herculis filiis . . . hoc asylum etiam Romulus imitatus est.*"

3. According to Plutarch: "Not long after the first foundation of Rome they opened a sanctuary of refuge for all fugitives, which they called the temple of the god Asylaeus, where they received and protected all, delivering none back, neither the servant to his master, the debtor to his creditor, nor the murderer into the hands of the magistrate, saying it was a privileged place." Plutarch, "Romulus," in *The Lives of the Noble Grecians and Romans*, trans. John Dryden (New York: Modern Library, 1932), 19; Virgil, *Aeneid*, in *The Poems of Virgil*, trans. James Rhoades (London: Oxford University Press, 1921), Book 8.

4. *The Theodosian Code*, ed. Clyde Pharr (Princeton: Princeton University Press, 1952), 9.44. Hereinafter *C. Th.*

5. Augustine, *De civitate Dei* 1.1 and 4. An English translation is The *City of God*, ed. and trans. R. W. Dyson (Cambridge: Cambridge University Press, 1998), Book 1, Chapter 1, 4. For a very readable account of the sack of Rome in 410, see Michael Kulikowski, *Rome's Gothic Wars: From the Third Century to Alaric* (Cambridge: Cambridge University Press, 2007).

6. *Acta Conciliorum Oecumenicorum*, ed. Eduard Schwartz, 5 vols. (Berlin and Leipzig, 1927–1932), 1:1:4, 61. The same language also appears in the prologue of legislation issued by Theodosius in 431. See *Corpus Legum ab Imperatoribus Romanis ante Iustinianum Latarum*, ed. Gustav Haenel (Leipzig, 1857–60), 241. The body of the law is found in *C. Th.* 9.45.4, but the prologue is not included by modern editors.

7. *Concilium Matisconense* (Mâcon) (585), c. 8, in *Concilia Galliae, 511–695*, ed. Caroli de Clercq (Turnhout: Corpus Christianorum Series Latina, 1963), 148a:243: "*Si enim mundani principes suis legibus censuerunt, ut, quicumque ad eorum statuas fugiret, inlesus habeatur, quanto magis hi permanere debeant indemnati, qui patrocinia immortalis regni adepti sunt celestis?*"

8. For recent attempts to locate the origins of sanctuary in legal enactments of the late Roman Empire, see Hanspeter Ruedl, "Ad ecclesiam confugere: Die kaiserliche Asylgesetzgebung in der Spätantike," in *Tradition—Wegweisung in die Zukunft: Festschrift für J. Mühlsteiger* (Berlin: Duncker und Humblot, 2001), 133–45; Johannes Hermann, "Cod. Theod. 9, 45: De his, qui ad ecclesias confugiunt," in *Beiträge zur Rechtsgeschichte: Gedächtnisschrift für Hermann Conrad*, ed. Gerd Kleinheyer and Paul Mikat (Munich: Ferdinand Schöningh, 1979), 271–82; an earlier such attempt is M. F. Martroye, "L'asile et la législation impérial du IV au VI siècle," in *Mémoires de la société nationale des antiquaires de France* (1918), series 8, vol. 5, 158; the most authoritative monograph on the subject remains Pierre Timbal, *Le droit d'asile* (Paris: Sirey, 1939). More attentive to the problems that inhere in scholarly attempts to seek strictly legislative origins of sanctuary law are Anne Ducloux, *Ad Ecclesiam Confugere: Naissance du droit d'asile dans les églises (IVe–milieu du Ve s.)* (Paris: De Boccard, 1994), and Harald Siems, "Asyl in der Kirche? Wechsellagen des Kirchenasyls im Mittelalter," in *Das antike Asyl: Kultische Grundlagen, rechtliche Ausgestaltung und politische Funktion*, ed. Martin Dreher (Cologne: Böhlau Verlag, 2003).

9. Louis Thomassin, *Ancienne et nouvelle discipline de l'Eglise* (Paris: Chez François Montalant, 1725), part 2, bk. 3, chap. 95, 2:1846.

10. Thomassin was referring to the so-called Ten Laws attributed to Constantine, which contained a provision for protecting sanctuary seekers in Christian churches.

11. Thomassin, *Ancienne et nouvelle discipline de l'Eglise*. A fragment of the council's request exists, but there is no indication of any imperial response.

12. Jacobus Menochius, *De ivrisdictione, imperio et potestate ecclesiastica ac secvlari libri tres. Accessit liber quartus De immunitate ecclesiae, pro ad eam confugientibus* (Geneva: J. A. Cramer & P. Perachon, 1695), fol. 298.

13. Ibid., fol. 297.

14. See, for example, the sixteenth-century Italian lawyer Alciatus, *de presumptiones*, 33.1–5 in *Tractatus Universi Juris* (Venice: Franciscus Zilettus, 1584–86), 4:342.

15. Antonius Mattheas, *On Crimes: A Commentary on Books XLVII and XLVIII of the Digest* (1684), trans. and ed. M. L. Hewett (Cape Town: Juta, 1986), 4:632: "*ex paganismo ad religionem.*"

16. Samuel Pegge, "A Sketch of the History of Asylum, or Sanctuary," *Archaeologia* (London: Society of Antiquities of London, 1787), 8:1.

17. Ibid.

18. Aemilius Ludwig Richter, *Lehrbuch des Katholischen und Evangelischen Kirchenrechts* (Leipzig: B. Tauchnitz, 1858), 708. See also Charles de Beaurepaire, "Essai sur l'asile religieux dans l'empire romain et la monarchie française," in *Bibliothèque de l'École des Chartes* (Paris: Librairie Droz, 1853–54), 4:351–75, 573–91.

19. P. Perdrizet, "Asiles gréco-égyptiens et asiles romans," in *Annales du service des antiquités de l'Égypte* (Cairo: Le Service, 1920), 20:252–55. It is "in Egypt that one should search for the origin of Christian asylums."

20. Stengel, "Asylon," in *Paulys Real-Encyclopädie der classischen Altertumswissenschaft*, ed. August Friedrich von Pauly and Georg Wissowa (Stuttgart: 1884–1972), vol. 2, part 2, col. 1881ff. suggests Greek roots, as does Rudolf Bindschedler, *Kirchliches Asylrecht (immunitas ecclesiarum localis) und Freistätten in der Schweiz* (Amsterdam: P. Schippers, 1965); reprinted from *Kirchenrechtliche Abhandlungen* (Stuttgart: F. Enke, 1906), 32:7–8.

21. Stephan Brassloff, "Zu den Quellen der byzantinischen Rechtsgeschichte," *Zeitschrift der Savigny-Stiftung für Rechtsgeschichte* 25 (1904): 313n1.

22. Paul Hinschius, *Das Kirchenrecht der Katholiken und Protestanten in Deutschland* (Graz: Akademische Druck- u. Verlagsanstalt, 1888, reprint 1959), 4:382–83.

23. E. Herman, "Asile dans l'église orientale," in *Dictionnaire de droit canonique* (Lyon: J. Duplain, 1935), 1:1084.

24. Timbal, *Le droit d'asile*, 32 and 55n3.

25. Martin Luther, *Traktat über das Asylrecht*, ed. Barbara Emme and Dietrich Emme (Regensburg: Verlag Dietrich Emme, 1985). The editors discuss the dispute over Luther's authorship at 7–8.

26. Nicolas Mylerus von Ehrenbach, *De Asylorum jure* (Stuttgart: Johannis Wyrichl Rösslini, 1663), fol. 37.

27. Zeger Bernhard van Espen, "*Dissertatio canonica de intercione sive interventione episcoporum pro reis apud princes et magistratus civiles et de confugientibus ad ecclesias sive de immunitate locali, sue asylo templorum,*" in *Jus ecclesiasticum universum* (Venice: Johannes Petri Gibert, 1769), vol. 9.

28. François I, "Ordonnance de Villers-Cotterêts, Ordonnance générale en matière de justice et de police," in *Ordonnances des rois de France, Règne de François Ier*, ed. R. Mousnier (Paris, 1983), vol. 9, part 3, 553.

29. P. Timbal, *Le droit d'asile* (Paris: Sirey, 1939), 434.

30. For instance, see J. Gröll, *Die Elemente des kirchlichen Freiungsrechtes* (Amsterdam, Verlag P. Schippers, 1965, reprint. from 1911), 256–57; Beaurepaire, "Essai sur l'asile religieux dans l'empire romain et la monarchie française," in *Bibliothèque de l'École des Chartes* (Paris: Librairie Droz, 1853), 351.

31. Hinschius, *Das Kirchenrecht*, 382.

32. See, e.g., the research of Hanspeter Ruedl, "Ad ecclesiam confugere: Die kaiserliche Asylgesetzgebung in der Spätantike," in *Tradition—Wegweisung in die Zukunft*, 133–145.

33. Ducloux, *Ad ecclesiam confugere*; see also Beatrice Caseau, "A Case Study for the Transformation of Law in Late Antiquity: The Legal Protection of Churches," in *Confrontation in Late Antiquity: Imperial Presentation and Regional Adaptation*, ed. Linda Jones Hall (Cambridge: Orchard Academic, 2003). Caseau is critical of Ducloux but reaches some similar conclusions about the multifaceted origins of sanctuary law.

34. Ducloux, *Ad ecclesiam confugere*, 253–54.

35. Ibid., 6.

36. Ibid., 34: "*L'héritage païen est donc flagrant, même si le fondement religieux de l'asile chrétien en fait une institution totalement différente de son ancêtre grec. C'est l'amalgame entre asylie païenne et asile chrétien.*"

37. Harald Siems, "Zur Entwicklung des Kirchenasyls zwischen Spätantike und Mittelalter," in *Libertas: Grundrechtliche und rechtstaatliche Gewährungen in Antike und Gegenwart: Symposion aus Anlaß des 80. Geburtstages von Franz Wieacker* ed. Okko Behrends and Malte Diesselhorst (Ebelsbach: Rolf Gremer, 1991), 139–86, 141.

38. Ibid.

39. R.A. Markus, *The End of Ancient Christianity* (Cambridge: Cambridge University Press, 1990), 139–55; and also his article, "How on Earth Could Places Become Holy? Origins of the Christian Idea of Holy Places," *Journal of Early Christian Studies* 2 (1994): 257–71. Hereinafter *JECS*.

40. Markus, *End of Ancient Christianity*, 141. Markus argues that early Christian theology was characterized by its insistence that God "was wholly present everywhere at once, allowing no site, no building or space any privileged share of holiness." But see Christine Shepardson, "Controlling Contested Places: John Chrysostom's *Adversus Iudaeos* Homilies and the Spatial Politics of Religious Controversy," *JECS* 15, no. 4 (2007): 483–516.

41. Augustine, *Patrologia Latina*, ed. J-P. Migne et al. (Paris, 1844–91), 38:1471–72 (hereinafter *PL*): "*Celebritas hujus congregationis, dedicatio est domus orationis. Domus ergo nostrarum orationum ista est, domus Dei nos ipsi. Si domus Dei nos ipsi, nos in hoc saeculo aedificamur, ut in fine saeculi dedicemur.*"

42. John Chrysostom, *Homilia de capto Eutropio et de divitiarum vanitate*, in *Patrologiae cursus completus Series Graeca*, 52:397. Hereinafter *PG*.

43. Shepardson, "Controlling Contested Places."

44. Beatrice Caseau, "A Case Study for the Transformation of Law in Late Antiquity: The Legal Protection of Churches," in Hall, *Confrontation in Late Antiquity*.

45. Peter Brown, *The Cult of the Saints: Its Rise and Function in Latin Christianity* (Chicago: University of Chicago Press, 1981).

46. The Council of Orange (441), chap. 5 in *Concilia Galliae, a. 314–a. 506*, ed. C. Munier (*CCSL*, 148), 79.

47. *Corpus Legum*, 241.

48. Harold Siems, "Asyl in der Kirche? Wechsellagen des Kirchenasyls im Mittelalter," in Dreher, *Das Antike Asyl*, 268.

49. There are reasons to be suspicious of the constitution. It does appear in a ninth-century text of Florus of Lyon (*PL* 119:421), but this leaves the very real possibility that the text was a Carolingian-era forgery.

50. Orosius, *Historiarum adversum paganos*, ed. C. Zangemeister (Hildesheim: G. Olms, 1967), 7.39.

51. Augustine, *De civitate Dei*, 1.3.

52. Council of Sardica (ca. 343), c. 7, in *Concilia Galliae, a. 314–a. 506*. This is chap. 8 in the text of Dionysius and Isodore, though some editions number it by the Greek text as chap. 7: "*Honestum est autem, ut episcopi intercessionem his praestant qui iniqua vi opprimuntur aut si vidua affligatur aut pupillus exspolietur.*" The quoted text follows Isidore's use of "*pupillis*" (orphans) rather than "*laicis*" (laity) although the latter has some support in the Greek texts of this council.

53. See, e.g., Isaiah 1:17 in the Old Testament and James 1:27 in the New Testament.

54. "The Letter of St. Clement of Rome to the Corinthians," in *The Apostolic Fathers, Volume I*, trans. Francis X. Glimm (New York: Cima, 1947), 51. The date and authorship of the letter are disputed, with some arguing for a second-century date. Eusebius judged the letter spurious (*Hist. Eccl.* 3.37), though it does appear in the fifth-century *Codex Alexandrinus* of the whole Bible.

55. Council of Sardica, c. 7, in *Concilia Galliae, a. 314–a. 506*, CCSL 148.

56. I Timothy 2:1.

57. I Timothy 2:2.

58. I Timothy 2:5.

59. As Ramsay MacMullen has shown, bishops by the fourth century might have considerable social standing and influence in imperial courts. See *Christianizing the Roman Empire* (New Haven: Yale University Press, 1984), 52–58.

60. Gröll, *Elemente des Kirchlichen Freiungsrechtes*, 122 where this development is related to the increasingly legal nature of determining qualification for clerical office: "*Je mehr sich nun die Rechtsnatur dieser Klerikerqualifikation entwickelte, desto mehr wurde schon von diesem Gesichtpunkte aus die Interzession eine Rechtspflicht.*"

61. The relevant portion of Macedonius's letter reads: "*Officium sacerdotii vestri esse dicitis intervenire pro reis, et nisi obtineatis, offendi, quasi quod erat officii vestri minime reportetis. Hic ego vehementer ambigo utrum istud ex religione descendat. Nam si a Domino peccata adeo prohibentur, ut ne poenitendi quidem copia post primam tribuatur; quemadmodum nos possumus ex religione contendere ut nobis qualecumque illud crimen fuerit, dimittatur? quod utique, cum impunitum volumus, probamus. Et si constat non minus auctorem quam probatorem teneri in omnibus quae peccantur, certum est nos culpae societate vinciri, quoties eum impunitum esse cupimus, qui culpae tenetur obnoxius. Tum praeterea accedit hoc quod gravius est. Nam omnia peccata videntur veniabiliora, cum is qui reus est correctionem promittit: verum nunc, ut mores nostri sunt, et sceleris poenam cupiunt homines sibi relaxari, et id propter quod scelus admissum est, possidere. Pro his quoque interveniendum putat sacerdotium vestrum, de quibus adeo futuri nulla spes est, ut etiam in praesenti eadem criminis ratio perseveret. Nam qui tam pervicaciter tenet propter quae crimen admisit, ostendit se, ubi licentia fuerit, similia peccaturum.*" Ep. 152, *Epistulae 124–184*, ed. A. Goldbacher in *Corpus Scriptorum Ecclesiasticorum Latinorum* (hereinafter *CSEL*), 44: 250 (Vienna: Hoelder-Pichler-Tempsky, 1904). (*PL* 33:653).

62. "*Nullo modo ergo culpas quas corrigi volumus, approbamus, nec quod perperam committitur, ideo volumus impunitum esse, quia placet; sed hominem miserantes, facinus autem seu flagitium detestantes, quanto magis nobis displicet vitium, tanto minus volumus inemendatum interire vitiosum. Facile enim est atque proclive malos odisse, quia mali sunt: rarum autem et pium eosdem ipsos diligere, quia homines sunt; ut in uno simul et culpam improbes, et naturam approbes, ac propterea culpam iustius oderis, quod ea foedatur natura quam diligis. Non est igitur iniquitatis, sed potius humanitatis societate devinctus, qui propterea est criminis persecutor, ut sit hominis liberator. Morum porro corrigendorum nullus alius quam in hac vita locus est; nam post hanc, quisque id habebit quod in hac sibimet conquisierit. Ideo compellimur humani generis caritate intervenire pro reis,*

ne istam vitam sic finiant per supplicium, ut ea finita non possint finire supplicium." Ep. 153, *CSEL* 44:262; *PL* 33:653.

63. "*Nam quosdam quorum crimina manifesta sunt, a vestra severitate liberatos, a societate tamen removemus altaris, ut poenitendo placare possint quem peccando contempserant, seque ipsos puniendo. Nam nihil aliud agit quem veraciter poenitet, nisi ut id quod mali fecerit, impunitum esse non sinat: eo quippe modo sibi non parcenti ille parcit, cuius altum iustumque iudicium nullus contemptor evadit. Quod si iniquis et scelestis ille parcendo, eisque vitam salutemque largiendo, etiam plerisque eorum quos novit non acturos poenitentiam, tamen exhibet patientiam; quanto magis nos in eos qui correctionem promittunt, et utrum faciant quod promittunt incerti sumus, misericordes esse debemus, ut rigorem vestrum pro eis intercedendo flectamus, pro quibus et Dominum, quem nihil de moribus eorum etiam futuris latet, non tamen impudenter, quia hoc ipse praecepit, oramus!*" Ep. 153, *CSEL* 44:262; *PL* 33:653.

64. Stephan Kuttner, *Kanonistische Schuldlehre von Gratian bis auf Die Dekretalen Gregors IX: Systematisch auf Grund der handschriftlichen Quellen dargestellt* (Vatican City: Biblioteca Apostolica Vaticana, 1935), 1–59.

65. Jaroslav Pelikan, *The Christian Tradition: A History of the Development of Doctrine* (Chicago: University of Chicago Press, 1971), 1:285.

66. John Chrysostom, Homily 15.5 in *epist. II ad Cor.* (pertaining to II Corinthians 7: 13) (*PG* 61:510).

67. Cyprian, *Opera Omnia* in *PL* 4:863 (1865).

68. Cyprian, *Letters*, 55, trans. Rose Bernard Donna (Washington: Catholic University of America Press, 1964), 51:142.

69. Pelikan, *The Christian Tradition*, 2:32.

70. Francis X. Murphy, "Penitential Controversy," in *The New Catholic Encyclopedia* (New York: McGraw-Hill, 1967).

71. Ep. 153, *CSEL* 44:262; *PL* 33:655.

72. Hefele, *Histoire des conciles*, 2, part 2, 737–42; Duchesne, *Histoire ancienne de l'Eglise*, 2:15.

73. Council of Sardica, c. 7, in *Concilia Galliae, a. 314–a. 506*: "*Sed quoniam saepe contingit, ut ad misericordiam Ecclesiae confugiant, qui injuriam patiuntur, aut qui peccantes in exilio vel insulis damnantur; aut certe quamcunque sententiam excipiunt, subveniendum est his et sine dubitatione petenda indulgentia.*"

74. For the most part, the close connection between ecclesiastical sanctuary and episcopal intercession has been recognized in the historical scholarship. E.g., Timbal, *Le droit d'asile*, 32 and 55n3. See also De Beaurepaire, "Essai sur l'asile religieux dans l'Empire Romain et la monarchie française," *Bibliothèque de l'Ecole de Chartres* (Paris: Librairie Droz, 1853–55), 4:162ff.; Hinschius, *Das*

Kirchenrecht der Katholiken und Protestanten, 4:300 (Berlin: I. Guttentag, 1888); J. Gröll, *Die Elemente des kirchlichen Freiungsrechtes* (Amsterdam: Verlag P. Schippers, 1965), 125. Other writers had also stressed the close link between clerical intercession and the sanctuary protections offered by Christian churches. See, e.g., E. Loening, *Geschichte des Deutschen Kirchenrechts* (Strassburg: K. J. Truebner, 1878), 318–19, and P. Hinschius, *Das Kirchenrecht der Katholiken und Protestanten* (Berlin: I. Guttentag, 1869–97), 383. See, e.g., the review of Timbal's book by Franz Gescher in the *ZSS KA* (1940), 29:466, which stressed the importance of Timbal's having traced sanctuary to a Christian source (as well as the debt Gescher felt that this view owed to earlier German scholars such as P. Hinschius).

Martroye, however, took exception to such a close juridical linking: "*Le fondement juridique de l'asile ne se trouve pas dans le droit d'intercession.*" While he notes that both intercession and sanctuary were both useful "*moyens d'action au service de la bienfaisant influence des évêques*" he seeks to separate the two, presumably on grounds that their positive legislative recognition in imperial Roman law occurred separately and that intercession is granted by persons while sanctuary derives from a place. "L'asile dans la législation impériale du IV au VI siècle," in *Mémoires de la société nationale des antiquaires de France* (Paris: Société Nationale des Antiquaires de France, 1918), 75:160. He is followed on this by Herman, "Asile dans l'église orientale," in *Dictionnaire de droit canonique* (Lyon: J. Duplain, 1935), 1:1084.

75. These events probably took place around 410 or 411. Ep., 115, *CSEL*, 33: 661: "*Ad Hipponiensem ecclesiam confugit et ibi erat, ut confugientes solent, expectans quo modo per intercessionem nostram sua negotia terminaret.*" The fugitive was named Faventius, and he appears in letters 113–16 of Augustine. *CSEL* 34:659–62. Faventius was arrested when he left the church one day, but Augustine continued to intercede for him with imperial and ecclesiastical officials by letter after he was sent to Numidia. The extant sources do not tell us how the affair ended.

76. *CSEL* 57:652; *PL* 33:1092.

77. Timbal (*Le droit d'asile*, 18) and Martroye ("L'asile et la législation impérial," 66) both assumed the debt was private. Ducloux (*Ad ecclesiam confugere*, 147) concluded the debt was to the public fisc, but argues that even if it were a private debt, the agents who come for Fascius would not have been able to use corporal forms to coerce payment of the debt.

78. The *PL* text suggests the debt was private because it uses the term *oppigneratores*, which can mean a private surety, *PL* 33:1092. On the other hand the *CSEL* gives *opinatores*, which Ducloux and others, have read to imply a fiscal responsibility, and thus a public debt, *CSEL* 57:652. See also Ducloux, *Ad ecclesiam confugere*, 145–49.

79. *C. Th.* 9.45.1.

80. *C. Th.* 9.45.3. Ducloux is of the opinion that this law only had effect in the eastern empire because of an effective estrangement between the two halves of the empire during the years 398–99. Ducloux, *Ad ecclesiam confugere*, 146n5.

81. Augustine knew how to invoke imperial law when it was known to him and useful in a given circumstance. See, for instance, his apparent invocation of a 408 law prohibiting pagan celebrations (known to us as Sirmondian Constitution 14) in Letter 91.8. See Erika Hermanowicz, "Catholic Bishops and Appeals to the Imperial Court: A Legal Study of the Calama Riots in 408," *JECS*, 12:481–521 (2004).

82. Letter 28*, *Sancti Aurelii Augustini Opera: Epistolae ex duobus codicibus nuper in lucem prolatae*, ed. Johannes Divjak, *CSEL* 88 (Vienna, 1981).

83. Letter 28*, *CSEL* 88 "*legit mihi ipsum commonitorium memoratus tribunus, quod ego verum esse non credidi. . . . non autem dedit aut id gestis municipalibus allegavit.*"

84. See the discussion in in Chapter 2, "Roman Sanctuary Legislation: The Theodosian Code," concerning the difficulties this particular text has presented to historians trying to locate the earliest legislative sanction for sanctuary in late imperial Roman law. If Mommsen's reconstruction of the text is permissible—though some scholars doubt that it is—Augustine could have known of the law and perhaps invoked it in favor of Victorinus *C. Th.* 16.8.19, ed. Pharr 469n38.

85. Ducloux, *Ad ecclesiam confugere*, 157.

86. *C. Th.* 9.40.16.

87. Ducloux makes some efforts to do so (*Ad ecclesiam confugere*, 146–47) before concluding that the evidence cannot support the claim that Augustine acted with the 409 law in mind. Timbal (*Le droit d'asile*, 66) agrees.

88. *Oratio 43, in laudem Basilii Magni*, PG 36:513–516.

89. Eutropius, *Brevarium* 10.9.4, in MGH, *Chronica Minora* 1:237; Socrates of Constantinople (also known as Socrates Scholasticus), *Historia Ecclesiastica*,2.25 *ed.* G. C. Hansen, in *Die Griechischen Christlichen Schriftsteller, vol. 1* (Berlin:Akademie Verlag, 1995); Zonaras, *Epitome Historiarum*, 6:192–93 (ed. J. Smith, Leipzig: Bibliotheca Scriptorum Graecorum et Romanorum Teubneriana, 1870) has Constant flee to and be dragged from a *naos* (Greek: temple), though this may have designated an *ecclesia* as well. See Moreno Morani, "Sull'espressione linguistica dell'idea di 'santuario' nelle civiltà classiche," in *Santuari e politica nel mondo antico*, ed. Marta Sordi (Milan: Università Cattolica del Sacro Cuore, 1983). But cf., Ducloux, *Ad ecclesiam confugere*, 37.

90. Theodoret, *The Ecclesiastical History, Dialogues and Letters of Theodoret* in *Nicean and Post-Nicean Fathers* (2nd. Series), ed. Philip Schaff and Henry Wace (Edinburgh: Continuum International, 1980), 3:75.

91. Ducloux, *Ad ecclesiam confugere*, 53–80.

92. *C. Th.* 9.45.1, where public debtors are excluded from the privilege.
93. *C. Th.* 9.45.5.
94. Ducloux, *Ad ecclesiam confugere*, 79.
95. See, Augustine's Letter 11* (*CSEL* 88), where a mob protected a monk, even though he was rather unpopular, against a man who wanted to drag him from the church where he sought sanctuary and kill him. See, on this event, Michael Kulikowski, "Fronto, the Bishops, and the Crowd: Episcopal Justice and Communal Violence in Fifth-century Tarraconensis," *Early Medieval Europe* (2002), 2:295–320.
96. He is the only eunuch known to have reached this rank. Eunuchs were prevented by imperial law from holding the consulship.
97. Arcadius is depicted in the surviving sources as feeble and ineffectual. Synesius, *De regno* (*PG* 66:1050). Eutropius, on the other hand, appears able, but grasping and nearly universally despised. Helge Schweckendiek, *Claudians Invektive gegen Eutrop: Ein Kommentar* (Hildesheim: Olms-Weidmann, 1992); *The Prosopography of the Later Roman Empire II*, ed. J. R. Martindale (Cambridge: Cambridge University Press, 1971).
98. Zosimus, *Historia Nova in* François Paschoud, *Zosime: Histoire Nouvelle* (Paris: Les Belles Lettres, 1971) 5.8; Sozomenus, *Historia Ecclesiastica*, 8.7 *PG* 67:1534.
99. John Chrysostom, *Homilia in Eutropium*, *PG* 52:393 and *Homilia de capto Eutropio et de divitiarum vanitate*, *PG* 52:397.
100. Chrysostom, *Homilia in Eutropium*, *PG* 52:393.
101. Ibid.
102. Ibid.; *PG* 52:394.
103. *C. Th.* 9.45.1.
104. *C. Th.* 9.45.2.
105. *C. Th.* 9.45.3.
106. Ibid.
107. Tony Honoré, *Law in the Crisis of Empire, 379–455 AD* (Oxford: Clarendon Press, 1998), 77–78, 81–83, 88–90.
108. Martroye, "L'asile dans la législation impériale du IV au VI siècle," 193ff; But cf. Ducloux, *Ad ecclesiam confugere*, 65.
109. *Codex Justinianus* (Hereafter *CJ*) 1.4.7 (restricting the judicial power of bishops in civil matters and restricting the right of litigants in such cases to choose bishops as judges); *C. Th.* 9.40.16 (forbidding clerics to intercede on behalf of condemned criminals); *C. Th.* 16.2.32 (concerning clerical responsibility for debts); *C. Th.* 16.2.33 (regarding episcopal oversight of clergy); *C. Th.* 9.45.3 (causing, among other things, clergy to be responsible for the debts of fugitives they protect).
110. Chrysostom, *Homilia in Eutropium*, *PG* 52:394.

111. Ibid.

112. Chrysostom, *Homilia de capto Eutropio*, *PG* 52:397.

113. Zosimus, *Histoire Nouvelle*, 5.18.1.

114. Chrysostom, *Homilia de capto Eutropio*, *PG* 52:397.

115. Houlou, "Le droit pénal chez Saint Augustin," *Revue Historique du Droit Français et Etranger* (1974), 21–22: "*et c'est là la pensée profonde d'Augustin, le but du droit d'asile* [*est*] . . . *de rendre possible l'intercessio.*"

116. Augustine, Ep. 160, *CSEL* 44:281.

2. ROMAN ARISTOCRATIC TRADITIONS, IMPERIAL PENAL LAW, AND SANCTUARY

1. Pierre Timbal, *La droit d'asile* (Paris: Sirey, 1939), 25–26. Timbal's account rests in a long historical tradition of idealizing Roman law and governance. See, e.g., Paganinus Gaudentius, *De moribus saeculi Justinianei* (Strasbourg: Frederic Spoor, 1654), whom Timbal cites.

2. Theodor Mommsen, *Römisches Strafrecht* (Leipzig: Duncker & Humblot, 1899), 459–60. Mommsen speaks of an "indulgence" toward "foreign institutions" such as sanctuary "under the regime of the Republic."

3. Instances where imperial Rome grants sanctuary rights to Greek temples in the provinces can be found in *Ancient Roman Statutes*, ed. and trans. Allan Chester Johnson, Paul Robinson Coleman-Norton, and Frank Card Bourne (Austin: University of Texas Press, 1961), nos. 20, 21, 68.

4. Livy, *Ab urbe condita*, ed. A. McDonald (Oxford: Oxford University Press, 1965), 35.51. See Timbal, *Le droit d'asile*, 25–30.

5. Tacitus, 3.36, in Francis Goodyear, *The Annals of Tacitus* (New York: Cambridge University Press, 1972).

6. See Martin Dreher, "Das Asyl in der Antike von seinen griechischen Ursprüngen bis zur christlichen Spätantike," in *Tyche: Beiträge zur Alten Geschichte Papyriologie und Epigraphik* 11 (1996): 79–96. Dreher also stresses continuity in asylum practices between pre-Christian and Christian practices.

7. Dio Cassius, 48.19 in *Histoire Romain*, eds. Marie-Laure Freyburger et Jean-Michel Roddaz (Paris: Les Belles Lettres, 1991).

8. Gaius, 1.53, in *The Institutes of Gaius*, eds. William Gordon and O.F. Robinson (Ithaca: Cornell University Press, 1988); *The Theodosian Code*, ed. Clyde Pharr (Princeton: Princeton University Press, 1952), 9.44.1; D. 1.6.2 and 1.12.1.1 (hereinafter *C. Th.*); notice how this closely mirrors the tradition already memorialized by Aeschylus's account of Orestes and the statue of Athena.

9. *C. Th.* 9.44.1; see also Arrido Diego Manfredini, "'Ad ecclesiam confugere,' 'ad statuas confugere' nell'età di Theodosio I," in *Atti di Accademia Romanistica Constantiana. VI Convegno Internazionale* (Perugia, 1986), 39–58; Richard

Gamauf, "Ad statuas confugere in der frühen römischen Kaiserzeit," in *Das antike Asyl: Kultische Grundlagen, rechtliche Ausgestaltung und politische Funktion*, ed. Martin Dreher (Cologne: Böhlau Verlag 2003), 177.

10. Tacitus, *Annals*, 1:39.

11. See, for instance, the discussion in Mommsen, *Römisches Strafrecht*, 473ff.

12. Wolfgang Kunkel, *Untersuchungen zur Entwicklung des römische Kriminalverfahrens in vorsullanischer Zeit* (Munich: C. H. Beck, 1962); Richard Bauman, *Crime and Punishment in Ancient Rome* (New York: Routledge, 1996); and Winfried Nippel, *Public Order in Ancient Rome* (Cambridge: Cambridge University Press, 1995).

13. Mommsen, *Römisches Strafrecht*, 462–68.

14. Nippel, *Public Order in Ancient Rome*, 10–12; 48–52; and O. F. Robinson, *The Criminal Law of Ancient Rome* (Baltimore: Johns Hopkins University Press, 1995), 6–11.

15. Even among the magistrates employing the *intercessio*, we might say they thought "of their functions as a personal honor more than a public 'mission' or responsibility." P. Veyne, *Le pain et le cirque: Sociologie historique d'un pluralisme politique* (Paris: Seuil, 1976), 386 (where he is describing oligarchies of the republican era); Ramsay MacMullen, *Corruption and the Decline of Rome* (New Haven: Yale University Press, 1988), 79. Note the observations of Tacitus that when the emperor was present at court, the solicitations of many powerful men were denied: "while equity gained, liberty suffered." *Annals*, 1.75.1: "*libertas corrumpebatur.*"

16. Cicero, *Oration Pro P. Quinctio*, ed. Michael Reeve (Leipzig: BG Teubner, 1992) 22.72.

17. MacMullen, *Corruption and the Decline of Rome*, 93.

18. Libanius scornfully contrasted the benefices he freely disposes *on his dependents* with those bestowed upon just anyone and conditioned on "payment as though for meat and vegetables!" And likewise he was outraged by a powerful man who sold his influence for "silver, gold, clothes, a slave, a horse, or whatever pleases the belly" to anyone willing to pay. See Libanius, *Selected Works, II: Selected Orations*, ed. A. F. Norman (Cambridge, Mass.: Loeb Classical Library, 1977), 46.

19. *C. Th.* 1.27.1.

20. *Selected Letters of Pliny the Younger* (Boston: Perkins, Marvin and Co., 1835), 70.

> *Libertus tuus, cui succensere te dixeras, venit ad me, advolutusque pedibus meis, tamquam tuis haesit. Flevit multum, multumque rogavit, multum etiam tacuit; in summa, fecit mihi fidem poenitentiae. Vere credo emendatum, quia deliquisse*

se sensit. Irasceris, scio; et irasceris merito, id quoque scio; sed tunc praecipua mansuetudinis laus, cum irae causa iustissima est. . . . remitte indulgentiae tuae; ne torseris illum, ne torseris etiam te. Torqueris enim, cum tam lenis irasceris.

21. John Procopé, "Greek and Roman Political Theory," in *The Cambridge History of Medieval Political Thought*, ed. J. H. Burns (New York: Cambridge University Press, 1988), 26–27.

22. *The Pythagorean Texts of the Hellenistic Period*, ed. H. Thesleff (Abo, Finland: Abo akademi, 1965).

23. St. Clement, *The First Epistle of Clement to the Corinthians*, in *The Apostolic Fathers, Volume I*, trans. Francis X. Glimm (New York: Cima, 1947), 55.

24. *C. Th.* 9.24.4 and 5; also *C. Th.* 13.7.2.

25. *C. Th.* 12.1.50.

26. *C. Th.* 12.1.96.

27. Hans Langenfeld, *Christianisierungspolitik und Sklavengesetzgebung der römischen Kaiser von Konstantin bis Theodosius II* (Bonn: Habelt, 1977), 158.

28. John Chrysostom, *PG* 52: 615.

29. Ramsay MacMullen has shown that many other powerful ones had fortresses as well; *Corruption and the Decline of Rome*, 72–73.

30. Orosius, 7.39 in *Historiarum adversum Paganos Libri VII*, CSEL 5:544–46.

31. See Amnon Linder, "Constantine's Ten Law Series" in *Schriften*, in MGH (Hannover: Hahnsche Buchhandlung, 1988), 33, II, 491–507; Harald Siems, "Zur Entwicklung des Kirchenasyls zwischen Spätantike und Mittelalter," in *Libertas: Grundrechtliche und rechtstaatliche Gewährungen in Antike und Gegenwart: Symposion aus Anlaß des 80. Geburtstages von Franz Wieacker*, ed. Okko Behrends and Malte Diesselhorst (Ebelsbach: R. Gremer, 1991), 157. Siems gives a helpful discussion of the significance of this text as a forgery for medieval compilers.

32. Linder, "Constantine's Ten Laws Series," 491.

33. Siems, "Zur Entwicklung des Kirchenasyls zwischen Spätantike und Mittelalter," 157.

34. The text is reproduced in Linder, "Constantine's Ten Laws Series," 495.

35. Siems, "Zur Entwicklung des Kirchenasyls zwischen Spätantike und Mittelalter," 157.

36. Gabriel Le Bras, "Asile," in *Dictionnaire d'histoire et de géographie ecclésiastiques*, ed. Alfred Baudrillart (Paris, 1930), 1036.

37. John Matthews, *Laying Down the Law: A Study of the Theodosian Code* (New Haven: Yale University Press, 200), 168–99; Tony Honoré, *Law in the Crisis of Empire, 379–455 AD* (Oxford: Clarendon Press, 1998), 58–96; 212–27; Jill Harries, *Law and Empire in Late Antiquity* (New York: Cambridge University Press, 1999), 19–31.

38. See the interesting discussion in Harries, *Law and Empire*, 56–76.

39. Harries, *Law and Empire*, 77–82.

40. *C. Th.* 9. 45. 1: "*Publicos debitores, si confugiendum ad ecclesias crediderint, aut ilico extrahi de latebris oportebit aut pro his ipsos, qui eos occultare probantur, episcopos exigi. Sciat igitur praecellens auctoritas tua neminem debitorum posthac a clericis defendendum aut per eos eius, quem defendendum esse crediderint, debitum esse solvendum.*"

41. By the late empire, the class of capital crimes was growing, but it did not include debtors. Usually, capital punishment was reserved to crimes such as "sacrilege against the Imperial Majesty, crimes against the dead, sorcery, magic, adultery, ravishing, and homicide." *C. Th.* 9.38.1–12. Counterfeiting coins was eventually added as well. See *C. Th.* 9.38.6. The number of capital crimes increased dramatically during the fourth century.

42. Augustine, Ep. 153, in *Corpus Scriptorum Ecclesiasticorum Latinorum* (*CSEL* 44:250–262 (Vienna: Hoelder-Pichler-Tempsky, 1904).

43. Timbal, *Le droit d'asile*, 65.

44. *C. Th.* 9. 45. 2: "*Iudaci, qui reatu aliquo vel debitis fatigati simulant se Christianae legi velle coniungi, ut ad ecclesias confugientes vitare possint crimina vel pondera debitorum, arceantur nec ante suscipiantur, quam debita universa reddiderint vel fuerint innocentia demonstrata purgati.*"

45. A subsequent edict, issued in 416 (*C. Th.* 16. 8. 23) grants to those Jews simulating Christianity for purposes of gaining sanctuary protections, the opportunity to freely return to Judaism, implying both that those making earnest conversions could stay, and that simulated conversions remained a problem that gained imperial and ecclesiastical attention.

46. *Sancti Augustini tractatus sive sermones inediti ex codice Guelferbytano* (Zürich: Rascher, 1918), 100–101: "*Melius est ergo ut et nocentes in ecclesia muniantur, quam innocentes de ecclesia rapiantur.*" On this text, and its relation to Sermo 302 of Augustine, see G. Morin, "Sancti Augustini sermons post Maurinos reperti," in the *Miscellanea Agostiniana* 1:528 (Rome, 1930).

47. *C. Th.* 9. 45. 3. On "purple-die fish collectors," see "Murileguli," in *Paulys Real-Encyclopädie der classischen Altertumswissenschaft*, ed. August Friedrich von Pauly and Georg Wissowa (Stuttgart: 1884–1972), vol. 16, part 1, 662.

48. *C. Th.* 9.45.1–3.

49. See, e.g., Anne Ducloux, *Ad ecclesiam confugere: Naissance du droit d'asile dans les églises (IeV–milieu du Ve s.)* (Paris: De Boccard, 1994), 53–63; Timbal, *Le droit d'asile*, 55–94.

50. Gaius, *Inst.* 3.82.

51. Dig. 1.3.36, See also Harries, *Law and Empire*, 31–34.

52. Harries, *Law and Empire*, 33.

53. *CJ* 8.52.2.
54. Timbal, *Le droit d'asile*, 56.
55. John Chrysostom, *Homilia in Eutropium*, in *PG* 52:394.
56. Socrates Of Constantinople, *Hist. Eccl.* 6.5.
57. At least this is what M. F. Martroye thought; see "L'asile et la législation impérial du IV au VI siècle," in *Mémoires de la société nationale des antiquaires de France* (1918), series 8, vol. 5, 177–78. He was taken to task for such a suggestion by Timbal (*Le droit d'asile*, 32–55) and Ducloux (*Ad ecclesiam confugere*, 62).
58. *C. Th.* 9.45.3. See above.
59. Zosimus, *Histoire Nouvelle*, 5.18.1.
60. This was the position of Martroye ("L'asile et la législation impérial du IV au VI siècle," 177–78); Ducloux (*Ad ecclesiam confugere*, 67) disagrees strongly.
61. Ducloux (*Ad ecclesiam confugere*, 67) finds this unlikely.
62. For instance, *C. Th.* 9.45.3. *in medio*, "We no longer permit such persons to have the benefit of the law which did not forbid *decurions* to be clerics after surrender of their patrimonies had ensued."
63. Alan Cameron, *Claudian. Poetry and Propaganda at the Court of Honorius* (Oxford: Oxford University Press, 1970), 139–40; Honoré (*Law in the Crises of Empire*, 82) rightfully notes the "steady flow of well-constructed texts" that testify to Eutropius's skills as an administrator. Of course, administrative and legislative skills are not guarantees against self-serving legislation. The older view stressed Eutropius's tendency to satisfy his personal interests through imperial legislation and downplayed his administrative skill, See "Arkadios," in *Paulys Real-Encyclopädie der classischen Altertumswissenschaft*, 2:1141.
64. Sozomenus, *Ecclesiastical History* 8.7 in *A Select Library of Nicene and Post-Nicene Fathers*, eds. Philip Schaff and Henry Wace (New York: Christian Literature Company, 1890), 2:403.
65. At least Augustine thought the Donatists presumed thus in his Letter 105.6; See, on this, Erika Hermanowicz, "Catholic Bishops and Appeals to the Imperial Court: A Legal Study of the Calama Riots in 408," *Journal of Early Christian Studies*, 12:481–521 (2004).
66. Honoré, *Law in the Crises of Empire.*
67. Timbal, like Ducloux, found Martroye's supposition in this regard unconvincing. *Le droit d'asile*, 55–93.
68. *C. Th.* 16.8.19.
69. *C. Th.* 16.8.19: "*et idcirco iubemus, ne ecclesiis quisquam nocens vel cuiusquam abducere fideli ac devota deo praeceptione sancimus*" and continued "*sub hac videlicet definitione, ut, si quisquam contra hanc legem venire temptaverit, sciat, se ad maiestatis crimen esse retinendum.*"

70. *C. J.* 1.12.2. Mommsen, *Theodosiani libri XVI cum constitutionibus Sirmondianis* (Berlin: Weidmann, 1905), vol. 1, par. 2, 892. Pharr followed Mommsen in this regard. See also *Le Code Théodosien, Livre XVI*, ed. Élisabeth Magnou-Nortier (Paris: Cerf, 2002), which also accepts Mommsen's reconstruction. Martroye was unwilling to see in this text the first official recognition of a sanctuary right by the empire. *Mémoires de la société nationale des antiquaires de France*, 206.

71. *C. J.* 1.12.2 "*Fideli ac devota praeceptione sancimus nemini licere ad sacrosanctas ecclesias confugientes abducere*" and continuing "*sub hac videlicet definitione, ut, si quisquam contra hanc legem venire temptaverit, sciat se ad maiestatis crimen esse retinendum.*"

72. Timbal refused (*Le droit d'asile*, 74). Also Ducloux (*Ad ecclesiam confugere*, 157). Paul Hinshius, however, was willing to accept the text as authentic. See *Das Kirchenrecht der Katholiken und Protestanten in Deutschland* (Graz: Akademische Druck- u. Verlagsanstalt, 1888), 4:382.

73. Martroye, 206.

74. Sirm. Const. 13, (Pharr's edition).

75. Siems, "Zur Entwicklung des Kirchenasyls zwischen Spätantike und Mittelalter," 143. But see Langenfeld, *Christianisierungspolitik und Sklavengesetzgebung der Römischer Kaiser*, 124.

76. Élisabeth Magnou-Nortier, "Sur l'origine des constitutions Sirmondiennes," *Revue du Droit Canonique* 51 (2001): 279–303.

77. Ibid., 302.

78. Matthews, *Laying Down the Law*, 121–66.

79. Magnou-Nortier, "Sur l'origine des constitutions Sirmondiennes," *RDC* *51*:295.

80. *C. Th.* 9.45.4.

81. For a good discussion of the jurisprudential foundation of modern legal codification, see Roger Berkowitz, *The Gift of Science: Leibniz and the Modern legal Tradition* (Cambridge, Mass.: Harvard University Press, 2005).

82. For the specific methods of compiling the Theodosian code that support these conclusions, see generally Honoré, *Law in the Crises of Empire.*

83. Johannes Hermann, "Cod. Theod. 9, 45: De his, qui ad ecclesias confugiunt," in *Beiträge zur Rechtsgeschichte: Gedächtnisschrift für Hermann Conrad*, ed. Gerd Kleinheyer and Paul Mikat (Munich: Ferdinand Schöningh, 1979), 274; Hanspeter Ruedl, "Ad ecclesiam confugere: Die kaiserliche Asylgesetzgebung in der Spätantike," in *Tradition—Wegweisung in die Zukunft: Festschrift für J. Mühlsteiger* (Berlin, 2001),141. But cf. Ducloux, *Ad ecclesiam confugere*, 207, and Timbal, *Le droit d'asile*, 76–79.

84. C. Th. 9.45.4: *Arma quoque in quovis telo, ferro vel specie eos, qui confugiunt, minime intra ecclesias habere praecipimus, quae non modo a summi dei templis ac divinis altaribus prohibentur, sed etiam cellulis, domibus, hortulis, balneis, areis atque porticibus. Proinde hi, qui sine armis ad sanctissimum dei templum aut ad sacrosanctum altare sive usquam gentium sive in hac alma urbe confugiunt, somnum intra templum sive ipsum altare vel omnino cibum capere absque aliqua eorum iniuria ab ipsis clericis arceantur, designantibus spatia, quae in ecclesiasticis septis eorum tuitioni sufficiant, ac docentibus, capitalem poenam esse propositam, si qui eos conentur invadere. quibus si perfuga non annuit, neque consentit, praeferenda humanitati religio est et a divinis ad loca, quae diximus, turbanda temeritas. Hos vero, qui templa cum armis ingredi audent, ne hoc faciant, praemonemus; dein si telis cincti quovis ecclesiae loco vel ad templi septa vel circa vel extra sint, statim eos, ut arma deponant, auctoritate episcopi a solis clericis severius conveniri praecipimus, data eis fiducia, quod religionis nomine melius quam armorum praesidio muniantur. sed si ecclesiae voce moniti, post tot tantorumque denuntiationes, noluerint arma relinquere, iam, clementiae nostrae apud deum et episcoporum causa purgata, armatis, si ita res exegerit, intromissis, trahendos se abstrahendosque esse cognoscant et omnibus casibus esse subdendos. sed neque episcopo inconsulto, nec sine nostra sive iudicum in hac alma urbe vel ubicumque iussione armatum quemquam ab ecclesiis abstrahi oportebit, ne, si multis passim hoc liceat, confusio generetur.*

85. *Ibid.*

86. *C. Th.* 9.45.5.

87. *Ibid.*

88. *CJ* 1.12.5 (containing admonitions that churches were to be free from disruption and violence) and *CJ* 1.12.6 (fairly detailed reiteration the rights and responsibilities of debtors and slaves who fled to church, as well as their creditors and masters).

89. *Nov.* 17.7.

90. *Nov.* 37.10.

91. *Nov.* 17.7.

3. REASSESSING EARLY MEDIEVAL SANCTUARY LEGISLATION

1. Alcuin, *Epistolae Karolini Aevi II*, 247, ed. Ernst Dümmler et al. (Berlin: MGH, 1892–1925), 399–401. "*Hic vero infamis clericus, et accusatus et iudicatus et in custodiam missus et de custodia elapses, basilicam, quam nisi post paenitentiam ingredi non debuerat, contra legem ingressus, et adhuc, ut fertur, pervese vivere non cessans.*"

2. Luitpold Wallach, *Alcuin and Charlemagne: Studies in Carolingian History and Literature* (Ithaca, N.Y.: Cornell University Press, 1959), 109; and also Wallach's "A Manuscript of Tours with an Alcuinian Incipit," *Harvard Theological Review* 51 (1958): 258.

3. *Epistolae* 245 (MGH, *Epistolae* 394). For a detailed account of the circumstances that gave rise to the dispute between Alcuin and Charlemagne, and a discussion of the letters that record the dispute, see Rob Meens, "Sanctuary, Penance, and Dispute Settlement Under Charlemagne: The Conflict Between Alcuin and Theodulf of Orléans over a Sinful Cleric," *Speculum* 82 (2007): 277–300; and Sam Collins, "*Domus Domini patet figura mysterii*: Architectural Imagination and the Politics of Place in the Carolingian Ninth Century" (Ph.D. diss., University of California, Berkeley, 2005).

4. Daniela Fruscione has exhaustively catalogued the law code references to early medieval sanctuary in her recent book, *Das Asyl bei den Germanischen Stämmen im Frühen Mittelalter* (Berlin: Böhlau Verlag, 2003).

5. Charles H. Riggs Jr., *Criminal Asylum in Anglo-Saxon Law* (Gainesville: University of Florida Press, 1963).

6. Patrick Wormald, *The Making of English Law: King Alfred to the Twelfth Century* (Oxford: Blackwell, 1999), vol. 1. Wormald was referring to English legislation, but his caution is fully applicable to the situation on the European continent as well.

7. Wallace-Hadrill, *Early Germanic Kingship* (Oxford: Clarendon Press, 1971), 32–44; Wormald, *The Making of English Law*, 29–30.

8. See *Pactus Legis Salicae*, ed. K. A. Eckhardt, *MGH: Legum* (1962–69), sectio I, vol. 4, pt. 1, ix–xlii.

9. Wormald, *The Making of Early English Law*, 53–70.

10. *The New Cambridge Medieval History*, ed. Rosamond McKitterick (Cambridge: Cambridge University Press, 1995), 2:845.

11. Wormald, *The Making of English Law*, 41.

12. Detlef Liebs, "Römische Juristen der Merowinger," in *Wirkung europäischer Rechtskultur: Festschrift für Karl Kröschell zu seinem 70. Geburtstag*, ed. Gerhard Köbler and Hermann Nehlsen (Munich: Beck, 1997), 635–66.

13. In many cases, overt Frankish influence can be found in the legal texts of these nations. Certainly Carolingians were responsible for the production and transmission of several of these legislative traditions. See Ian Wood's informative discussion in *The Merovingian Kingdoms* (London: Longman, 1994), 102–19, and Wormald, *The Making of English Law*, 44, who observed: "The Franks then were not so much creating law for subject peoples as coaching them in the value of having written law."

14. "De homicides, adulteris et furibus, si ad ecclesiam confugerint, id constituimus observandum, quod ecclesiastici canones decreverunt et lex Romana consitituit: ut ad ecclesiae atriis vel domum ecclesiae vel domum episcopi eos abstrahi omnino non liceat." CCSL 148a:4; Also, *Concilia*, *MGH* 1 (1869): 2. For other instances where kings summoned ecclesiastical councils, see Wood, *The Merovingian Kingdoms*, 104–5.

15. See, however, *Lex Visigothorum* 6.5.18, in *MGH Leges* (1902), sectio 1, tom. 1, 283, which ordered that the sanctuary seeking homicide be put in servitude to the kin of the one whom he had slain.

16. *Leges Burgundionum* 2.3, *MGH Legum*, vol. 2, part 1, p. 126 "Si vero ad ecclesiam servus homicidii reus forte confugerint, quia lex Theudosiani libro nono ad Antiochum data ab ecclesia nullum inermem permittit abduci, indulta vita, pro eo, quem occidit, ipse deserviat.". The reference to the Theodosian code is to 9.45.4 (AD 431).

17. *Leges Visigothorum* 9.3.1–4, ed. K. Zeumer, *MGH: Legum*, sectio 1, 1 (1902), 379–81.

18. "*Nullus latronem vel quamlibet culbabilem, sicut cum episcopis convenit, de atrio ecclesiae extrahere praesumat.*" *Pactus pro tenore pacis domnorum Childeberti et Chlotharii regum*, in *Capitularia Regum Francorum*, ed. A. Boretius and V. Krause, *MGH Legum*, sectio II, 1:6.

19. The Gelasian letter can be found in *Epistolae Romanorum Pontificum*, ed. Thiel (Braunsberg: E. Peter, 1868), 1:505 (fragment 41); it was eventually included in Gratian's *Decretum* at C. 17. q. 4. c. 32. See *Corpus Iuris Canonici*, ed. A. Friedburg and A. Richter (Leipzig: Bernhard Tauchnitz, 1879–81).

20. V Council of Orleans, chap. 22: "*sicut in antiquis constitutionibus tenetur scriptum*" In *Concilia Aevi Karolini, MGH Legum*, sectio III (1906–), 1:107.

21. See, e.g., the seminal work of Ernst Levy, *West Roman Vulgar Law: The Law of Property* (Philadelphia: American Philosophical Society, 1951). See also *Leges Visigothorum*, in *MGH: Leges*, ed. Karol Zeumer (1902); *Lex Romana Visigothorum*, ed. G. Haenel (Leipzig: Teubner, 1848).

22. See *Lex Romana Visigothorum*, 9.34, 208.

23. *Prologus Legis*, in the *Lex Baiuwariorum*, ed. E. de Schwind in *MGH Legum Sectio* I, V(2), p. 198, (1926). "*Moyses gentis Hebreae primus omnium divinas leges sacris litteris explicavit.*"

24. Ibid. "*Numa Pompilius, qui Romulo successit in regn, primus leges Romanis edidit. Deinde cum populus seditiosos magistratus ferre non possit, decemviros legibus scribendis creavit qui leges ex libris Solonis in Latinum sermonem translatas duodecim tabulis exposuerunt. . . . Deinde Caesar coepit id facere, sed ante interfectus est . . . Novae a Constantino coeperunt caesare . . . erantque permixtae et inordinatae.*

Postea Theodosius minor Augustus ad similitudinem Gregoriani et Hermogeniani codicem factum consitutionum a Constantini temporibus sub proprio cuiusque imperatoris titulo disposuit, quem a suo nomine Theodosianum vocavit."

25. *Etym.*, 5.1, *Isidori Hispalensis Episcopi Etymologarium sive Originum*, ed. W.M. Lindsay (Oxford: Clarendon Press, 1911), vol. 1. Discussions of the Bavarian prologue and the context of early medieval royal lawgiving can be found in Wood, *The Merovingian Kingdoms*, 115–19; Wormald, *The Making of English Law: King Alfred to the Twelfth Century*, vol. 1, 43ff.

26. *Bede's Ecclesiastical History of the English People,* 2.5, ed. and trans. B. Colgrave and R. A. B. Mynors (Oxford: Oxford Medieval Texts, 1969): "*iuxta exempla Romanorum.*" Wallace-Hadrill suggests that Bede's use of "Romans" here might refer to Frankish kings as well. See *Early Germanic Kingship in England and on the Continent*, 32–44; Wormald endorses and adds to this interpretation; see *The Making of English Law*, 29–30.

27. Exodus 21:14. Biblical quotations are taken from the King James Version.

28. I Kings 2:23–31; see also II Kings 11:15 where Athalia, the condemned daughter of Jezebel, was removed from the temple at the order of the priest: "She shall not be put to death in the house of the Lord."

29. See the informative discussion regarding use of biblical themes in Martin Heinzelmann, *Gregory von Tours (538–594): "Zehn Bücher Geschichte": Historiographie und Gesellschaftskonzept im 6. Jahrhundert* (Darmstadt: Wissenschaftliche Buchgesellschaft, 1994). One might consult also Bede, *The Ecclesiastical History of the English People*, 3.25, where the account of King Oswy's desperate campaign against the pagan warlord Penda harbors Old Testament themes of divinely inspired military victories. The classic statement on biblical influences on Frankish kingship is Ernst Kantorowicz, *Laudes Regiae: A Study in Liturgical Acclamations and Medieval Ruler Worship* (Berkeley: University of California Press, 1946).

30. Rabanus Maurus, in *PL* 108:907.

31. *PL* 108:907–8 (glossing Deuteronomy 19). Rabanus echoed a reading of this passage that St. Ambrose had put forward in his *De fuge saeculi*, *PL* 14:571.

32. Herrmann Wasserschleben, *Die Irische Kanonensammlung* (Aalen: Scientia-Verlag, 1966, 1885).

33. Ibid., 94.

34. Letters 245 and 246 in *Epistolae MGH*, 393 and 398.

35. Alfred, *Einleitung* 13, in Liebermann, *Die Gesetze der Angelsachsen* (Halle: M. Niemeyer, 1898–1912; Aalen: Scientia, 1960), 1:26–46. Most scholars assume Alfred himself translated the prologue to the Laws of Alfred from Latin sources. Some take umbrage at any suggestion to the contrary. See, for instance, Patrick Wormald's entry for Alfred in the *Oxford Dictionary of National Biography: From*

the Earliest Times until the Year 2000, ed. H. C. Matthew and Brian Harrison (Oxford: Oxford University Press, 2004), 1:718–23. See, however, the recent article by Malcolm Godden, who argues that Alfred was likely not the author of the Laws of Alfred or their prologue, and may not have necessarily been connected with the production of either. "Did King Alfred Write Anything?" *Medium Aevum* 76 (2007): 1–23. Godden's view is supported by Wilhelm Busse in "Die 'karolingische' Reform König Alfreds," in *Karl der Grosse und das Erbe der Kulturen*, ed. Franz-Reiner Erkens (Berlin: Akademie Verlag 2001), 169–84.

36. Felix Liebermann, *Gesetze der Angelsachsen*, 2:82, renders *friðstowe* as *Asylstätte* and "*locum quo fugere.*"

37. David Pratt, *The Political Thought of King Alfred the Great* (Cambridge: Cambridge University Press, 2007), 214.

38. Ibid., 219–221, 226.

39. The Gospel account is given in Matthew 21:12; Mark 11:15; Luke 19:45; John 2:15.

4. THE TRANSMISSION AND RECEPTION OF SANCTUARY LEGISLATION IN THE EARLY MIDDLE AGES

1. R. Dann, "Über den Ursprung des Asylrechts und dessen Überreste in Europa," *Zeitschrift für Deutsches Recht und Deutsche Rechtwissenschaft* (1840), 3:67; Wilhelm Wilda, *Das Strafrecht der Germanen* (Halle: C.A. Schwetschke und Sohn, 1842); H. Brunner, *Deutsche Rechtsgeschichte* (Leipzig: Duncker und Humblot, 1892), 610–11.

2. See Julius Goebel's underappreciated *Felony and Misdemeanor* (New York: Commonwealth Fund, 1937, 1976). For a very insightful discussion of Goebel and the older scholarship, see Patrick Wormald, *The Making of English Law: King Alfred to the Twelfth Century* (Oxford: Blackwell, 1999), 1:10–28.

3. *Pactus Legis Salicae/Lex Salica*, ed. Karl Eckhardt, in *MGH: Legum*, sectio I, IV (i–ii) (1962–69), 252–53 (under the heading *capitula legi Salicae addita*), and pt. 2, 180–81.

4. *Leges Alamannorum*, ed. Karl Lahmann (*MGH: Legum*, sectio I, V[1], 1888; 2nd ed., revised by Karl Eckhardt, 1966), sectio 1, tom. 5, pt. 1. See especially Karl Eckhardt's introduction. See also Ian Wood, "Jural Relations Between the Franks and Alamanni," in *Franks and Alamanni in the Merovingian Period: An Ethnographic Perspective*, ed. Ian Wood (Woodbridge: Boydell Press, 1998), 213–26, at 224.

5. For instance, see H. G. Richardson and G. O. Sayles, *Law and Legislation from Aethelberht to Magna Carta* (Edinburgh: University of Edinburgh Publica-

tions, 1966), 1–9; A. W. B. Simpson, "The Laws of Ethelbert," in *On the Laws and Customs of England*, ed. Morris Arnold et al. (Chapel Hill: University of North Carolina Press, 1981).

6. Wormald, *The Making of English Law*, 96–101; but see Lisi Oliver, *The Beginnings of English Law* (Toronto: University of Toronto Press, 2002), 16–17, for an argument in favor of ecclesiastical interpretation.

7. Wormald, *The Making of English Law*, 94.

8. *Ibid.*, 80–95.

9. See Jean Gaudemet's insightful analysis of the scholarly literature pertaining to the *Edictum Theodorici* in "Le Bréviaire d'Alaric et les Epitome," in *Ius Romanum Medii Aevi* (Milan: Giuffrè, 1965), pars I, 2, b, aa, ß, 6–8.

10. Hermann Nehlsen, *Rezension zu G. Vismara, Edictum Theoderici* (1969), *ZSS GA* 86: 246–60.

11. F. C. Savigny, *Geschichte des römischen Rechts im Mittelalter*, 2nd ed. (Heidelberg, 1834–51), 2:138.

12. Frederick Bluhme, *Edictum Theodorici Regis*, ed. J. Baviera, in S. Riccobono et al., *Fontes Iuris Romani Anteiustiniani*, 2nd ed. (Florence, 1968–69), 2:683–710.

13. Giulio Vismara, *Edictum Theoderici*, in *Ius Romana Medii Aevi* (Milan, 1967), I 2 b; A. d'Ors, *Estudios Visigóticos II: El Código de Eurico* (Rome and Madrid: Cuadernos del Instituto Juríco Español, 1960), 8.

14. F. Beyerle, "Zur Frühgeschichte der westgotischen Gesetzgebung," in *ZSS GA* (1950), 67:1. Beyerle saw the efforts of Theodoric II as a codification rather than an edict, a view contradicted by Vismara. Cf. Hermann Nehlsen, *ZSS GA* (1969), 86:246–60, who renovates the view that the Edictum should be attributed to the Ostrogoth Theodoric the Great. Above all, see on the state of the debates Claus Dieter Schott, "Der Stand der Leges-Forschung," *Frühmittelalterliche Studien* (1979), 13:28, esp. 32–35.

15. Beyerle, "Zur Frühgeschichte der westgotischen Gesetzgebung," in *ZSS GA* (1950), 67:1; cf. P. Rasi, "Sulla paternità del c.d. Edictum Theodorici Regis" (1953), 145 *Arch. Giur.* 105.

16. "*Vulcanae insulae perpetua relegatione damnamus, ut et secrato templo reverentiam habuisse videamur nec vindictam criminosus evadat in totum, qui innocenti non credidit esse parcendum.*" *Variae*, ed. Theodor Mommsen, III, 47, in *MGH Variae* (1894), AA 12, 102.

17. See Daniela Fruscione, *Das Asyl bei den germanischen Stämmen im frühen Mittelalter* (Berlin: Böhlau Verlag, 2002).

18. *E. Th.* in *MGH*, 5:160: "*Si servus cuiuslibet nationis ad quamlibet ecclesiam confugerit, statim domino veniam promittente reddatur: nec enim ultra unum diem ibidem residere praecipimus. Qui si exire noluerit, vir religious archdiaconus eiusdem ecclesia, vel presbyter atque clerici, eundem ad dominum suum*

exire compellant, et domino indulgentiam praestanti sine dilatione contradant. Quod si hoc suprascriptae religiosae personae facere forte noluerint, aliud mancipium euisdem meriti domino dare cogantur: ita ut etiam illud mancipium, quod in ecclesiae latebris commoratur, si extra ecclesiam potuerit comprehendi, a domino protenus vindicetur."

19. *C. Th.* 9.45.5.

20. *E. Th.c. 70.*

21. Ibid.

22. E. Th. c. 71, "*Si quis in causa publici debiti ad ecclesiam quamlibet convolaverit, archidiaconus eum compellat egredi . . . aut si hoc facere noluerit, eius substantiam, quam ad ecclesiam detulit, sine mora contradat. Quod nisi fecerit, quanti interest utilitatis publicae, archidiaconus cogatur exsolvere.*" See also *Nov.* 17.7.1, which also speaks of public utility in connection with exacting the debts of sanctuary seekers.

23. *C. J.* 1.12.6.

24. See Chapter 2.

25. "*Si quis de ecclesiis, id est locis religiosis, homines traxerit, vel aliquid violenter crediderit auferendum, capite puniatur.*"

26. *C. Th.* 9.45.4.

27. Jean Gaudemet, "Le bréviaire d'Alaric et les epitome," 37–41.

28. *Leg. Vis.* 9.3.1. "*Nullus de ecclesiam ausus sit aliquem violenter abstraere, nisi ad ecclesiam confugiens armis se fortasse defensare voluerit.*" Cf. *C. Th.* 9.45.4.

29. *Leg. Vis.* 9.3.2. "*Qui ad ecclesiae porticos confugerit et non deposuerit arma, que tenuit, si fuerit occisus, percussor in loco sancto nullam fecit iniuriam nec ullam calumniam pertimescat.*" Cf. *C. Th.* 9.45.4.3 and 5.

30. D'Ors, *Estudios Visigoticos* II, 181.

31. Ibid.

32. *Leg. Vis.* 9.3.3. "*Si quis de altaribus servum aut debitorem, non traditum sibi a sacerdote vel ab ecclesiae custodibus, violenter abstraxerit, si onestoris loci persona est, ubi primum iudici de eo fuerit relatum, altario, cui iniurioso fuit, cogatur absolvere solidos C, inferioris loci persona det solidos xxx. Quod si non habuerit, unde componat, correptus a iudice in conventu C flagella suscipiat. Dominus vero servum, sive creditor debitorem recipiat excusatum.*"

33. *Leg. Vis.* 9.3.4. "*De homicides autem . . . in eorum titulis leges sunt requirende.*"

34. *Leg. Vis.* 6.5.16.

35. *Leg. Vis.* 6.5.16 also provided that the homicide could be given over to the family of the one he killed. They could do to him as they wished, save killing him. See also *Leg. Vis.* 6.5.18, which dealt specifically with cases of intrafamilial homicide.

36. c. 15, *Pactum pro tenore pacis*, in *MGH Capitularia Regum Francorum* 1:6. "*Quod si cujuslibet servus deserens dominum suum ad ecclesiam confugerit, ubi primum dominus ejus advenerit, continuo excusatus reddatur.*"

37. *Pactus Legis Salicae, Lex Salica*, ed. K. A. Eckhardt (*MGH: Legum*, sectio 1, 4, pt. 1, 252 [1962–69]): "*Nullus latronem vel quemlibet culpabilem, sicut cum episcopis convenit, de atrio ecclesiae extrahere praesumat. Quod si sunt ecclesiae, quibus atriae clausae non sint, utrasque partibus parietem terrae spatium aripennis pro atrium observabitur; [et] nullus confugiens foris antedicta loca pro operarum cupiditate educat; quod si fecerit et capti fuerint, ad dignum sibi supplicium domin[or]um censuimus.*"

38. *Id.*; Katherine Fisher Drew gives *arpennis* as "a measure of 120 feet." *The Laws of the Salian Franks* (Philadelphia: University of Pennsylvania Press, 1991), 237n81.

39. *Leges Alamannorum*, 3.1 in *MGH: Legum*, sectio I , V, part 1.

40. Ibid. This procedure whereby the lord gives a monetary surety can be seen also in an earlier Merovingian sanctuary provision. See the *Pactus pro tenore pacis domonorum Childeberti et Chlothari regum*, chap. 15 in *Capitularia Regum Francorum*, MGH *Legum* sectio II,(1883–97), 1:4.

41. Ibid.

42. Council of Orleans (511), in *Concilia Galliae: 511–695*, ed. Caroli de Clercq (*CCSL*, 1963), 5–6. "*Servus qui ad ecclesia pro qualibet culpa confugerit, si a domino pro admissa culpa sacramenta susciperit, statim ad servitium domini redire cogatur . . . exire nolentem a domino liceat occupari.*"

See also the Council of Lerida (524), 8, "*Nullus clericorum servum aut discipulum suum confugientem ad ecclesiam extrahere audeat vel flagellare presumat. Quod si fecerit, donec digne peniteat, a loco, cui honorem non dedit, segregetur.*" G. D. Mansi, *Sacrorum conciliorum nova* (Paris: H. Welter, 1901–27), 8:613.

43. A. Theil, *Epistolae Romanorum Pontificum Genuinae* (Braunsberg, 1868), 505.

44. C. 17.4.32.

45. *Leg Vis.* 9.3.4.

46. Ibid.

47. This canon was included in the *Decretum* at C. 17.4.9; it was also included in Burchard of Worms collection at 3.194 and Ivo of Chartres at 3.12.

48. The *Libri Historiarum X*, sometimes called the *Historia Francorum*, has been extensively studied for, among other things, the light it sheds on the workings of penal law in early medieval Gaul. Among useful studies, one might consult Jürgen Weitzel, "Strafe und Strafverfahren bei Gregor von Tours und in anderen Quellen der Merowingerzeit," in *Recht in frühmittelalterlichen Gallien: Spätantike Tradition und germanische Wertvorstellung*, ed. Harald Siems, Karin

Nehlsen-von Stryk, and Dieter Strauch (Cologne: Böhlau, 1995), 109–26; on sanctuary law specifically, see Anne Ducloux, "La Violation du droit d'asile par '*dol*' en Gaule, au VI siècle," *Antiquitae tardive* (Paris: Brepols, 1993), 1:207–19. In another interesting study, Peter Sawyer discusses some aspects of Gregory's text relating to blood feud, "The Bloodfeud in Fact and Fiction," in *Tradition og historieskivning*, ed. Kirsten Hastrup and Preben Meulengracht Sorensen (Aarhus: Aarhus universitetsforlag, 1987), 27–38.

49. *Gregorii episcopi Turonensis. Libri Historiarum X* (ed. Bruno Krusch and Wilhelm Levison), in *MGH: SS* (1951), rer. Merov. ii (Hanover, 1951) (Hereinafter, LH). 5.3 An accessible translation is *History of the Franks*, ed. Lewis Thorpe (Baltimore: Penguin Books, 1974).

50. Ibid.: "*non enim poteris eos accepere, nisi ut fidem facias de permanente eorum conjunctione; similiter et de omni poena liberi maneant repromittas.*"

51. Ibid.

52. *Pactus legis Salicae*, 25.7 in *MGH: Legum*, sectio I, 4, 1.

53. Council of Orleans (541), chap. 24: "*Quaecumque mancipia sub specie conjugii ad ecclesiae septa confugerint, ut per hoc credant posse fieri conjugium, minime eis licentia tribuatur aut talis conjunctio a clericis defensetur, quia pollutum est, ut, qui sine legitima traditione conjuncti pro religionis ordine statuo tempore se ab ecclesiae communione suspendunt, in sacris locis turpi concubito misceantur. De quare decernimus, ut, a parentibus aut a propriis dominis, prout ratio reddantur; postmodum tamen, parentibus atque dominis libertate concessa, si eos voluerint propria voluntate conjugere.*" *Concilia Galliae: 511–695*, CCSL 148a, p. 138.

54. *LH* 5.3. (A brief account of this episode in Gregory of Tours is also discussed in Timbal, *Le droit d'asile*, 104.)

55. Ibid.: "*Qui cum sacerdote nuntiata fuissent, cuncurrit velociter; increpans hominem, vix obtenuit ut detegerentur. Verumtamen puerum vivum extraxit, puellam vero repperit suffocatam.*"

56. Council of Orleans (511), chap. 22: "*Enimvero si inmemor fidei dominus transcendisse convincitur quod juravit, ut is, qui veniam acciperat, probetur postmodum pro ea culpa qualicumque supplicio cruciatus, dominus ille, qui inmemor fuit datae fidei, sit ab omnium communione suspensus.*" *Concilia Galliae: 511–695*, CCSL 148a, p. 156.

57. Council of Orleans (511), c. 3: "*sed posteaquam datis a domino sacramentis fuerit consignatus, si aliquid poenae pro eadem culpa, qua excusatur, probatus fuerit pertulisse, pro contemptu ecclesiae vel prevaricatione fidei a communione et convivio catholicorum, sicut superius compraehensum est* [i.e., from communion, from clerics, and the company of all Christians (c. 1)], *habeatur extraneus.*" *Concilia Galliae: 511–695*, CCSL 148a, p. 4–6.

58. *LH* 5.3.

59. Ibid. In *LH* 9.9, Gregory informs us that Rauching, complicit in a plot against the king, later had his brains dashed out.

60. *LH* 7.21.

61. Ibid.

62. *LH* 7.22.

63. Ibid.

64. Ibid.

65. See, for instance, *C. Th.* 9.45.4; cf. *Leg. Vis.* 9.34 and its *interpretatio.*

66. Council of Orleans (511), CCSL 148a, p. 4–6.

67. *LH* 7.22. For the Latin text, see *Liber Historiarum X*, ed. B. Krusch and W. Levison, in *MGH: SS* (1951), rer. Merov. ii, 7.22.

68. Exodus 21:14.

69. Literally, *obnoxius*, which carries also the sense of liable to punishment. Jacques Godefroy, a seventeenth-century editor of the Theodosian corpus, suggests *reos vel debitores* for *obnoxius. Codex Theodosianus cum perpetuis commentariis Jocabi Godefredi*, ed. J. D. Ritter (Leipzig: Sumptibus Maur. George Weidmann, 1736), 3:404.

70. "*De obnoxiis vero, si qui ambulaverint cum episcopo vel cum presbytero vel etiam diacono sive platea, sive in agro, sive in quolibet loco, nullo pacto eos retineri vel adduci iubemus, quoniam in sacerdotibus ecclesia constat.*" *Corpus Legum, ab imperatoribus Romanis ante Iustinianum latarum*, ed. G. Haenel (Leipzig: J. C. Hinrichs, 1857–60), 241.

71. Both Sirmond and Godefroy expressed serious doubts about authenticity of this edict. Godefroy suggests that the supposed imperial edict likely originated from later African or Gallic synods. *Codex Theodosianus*, 6:A2. Harald Siems, on the other hand, has suggested that the these judgments are overhasty; see "Zur Entwicklung des Kirchenasyls zwischen Spätantike und Mittelalter," in *Libertas: Grundrechtliche und rechtstaatliche Gewährungen in Antike und Gegenwart: Symposion aus Anlaß des 80. Geburtstages von Franz Wieacker*, ed. Okko Behrends and Malte Diesselhorst (Ebelsbach: Rolf Gremer, 1991), 146.

72. Gaudemet, it should be noted, does not seem to level any objections to the provision. See his *La formation du droit séculier et du droit de l'église aux IV–V siècles*, 2nd ed. (Paris: Sirey, 1979), 74.

73. *Capitulare Haristalense* (779), c. 8 in *Capitularia Regum Francorum*, ed. A Boretius and V. Krause, *MGH Legum*, sectio II (2 vols.) (1883–97), 1:48: "*Ut homicidas aut caeteros reos qui legibus mori debent, si ad ecclesiam confugerint, non excusentur, neque eis ibidem victus detur.*"

74. *Capitulare Haristalense* (779), c. 8, in *MGH, Capitularia*, 1:47, and Boretius's notes.

75. *Capitulatio de partibus Saxoniae* (782/3), c. 2, in *MGH Capitularia*, 1:68.

76. "Life of St. Cuthbert," chap. 37. A translation of this text can be found in *The Age of Bede*, ed. J. F. Webb, trans. D. H. Farmer (Harmondsworth: Penguin, 1965). See also, regarding this, a Bavarian legal text that speaks of sanctuary protections as provoking pursuers who "all the while vex the presbyter of the church or, if the presbyter has not ventured to give a response, the bishop." *Lex Baiwariorum*, 1.7, in *MGH: Legum*, ed. Ernst Schwind (1926), sectio 1, tom. 5.

77. The *Summa Perusina* has been edited and published by Frederico Patteta as "Adnotationes Codicum Domini Justiniani," in the *Bullettino dell'Istituto di Diritto Romano* (Rome: L. Pasqualucci, 1900), vol. 12. Patteta dates the Summa to the seventh century.

78. *C. Th.* 9.45.1; *C. J.* 1.12.1.

79. *C. Th.* 9.45.2: "*Iudaci, qui reatu aliquo vel debitis fatigati simulant se Christianae legi velle coniungi, ut ad ecclesias confugientes vitare possint crimina vel pondera debitorum, arceantur nec ante suscipiantur, quam debita universa reddiderint vel fuerint innocentia demonstrata purgati.*"

80. Siems, "Zur Entwicklung des Kirchenasyls zwischen Spätantike und Mittelalter," in *Libertas: Grundrechtliche und rechtstaatliche Gewährungen in Antike und Gegenwart: Symposion aus Anlaß des 80. Geburtstages von Franz Wieacker*, ed. Okko Behrends and Malte Diesselhorst (Ebelsbach: Rolf Gremer, 1991), 79. The gloss, he writes, "precisely inverts the rule," which is not quite the case.

81. "*De mancipiis christianis, quae in Judaeorum servitio detinentur, si eis, quod christiana religio vetat, a dominis imponitur aut si eos, quos de ecclesia excusatos tollent, pro culpa, quae remissa est, adfligere aut coedere fortasse praesumpserint et ad ecclesiam iterato confugerint, nullatinus a sacerdote reddantur, nisi praecium offeratur hac detur, quod mancipia ipsa valere pronuntiaverit just taxatio.*" *Concilia*, *MGH*, 1:78.

82. Ibid.

83. Orléans (541), c. 30; Mâcon (583), c. 1. CCSL 148a. Some precedent for this stance can be found in the Theodosian Code 16.9.1 (335).

84. Fourth Council of Arles (541), chap. 30. The Arlean Council did not put determination of the just price in the hands of slaves themselves. Burchard of Worms included this canon in his well-known decretal collection, but he cast the rule thus: "If pagan slaves of Jews flee to church, *and seek baptism,* or even refuge themselves with any Christian," they would be liberated with the aid of the church. Burchard, 4.87 "*De mancipiis Iudaeorum quae ad baptismum confugiunt*" (Cologne: Ex officina Melchioris Nouesiani, 1548), fol. 90a-91b.

85. See for example, *Leg. Vis.* 5.4.17.

86. Burchard, 4.87: "*Licet prioribus canonibus iam fuerit definitum, ut de mancipiis paganis quae apud Iudaeos sunt si ad ecclesiam confugerint, & baptismum*

petierint, etiam ad quoscunque Christianos refugerint, taxato, & oblato a fidelibus iusto precio ab eorum dominio liberentur: ideo statuimus hoc, ut tam iusta constitutio, ab omnibus catholicis observetur."

87. *LH* 4.14.

88. *Carolingian Chronicles, Royal Frankish Annals, and Nithard's Histories*, ed. Bernhard Walter Scholz (Ann Arbor: University of Michigan Press, 1970), 49–50.

89. Ibid., 56; A contemporaneous account of Charlemagne's campaigns around this time can also be found in the works of Einhard. See *Charlemagne's Courtier: The Complete Einhard*, ed. and trans. Paul Edward Dutton (Peterborough, Ont.: Broadview Press, 1998), 20–21.

90. Ibid., 166.

91. Rosamond McKitterick, *The Frankish Kingdoms Under the Carolingians, 751–987* (London: Longman, 1983), 61–63.

92. *Capitulatio de partibus Saxoniae*, chap. 1 and 2.

93. C. 6.

94. C. 7.

95. C. 8.

96. Alcuin, Letters 107 and 110 in MGH *Epistolae*. See also the discussion in Wood, *The Merovingian Kingdoms*, 319–20.

97. See Chapter 1.

98. See, e.g., the discussion of a sanctuary case by Luitpold Wallach in his *Alcuin and Charlemagne: Studies in Carolingian Literature and History* (Ithaca, N.Y.: Cornell University Press, 1958), 127; and Sam Collins, "*Domus Domini patet figura mysterii*: Architectural Imagination and the Politics of Place in the Carolingian Ninth Century" (Ph.D. diss., University of California, Berkeley, 2005).

99. See Collins, *Domus Domini patet figura mysterii*, 238; Wallach, in *Alcuin and Charlemagne*, estimated that in all the case produced twenty different pieces of correspondence. As Collins notes, at 239n22, this estimate may be too high.

100. Ep. 4, *MGH Epistolae*, 393–98.

101. Ep. 4, *MGH Epistolae*, 400n247.

102. See Collins, *Domus Domini patet figura mystericii*, Chapter 4.

103. For a suggestion that the unnamed fugitive that Alcuin defended may have killed one of Theodulf's men, see Collins, *Domus Domini patet figura mysterii*.

104. *Capitulare Haristalense* (779), c. 8, in *MGH Capitularia*, 1:48.

105. This is the view taken by Meens in "Tumult in Tours." See also Meens, "Sanctuary, Penance and Dispute Settlement Under Charlemagne: The Conflict between Alcuin and Theodulf of Orléans Over a Sinful Cleric," *Speculum* 82 (2007): 277, and Collins, *Domus Domini patet figura mysterii.*

106. *Capitulare legibus additum* (803), c. 3, in *MGH Capitularia*, no. 39, 113.

107. Rob Meens, "Sanctuary, Penance, and Dispute Settlement under Charlemagne."

108. *Capitulare legibus additum* (803), chap. 2, in *MGH Capitularia*, cap. 1, no. 39, 113. While other writers had given up altogether on finding a satisfactory resolution to the apparent conflicts between the rules issued in the Saxon capitularies and, for example, the Tours case, Timbal is at pains to reconcile the seeming contradictions between the Saxon capitulary and earlier Carolingian sanctuary rules (*Le droit d'asile*, 143, particularly n. 3). Such attempts seem destined to fail if for no other reason than they try to measure medieval legislation by the standards of modern assumptions about promulgating laws.

5. SANCTUARY, BLOOD FEUD, AND THE STRENGTH OF ANGLO-SAXON GOVERNMENT

1. Katherine Fisher Drew, "Legal Materials as a Source for Early Medieval Social History," *Rice University Studies* 60 (1974): 33, 34–35: "The institutions probably least affected by Roman contacts were limited to criminal law and family law, and of the two the Germanic concept of criminal law proved considerably more resistant to Roman influence than did family law."

2. *MGH Legum* sectio I, tom. 2, pars. 1 *Leges Burgundionum*, ed. L.R. de Salis (Hanover, 1892), 126.

3. Ibid.: "*Et quia de preciis occisorum nihil evidenter Lex Romana constituit, dominus noster statuit observandum: ut si ingenuus ab ingenuo fuerit interemptus, et homicida ad ecclesiam confugerit, is ipse, qui homicidium admisit, cum medietate bonorum suorum occisi heredibus serviturus addicatur; reliqua medietas facultatis eius homicidae heredibus derelinquatur. [2.6] Si vero servus cuiuscumque occisus fuerit ab ingenuo, et ipse homicida ad ecclesiam convolaverit, secundum servi qualitatem infra scripta domino eius precia cogatur exsolvere, hoc est: pro actore C solidi. Pro ministeriale LX solidi, pro aratore aut porcario XXX, pro aurifice electo C, pro fabro ferrario L, pro carpentario XL solidi inferantur. Hoc ex praecepto domini Regis convenit observari.*"

The *MGH* editor gives Gundobad as the referent for *noster dominus*. Wormald suggests that Sigismund is more likely the promulgator of the Burgundian laws. See his "'Inter Cetera Bona Genti Suae': Law-Making and Peace-Keeping in the Earliest English Kingdoms," in *Legal Culture in the Early Medieval West* (London: Hambeldon Press, 1999), 190. This Burgundian text is interesting, among other reasons, because the supposed shortcoming of the Theodosian Code (failing to specify compensation payments) suggests that the text was being read for practical application.

4. Patrick Wormald, *The Making of English Law*, 39; cf. Peter Sawyer, "The Bloodfeud in Fact and Fiction," in *Tradition og historieskivning*, ed. Kirsten Hastrup and Preben Meulengracht Sorensen (Aarhus: Aarhus Universitetsforlag, 1987), 27–38.

5. *Lex Frisionum, Additio Sapientum*, 1.1, ed. K. A. Eckhardt and W. A. Eckhardt (MGH Fontes Iuris Germanici Antiqui in usum scholarum XII, 1982) "*Homo faidosus pacem habeat in ecclesia, in domo sua, ad ecclesiam eundo, de ecclesia redeundo, ad placitum eundo, de placito redeundo. Qui hanc pacem effregerit et hominem occiderit, novies XXX soli[dos] comp[onat].*" The heading *Additio Sapientum* appears to have been added by the *Lex Frisionum*'s early modern editors.

6. These matters received much attention from nineteenth-century German historians. See, e.g., Paul Frauenstädt, *Blutrache und Todtschlagsühne im deutschen Mittelalter* (Berlin: Duncker und Humblot,1881); Wilhelm Wilda, *Das Strafrecht der Germanen* (Halle: C. A. Schwetschke und Sohn, 1842). See also Julius Goebel, *Felony and Misdemeanor* (New York: Commonwealth Fund, 1937) for some very helpful correctives.

7. *Alf* 2, in *Die Gesetze der Angelsachsen* (hereafter, *Gesetze*), ed. Felix Liebermann (Halle, 1903–16), 1:48–49: "*Gif hwa þara mynsterhama hwelcne for hwelcere scylde gesece, þe cyninges feorm to belimpe, oððe oðerne frione hiered þe árwyrðe sie, age he þreora nihta fierst him to gebeorganne, buton he ðingian wille.*"

8. *Alf* 2,1 in *Gesetze*: "*Gif hine mon on ðam fierst geyflige mid slege oððe mid bende oððe þurh wunde, bete þara æghwelc mid ryhte ðeodscipe, ge mid were ge mid wite, 7 þam hiwum hundtwelftig scill. ciricfriðes to bote 7 næbbe his agne forfongen.*"

9. *Alf* 5 in *Gesetze*.

10. *Alf* 5 in *Gesetze*: "*Eac we settað æghwelcere cirican, ðe biscep gehalgode, ðis frið: gif hie fáhmon geierne oððe geærne, þæt hine seofan nihtum nan mon út ne teo. Gif hit þonne hwa dó, ðonne sie he scyldig cyninges mundbyrde 7 þære cirican friðes (mare, gif he ðær mare ófgefo), gif he for hungre libban mæge, buton he self útfeohte.*"

Note that *fahman*, which literally translates as "foeman," is formed from "*fah*," which carries the sense of foe, but also of "accursed." Its use here suggests just how difficult it is to disentangle feuding practices from criminal procedure in Anglo-Saxon law.

11. *Alf* 5.2, in *Gesetze*: "*Gewite ðære cirican ealdor, þæt him mon on þam fierste mete ne selle.*"

12. *Alf*, 5.3 in *Gesetze*: "*Gif he self his wæpno his gefan utræcan wille, gehealden hi hine XXX nihta 7 hie hine his mægum gebodien.*"

13. See, e.g., "Asser's Life of King Alfred," in *Alfred the Great*, ed. and trans. Simon Keynes and Michael Lapidge (New York: Penguin Books, 1983), chap. 49, 82–83.

14. *Alf* 42 in *Gesetze*: "*Eac we beodað: se mon se ðe his gefan hamsittendne wite, þæt he ne feohte, aer ðam he him ryhtes bidde.*"

15. *Alf* 42.1 in *Gesetze*: "*Gif he mægnes hæbbe, þæt he his gefan beride 7 inne besitte, gehealde hine VII niht inne 7 hine on ne feohte, gif he inne geðolian wille; 7 þonne ymb VII niht, gif he wille on hand gan 7 wæpenu sellan, gehealde hine XXX nihta gesundne 7 hine his mægum gebodie 7 his friondum.*"

16. II Edm. 1,1–1,3 in *Gesetze*; II Edg. 5.3 in *Gesetze*.

17. Karl P. Wentersdorf, "The Situation of the Narrator in the Old English Wife's Lament," *Speculum* 56 (1981): 492–516.

18. *Wulfstan's Canons of Edgar*, ed. Roger Fowler (London: Oxford University Press for the Early English Text Society, 1972), chap. 16, cited and translated in Wentersdorf, "The Old English Wife's Lament," 505.

19. *Norðhymbra preosta lagu* (Northumbrian Priests' Law), c. 54, in *Gesetze* 1:383.

20. Burchard, 3.193: "*Similiter in Matiscensi synodo decretum est, ut hi qui fugiunt suos inimicos, aut in ecclesiam, aut in atrium ecclesiae, aut in domum episcopi, aut in claustrum regularium, non inde abstrahantur, nisi prius super sacra accepta securitate a persequutoribus de morte, de debilitate, & omni poenarum genere, sint securi, . . . ita ut ei, cui rei criminosi fuerint, de statisfactione conveniant. Quod si is qui super sacra prius iuraverat, post convictus fuerit iuramentum violasse reus periurii communione privetur, quousque satisfaciat.*"

21. Timbal, *Le droit d'asile*, 185.

22. *Lex Frisionum, Additio Sapientum* 1.1.

23. *Alf.* 5.4: "*Eac cirican frið: gif hwelc mon cirican gesece for ðara gylta hwylcum, þara ðe ær geypped nære, 7 hin ðær on Godes naman geandette, sie hit healf forgifen.*"

24. *Capitulatio de partibus saxoniae* in *Capitularia*, MGH *Capitularia*, c. 14.

25. *Lex Baiwariorum* in *MGH: Legum*, sectio 1, tom. 5, chap. 1.7: "*Nulla sit culpa tam gravis, ut vita non concedatur propter timorem Dei et reverentiam sanctorum, quia Dominus dixit; 'Qui dimiserit, dimittetur ei,; qui non dimiserit, nec ei dimittetur.'*" The portion of the text in embedded quotes is a rendering of Matthew 6: 14 and 15, which follows immediately after the Lord's Prayer in the Gospels. In the Vulgate: "*Si enim dimiseritis hominibus peccata eorum dimitttet et vobis Pater vester caelistis delicta vestra. Si autem non dimiseritis hominibus nec Pater vester dimittet peccata vestra.*"

26. Cf. Thomas Oakley, *English Penitential Discipline and Anglo-Saxon Law in Their Joint Influence* (New York: AMS Press, 1923), 141ff.

27. Frederic Maitland, *Domesday Book and Beyond* (New York: Cambridge University Press, 1907), 283.

28. Frederick Pollock and Frederic Maitland, *The History of English Law Before the Time of Edward I* (Boston: Little, Brown and Co., 1899), 2:450–52.

29. The phrase is Wormald's. "Maitland and Anglo-Saxon Law: Beyond Domesday Book," in *The History of English Law: Centenary Essays on "Pollock and Maitland," Proceedings of the British Academy* (New York: Oxford University Press, 1996), 89:1–20, quoted at 6. The most sustained and well-supported form of this argument is in Wormald's *The Making of English Law*. See also James Campbell, "The Late Anglo-Saxon State: A Maximum View," *Proceedings of the British Academy* 87:39–65, though Campbell places the emergence of a strong Anglo-Saxon state even before the reign of Alfred.

30. Hyams, *Rancor and Reconciliation in Medieval England* (Ithaca, N.Y.: Cornell University Press, 2003), 98ff. where he neatly summarizes Wormald's case.

31. Julius Goebel, *Felony and Misdemeanor*, 339–78; Naomi Hurnard, "The Anglo-Norman Franchises," *English Historical Review* 64 (1949): 289–323, 433–60.

32. *I Atr* 1:10–11, and 4–4:1, *Gesetze* 1:218–19 and 220–21; *III Atr* 3:1–2 *Gesetze* I:228–29; *II Cn* 20–20a, 31–31:1, *Gesetze* 1:322–3, 334–35.

33. *II Cn* 21 in *Gesetze* 1:324–25.

34. *Alf* 1 in *Gesetze* 1:90; there was a Carolingian antecedent; see Walter Kienast, *Unternaneneid und Treuvorbehalt in Frankreich und England* (Weimar, 1952), 15ff.

35. See Patrick Wormald, "A Handlist of Anglo-Saxon Lawsuits," *Anglo-Saxon England* 17 (1988): 241–81, and "Domesday Lawsuits: A Provisional List and Preliminary Comment," in *England in the Eleventh Century*, ed. Carola Hicks (Harlaxton: Harlaxton Medieval Studies, 1992), 61–102; See Hyams's useful cautions about use of the word "crime" in medieval English law before and after the Conquest in *Rancor and Reconciliation*, 155–86.

36. Wormald, "Maitland and Anglo-Saxon Law: Beyond Domesday Book," 15–17.

37. Andrew Reynolds, *Later Anglo-Saxon England: Life and Landscape* (Charleston, S.C.: Tempus, 1999), 105–10.

38. *II Cn* 30:1–9 involves a series of accusatory and proof-taking procedures that eventually remove an accused thief from the protection of his lord and make him answerable to the king and "to the whole nation."

39. Simon Keynes, "Crime and Punishment in the Reign of King Æthelred the Unready," in *People and Places in Northern Europe, 500–1600: Essays in Honor of Peter Hayes Sawyer*, ed. Ian Wood and Niels Lund (Rochester, N.Y.: Boydell and Brewer, 1990), 67–81; and more recently Hyams, *Rancor and Reconciliation*, 101–2.

40. Hyams, *Rancor and Reconciliation*, 103.

41. Wormald, "Maitland and Anglo-Saxon Law: Beyond Domesday Book," 19.

42. The ability to bring the most powerful within the reach of the rule of law is probably not a felicitous category of analysis for modern states either.

43. Gervase Rosser already made suggestions in this direction. "Sanctuary and Social Negotiation," in *The Cloister and the World: Essays in Medieval History Presented to Barbara Harvey*, ed. John Blair and Brian Golding (Oxford: Oxford University Press, 1996), 59–79.

44. *IV AS* 6, in *Gesetze* 1:171) from the H ms., which only survives in a fragment. "*[6.1] 7 we gecwædon æt Ðunresfelda on þæm gemote, gif hwilc þeof oððe reafere gesohte þonne cing oþþe hwylce cyrican 7 ðone biscop, þæt he hæbbe nigon nihta first. [6.2] 7 gif he ealderman oððe abbud oþþe ðegen sece, hæbbe ðreora niht first. 7 gif hine hwa lecge binnan ðæm fyrste, þonne gebete he ðæs mundbyrde ðe he ær sohte, oþþe he hine twelfa sum ladige, þæt he þa scone nyste. 7 sece swylce scone swylce he sece, þæt he ne sy his feores wyrðe, butan swa feola nihta swa we her beufan cwædon. [6.3] 7 se ðe hine ofer þæt feormige, sy ðæs ilcan wyrðe þæs ðe se ðeof, butan he hine ladian mæge, ðæt he him nan facn ne nane ðyfþe on nyste.*" An English-language edition of this fragment appears in F. L. Attenborough, *The Laws of the Earliest English Kings* (Cambridge: Cambridge University Press, 1922), 150–51.

45. Hyams, *Rancor and Reconciliation*, 95.

46. *Alf* 5, *Gesetze* 1:51.

47. See, for example, the quadripartitus version of *Alf* 5, *Gesetze* 1:51.

48. D. H. Green, *Language and History in the Early Germanic World* (New York: Cambridge University Press, 1998), 42–43.

49. Julius Goebel, *Felony and Misdemeanor*, 427n331. Goebel suggests Frankish origins for *grið*.

50. *A Gu* prologue, *Gesetze* 1:126.

51. *E Gu 1*, *Gesetze* 1:128. See Dorothy Whitelock, "Wulfstan and the So-Called Laws of Edward and Guthrum," *HER* 56 (1941): 1–21; Wormald, *The Making of English Law*, 389–90.

52. *E Gu 1*, *Gesetze* 1:128..

53. *IV As* 6.2; see also Goebel, *Felony and Misdemeanor*, 428. As we saw in Alfred's laws, these sorts of practices were closely related to the sort of protections that attached to houses in Anglo-Saxon law. See Rebecca Coleman, "Hamsocn: Its Meaning and Significance in Early English Law," *The American Journal of Legal History* 25 (1981): 95–110.

54. *Grið* [4], *Gesetze* 1:470). "*7 þus it stod on ðam dagum inne mid Englum, ðæt, gyf feorhscyldig man cyning gesohte, arcebiscop oððon æþeling, þonne ahte ne nigon nihta grið feore to gebeorge, butan him se cyng rumran fyrstes geunnan wolde. [5] 7 gyf he gesohte leodbiscop oððe ealdorman oððon healicne heafodstede, þonne ahte he VII nihta grið, butan man leng geunnan wolde.*" In his commentary, Liebermann describes this collection thus: "This piece claims nothing more

than a private collection. . . . The contents hoped for no legal or judicial value." Liebermann's commentary on *Grið, Gesetze*, 3:264. But cf. Wormald, *The Making of English Law*, 390–95.

55. "The Sanctuary of St. Cuthbert," in *St. Cuthbert, His Cult and Community to AD 1200*, ed. Gerald Bonner, David Rollason, and Clare Stancliffe (Woodbridge: Boydell and Brewer, 1989), 425–36.

56. *I Cn* 2.2; Gesetze 1:281; A translation can be found in A. J. Robertson, *The Laws of the Kings of England from Edmund to Henry I* (New York: Cambridge University Press, 1925), 155.

57. *I Cn* 2.5. *Gesetze* 1:282.

58. *I Cn* 3.2. *Gesetze* 1:282–3.

59. *I Cn.* 3.2. *Gesetze* 1:282.

60. *Grið*, in *Gesetze* 1:470.

61. *VIII Atr.* 1, in *Gesetze* 1:264.

62. See Wormald, *The Making of English Law*, 394–95.

63. *II Cn* 30.3 in *Gesetze* 1:332–33; Wormald, *The Making of English Law*, 127.

6. SANCTUARY IN THE CENTURY AFTER THE NORMAN CONQUEST

1. Frederick Pollock and Frederic Maitland, *The History of English Law Before the Time of Edward I*, 2nd ed. (Boston: Little, Brown and Co., 1899), 1:79. See John Hudson, "Maitland and Anglo-Norman Law," in *Proceedings of the British Academy*, 89:21–46.

2. Pollock and Maitland, *The History of English Law*, 1:79.

3. *Leges Henrici Primi* (Hereinafter, LHP), ed. and trans. L. J. Downer (Oxford: Clarendon Press, 1972) is the critical edition. See Wormald's incisive treatment of the fated influences of the *LHP* in "Maitland and Anglo-Saxon Law," *Proceedings of the British Academy*, 89:1–20. It appears that the *Leges Henrici Primi* are least trustworthy when its author is making claims based on written texts. John Hudson, "Maitland and Anglo-Norman Law," *Proceedings of the British Academy*, 89:21–46.

4. *Leges Henrici Primi*, c. 12,1a.

5. *Leges Henrici Primi*, c. 12, 3.

6. See, e.g., Mark Hagger, "A Pipe Roll for 25 Henry I," *English Historical Review* 122 (2007): 133–40.

7. Hudson, "Maitland and Anglo-Norman Law," 44; Wormald, "Maitland and Anglo-Saxon Law," 7–12; and, in some detail, Hyams, *Rancor and Reconciliation in Medieval England* (Ithaca, N.Y.: Cornell University Press, 2003), 145–54.

But see John Gillingham, "1066 and the Introduction of Chivalry into England," in *Laws and Government in Medieval England and Normandy: Essays in Honor of Sir James Holt*, ed. George Garnett and John Hudson (New York: Cambridge University Press, 1994), 31–55; and his "The Beginning of English Imperialism," *Journal of Historical Sociology* 5 (1992): 392–409; as well as his "Conquering the Barbarian: War and Chivalry in Twelfth-Century Britain," *Haskins Society Journal* 4 (1992): 67–84. In short, Gillingham has argued that the Conquest marked a demonstrable change in English culture, penal law included. Gillingham noted a post-Conquest marginalization of the blood feud and a softening of the afflictive punishments deployed by royal justice. He attributed these developments to the chivalric values the Normans brought with them. Gillingham's arguments seem to find the most traction when he examines the intellectual and ecclesiastical elite of Anglo-Norman England, and in regard to royally prosecuted warfare.

8. Wormald, "Maitland and the Anglo-Saxon Law," 14.

9. Bruce Roland O'Brien, "From *moðor* to *Murdrum*: The Pre-Conquest Origin and Norman Revival of the Murder Fine," *Speculum* 71:321–57; and his *God's Peace and King's Peace: The Laws of Edward the Confessor* (Philadelphia: University of Philadelphia Press, 1999); See also James Campbell, "The Late Anglo-Saxon State: A Maximum View," *Proceedings of the British Academy* 87:39–65; Wormald, "Maitland and Anglo-Saxon Law," *Proceedings of the British Academy* 89:1–20; and his "Giving God and King Their Due: Conflict and its Regulation in the Early English State," in *La Giustizia nell'alto medioevo* (Spoleto: Presso la Sede del Centro, 1996), 11–17, and his *Making of English Law*, particularly 306–7.

10. Hyams, *Rancor and Reconciliation*, 111–86.

11. The charter has been reproduced in print many times, and can claim the distinction of being the only piece of legislation in the early medieval West to survive in its original form. Its original seal also survives. See Wormald, *The Making of English Law*, 398; *Regesta Regum Anglo-Normannorum: The Acta of William I 1066–1087*, ed. David Bates (Oxford: Clarendon Press, 1998), no. 180, 593. Wormald rightly notes that the charter echoed certain writs issued by Anglo-Saxon kings to boroughs.

12. *Regesta Regum Anglo-Normannorum: The Acta of William I*, 593 (no. 180).

13. See, e.g., *Regesta Regum Anglo-Normannorum*, 111–14 (nos. 1, 2, 3).

14. See Wormald's discussion and rehabilitation of twelfth-century Anglo-Norman legal tracts in *The Making of English Law*, 395–415.

15. *Willelmi I, Articuli*, c. 7 in *Gesetze* 1:488; See Wormald, *The Making of English Law*, 402–03.

16. *Leis Willelme, prol.*, in *Gesetze* 1:492.

17. On the whole, the twelfth-century Norman compilers responsible for these texts probably deserve more credit than previous generations of historians have afforded them for their efforts. Richardson and Sayles were probably the harshest critics of these collections (*Law and Legislation*, 121–23). Wormald makes a vigorous attempt at rehabilitating the collections in *The Making of English Law*, 407–15. Concerning the *Articuli*, Wormald (*The Making of English Law*, 403), says, "The 'Articles' were hardly a legislative act of the Conqueror's in the same sense as" the London Charter and probably had "private origins," though some provisions of the *Articuli* (including chap. 3) may have reflected reports of contemporary royal decrees. The *Leis*, according to Wormald (409) are an intellectual exercise.

18. *ECf.* 5 in *Gesetze* 1:630. The prologue of the text makes explicit that the laws were recorded after the Conquest and with the aid of "*Anglos nobiles, sapientes et lege sua eruditos.*"

19. For an addition and translation of the Laws of Edward the Confessor, see Bruce R. O'Brien, *God's Peace and King's Peace: The Laws of Edward the Confessor* (Philadelphia: University of Pennsylvania Press, 1999), 158–203; see also the discussion in Wormald, *The Making of English Law*, 409–11.

20. See the account of Orderic Vitalis in *The Ecclesiastical History of Orderic Vitalis*, ed. and trans. Marjorie Chibnall (Oxford, 1968–80), 5:5; the canons of the council have been printed. J. Teulet, *Layettes du Trésor des Chartes* (Paris: Archives Nationales, 1863–75), no. 22; see also Haskins, *Norman Institutions*, 30–38.

21. Gillingham, "1066 and the Introduction of Chivalry in England," in *Law and Government in Medieval England and Normandy: Essays in Honour of Sir James Holt*, 31–55.

22. See, e.g., *Wl Lond.* 2 in *Gesetze* 1:485:

> I mandate and by royal authority enjoin that no bishop or archdeacon hold pleas of episcopal laws in the hundreds any further, neither bring a cause which pertains to the regulation of souls to the judgment of secular men. But whosoever has been sued according to episcopal laws for whatever cause or wrong (under church law), . . . let him respond at the place chosen and named by the bishop, and not according to the hundred law, but according to the canons and episcopal laws let him make right with God and the bishop.

23. Timbal, *Le droit d'asile*, 454.

24. See, e.g., John Hudson, *The Formation of the English Common Law* (Oxford: Oxford University Press, 1996), 158.

25. Hyams's (*Rancor and Reconciliation*, 94–99) recent findings of the feudlike context of sanctuary claims in the century following the Conquest accord very closely with my own.

26. John of Worcester, *The Chronicle of John of Worcester*, ed. R. R. Darlington and P. McGurk (Oxford: Clarendon Press, 1995), 2:38–39.

27. John's account has several unique features, including the fact that it is the only source touching on these events that mentioned Robert taking sanctuary. In the Chronicle of Hyde account, Robert was simply seized, along with his men, put in prison, and sentenced to be executed. On his way to be executed, the Hyde account made Robert fall prostrate before a priest, beg absolution, and allow himself to be whipped as purgation for his sins before he was executed. Orderic Vitalis, whose portrait of Robert was not at all flattering (he describes Robert as a violent man who robbed peaceful merchants, plotted treacherously against his king, and was finally brought to a just end), said nothing of Robert taking sanctuary. *The Ecclesiastical History of Orderic Vitalis*, ed. Marjorie Chibnall (Oxford: Oxford Medieval Texts, 1968–80), 4:280, 284. Orderic's palpable dislike for Robert may have prompted him to leave out the sanctuary claim, but Orderic was generally attuned to breaches of sanctuary and expressed outrage when reporting them. See, e.g., *Hist.* 5.10; 6.11; 6.12.

28. Symeon of Durham *Historia Ecclesiae Dunhelmensis*, ed. David Rollason (Oxford: Oxford Medieval Texts, 2000), 260–62.

29. Dates for Earl Robert's death vary widely.

30. Reginald of Durham, *Libellus de admirandis beati Cuthberti virtutibus quae novellis patratae sunt temporibus*, ed. James Rayne (London: Surtees Society, 1835), 119–21; the case is also described in Hyams, *Rancor and Reconciliation*, 276–77.

31. The case might be compared to an instance of sanctuary recorded by Orderic Vitalis. William Pantulf was embroiled in a longstanding conflict in Normandy. He finally took sanctuary from his enemies in the church of St. Evroul. There he arranged to clear himself by the *judicium dei*. His enemies granted this, and he cleared himself of the ordeal, to the joyful praises of the onlooking monks. *Hist.* 2:24–25; also discussed by Hyams, *Rancor and Reconciliation*, 281.

32. *The Priory of Hexham, Its Chroniclers, Endowments and Annals*, ed. James Raine (London: Surtees Society, 1864–65), 1:176–77; a translation is found in van Caenegem, *English Lawsuits from William I to Richard I* (London: Selden Society, 1990), 1:306.

33. Bruce R. O'Brien, *God's Peace and King's Peace*, 65–70.

34. *Regesta Regum Anglo-Norannorum 1066–1154*, I, *Regesta Willelmi Conquestoris et Willelmi Rufi 1066–1100*, ed. H. W. C. Davis (Oxford: Oxford University Press, 1913), no. 62. Emphasis added.

35. For a fuller discussion of Battle Abbey and its context, see the introduction to *The Chronicle of Battle Abbey*, ed. and trans. Eleanor Searle (New York: Oxford University Press, 1980). On forgeries in the Middle Ages, see Giles Constable, "Forgery and Plagiarism in the Middle Ages," *Archiv für Diplomatik* 29 (1983): 1–41; see also Anthony Grafton, *Forgers & Critics: Creativity & Duplicity in Western Scholarship* (Princeton: Princeton University Press, 1990).

36. Eleanor Searle, *The Chronicle of Battle Abbey* (Oxford: Oxford University Press, 1980), 17–23.

37. *Regesta Regum Anglo-Normannorum: The Acta of William I* (1066–87), ed. D. Bates, nos. 15, 16: "Bello, quam fundavi ex voto ob victoriam quam mihi Deus ibidem contulit." Bates notes that "it is necessary to reserve judgment on this writ" (138) since its authenticity is an open question.

38. *The Chronicle of Battle Abbey*, ed. Eleanor Searle (Oxford: Oxford University Press, 1980), 69–71.

39. See ibid., 69n5 and 70n1.

40. *Leis Wl*, 1: "Ceo est a saver pais a seinte iglise. De quel forfeit que hom fet oust, e il poust venir a seinte iglise, oust pais de vie e de membre." In his translation of this text, Liebermann renders "saver" as "wissen" (i.e., "This is to know the peace of the holy church"), a reading also recommended by *Anglo-Norman Dictionary* fascicle 6, ed. William Rothwell (London: Modern Humanities Research Association, 1990). But "saver" can have also the sense of the English "save" or "preserve," a sense suggested by the context. See *Manual of Law French*, 2nd ed. (Aldershot: Scolar Press, 1990), ed. J. H. Baker.

41. Wormald, *The Making of English Law*, 409: "The main conclusion to be drawn about the *Leis* is perhaps this: what impressions one might otherwise derive from it as to the relevance of Anglo-Saxon law to twelfth-century practice are offset by its deference to Roman laws that are most unlikely to have come into court-room cognizance. For all that it was written in French, it was an intellectual exercise."

42. See Wormald, *The Making of English Law*, 410.

43. On the Laws of Edward the Confessor, see Bruce O'Brien, *God's Peace and King's Peace: The Laws of Edward the Confessor* (Philadelphia: University of Pennsylvania Press, 1999).

44. *E Cf*, 5 in 1:630: "*De reis ad ecclesiam confugientibus. Quicunque reus vel noxius ad ecclesiam pro presidio confugerit, ex quo atrium ingressus fuerit, securus sit et a nemine insequente ullo modo apprehendatur nisi per pontificem loci illius vel per ministros eius.*"

45. *E Cf*, 5.1 in *Gesetze* 1:630: "*Et si in fugiendo ad domum sacerdotis vel ad curiam eius diverterit, eandem securitatem et libertatem ibidem inveniat quam apud ecclesiam, dum tamen sacerdotis domus et curia in feudo ecclesiae consistant.*"

46. *E Cf,* 5.2 in *Gesetze* 1:630: "*Si latro est vel raptor, quod male ceperit, si ad manum est, reddat. Et si illud extirpauerit et de suo proprio quod reddat habuerit, in integrum ei a quo furatum est resituate.*"

47. *E Cf,* 5.3 in *Gesetze* 1:630: "*Si autem hoc egerit sepius et forte fortuitu ad ecclesiam sic sepius confugerit* (cf. *evaserit,* in some mss.), *ablatione reddita, provinciam forisiuret nec redeat.*"

48. *E Cf,* 5.3a in *Gesetze* 1:631: "*Et si redierit, quisquam eum recipere non presumat, nisi per consensum iusitiae* (cf. *iusticiarium* in some mss.) *regis.*"

49. *English Lawsuits from William I to Richard I,* ed. van Caenegem (London: Selden Society, 1990), vol. 1, 284n327.

50. *E Cf,* 6 in *Gesetze* 1:631.

51. Bruce O'Brien, *God's Peace and King's Peace: The Laws of Edward the Confessor* (Philadelphia: The University of Pennsylvania Press, 1999), 65–70.

52. Wormald, *The Making of English Law,* 410.

53. *Vita Sancti Cuthberti auctore Beda,* ed. Bertram Colgrave (New York: Cambridge University Press, 1940) 37.

54. H. H. E. Craster, "The Red Book of Durham," *English Historical Review* (1925), 40:524. See especially, David Hall, "The Sanctuary of St. Cuthbert," in *St. Cuthbert, His Cult and Community to AD 1200,* ed. Gerald Bonner, David Rollason, and Clare Stancliffe (Wolfeboro, N.H.: Boydell and Bewer, 1989), 425–36.

55. The evidence is ambiguous, but see Hall, "St. Cuthbert's Sanctuary," 430, who reads the payment as a fine for sanctuary-breach.

56. Simeon of Durham, *Historia Dunelmensis Ecclesiae,* ed. Thomas Arnold (1882, reprint 1962) in *Rerum Britannicarum Medii Aevi Scriptores,* vol. 75, pt. 1, 69–70; Hall, "The Sanctuary of St. Cuthbert," 431, traces the thirty-seven day rule directly to the laws of Alfred. Thirty-seven is the sum of days a fugitive could remain in the church (7) and the number of days a fugitive could be protected after leaving sanctuary while his kin arranged terms of settlement (30).

57. Ibid. at 70.

58. According to Thomas Arnold, in his introduction to the *Historia Dunelmensis Ecclesiae,* Simeon erased the name of Waltheof from his account of the donation of the church at Tynemouth because Waltheof had been executed by William I for treason (xiii).

59. On the political importance of St. Cuthbert after the Norman Conquest, see William Aird, *St. Cuthbert and the Normans: The Church of Durham, 1071–1153* (Rochester, N.Y.: Boydell Press, 1998).

60. Geoffrey of Monmouth, *Historia Regum Britanniarum,* ed. David Reeve (Rochester, N.Y.: Boydell and Brewer, 2007), 2.17.

61. Orderic Vitalis, *Historia Ecclesiastica,* 6.12.

62. William of Malmesbury, *Historia Novella*, ed. and trans. K. R. Potter (1955), chap. 470; O'Brien, *God's Peace and King's Peace*, 67.

63. See Chapter 5.

64. R. H. Forster, "Notes on Durham and Other North-Country Sanctuaries," *Journal of the British Archaeological Association* 11 (1905): 118.

65. Barbara Rosenwein, *Negotiating Space: Power, Restraint, and Privileges of Immunity in Early Medieval Europe* (Ithaca, N.Y.: Cornell University Press, 1999) 227–28.

66. BL, *Additions* ms. 10106, fol. 34b (spelling modernized). There are grounds to attribute this particular manuscript to William Evesham. See A. I. Doyle, "The work of a late 15th century English Scribe, William Evesham," *Bulletin of the John Rylands Library.* 39, no. 2 (March, 1957), 313–15.

67. Forster, "Notes on Durham and Other North-Country Sanctuaries," 118, 120.

68. These "peculiar sanctuaries" were located at: Abingdon, Armathwaite, Beaulieu, Battle Abbey, Beverley Colchester, Derby, Durham, Dover (St. Martin's Priory), Hexham, Lancaster, St.-Mary-Le-Bow (London), St.-Martin-le-Grand (London), Merton Priory, Northampton, Norwich, Ripon, Ramsey, Wells, Westminster, Winchester, York. Pegge did not disguise his glee that England was rid of such privileged places.

69. Thomas John d'Mazzinghi, *Sanctuaries* (Stafford: Halden & Sons, 1887), 16.

70. Norman Trenholme, *The Right of Sanctuary in England* (Columbia: University of Missouri Press, 1903), 47.

71. I. D. Thornley, "The Destruction of Sanctuary," in *Tudor Studies*, 184. Together, Thornley and Forster ("North County Sanctuaries") remain the best introductions to the question of chartered liberties and the difficulties of the sources.

7. SANCTUARY AND ANGEVIN LAW REFORMS

1. NA, JUST/1/37, m. 33r.

2. NA, JUST/1/37, m. 33r.

3. Hyams, *Rancor and Reconciliation*, 159.

4. R. C. Van Caenegem, "Public Prosecution of Crime in Twelfth-Century England," in *Church and Government in the Middle Ages: Essays Presented to C. R. Cheney on his 70th Birthday*, ed. C. N. L. Brooks, D. E. Luscombe, G. H. Martin, and D. Owen (New York: Cambridge University Press, 1976). John Hudson, *The Formation of the English Common Law: Law and Society in England from the Norman Conquest to Magna Carta* (London: Longman, 1996) downplays the importance of Henry II's reforms in the development of English law.

5. See Hugh Thomas, "Violent Disorder in King Stephen's England: A Maximum Argument," in *King Stephen's Reign, 1135–1154*, ed. Paul Dalton and Graeme White (Rochester, N.Y.: Boydell and Brewer, 2008), 139–70, and his discussion of the relevant historiography (139–40).

6. See Hyams, *Rancor and Reconciliation*, 155–74.

7. Ralph Pugh, *Imprisonment in Medieval England* (New York: Cambridge University Press, 1968), and Hyams's observations in *Rancor and Reconciliation*, 165.

8. Frank Barlow, *The Feudal Kingdom of England, 1042–1216* (New York: Longman, 1999), 314; Maurice Keen, *The Outlaws of Medieval Legend* (New York: Routledge and Kegan Paul, 1961), 10.

9. Pollock and Maitland, *The History of English Law*, 2:557.

10. S. F. C. Milsom, *The Historical Foundations of the Common Law*, 2nd ed. (London, 1981), 403.

11. T. F. T. Plucknett, *Edward I and the Criminal Law* (New York: Cambridge University Press, 1960), 87.

12. But note the extent to which Beccaria's views were anticipated by medieval jurists like Lucas de Penne. See Walter Ullmann, "The Idea of Crime," in *The Medieval Idea of Law as Represented by Lucas de Penne* (London: Methuen, 1946).

13. Hyams, *Rancor and Reconciliation*, 155.

14. Ibid., 157; Pollack and Maitland, *The History of English Law*, 2:467n1: "Many entries suggest that an appeal of felony often has its origin in a dispute about proprietary rights."

15. Henry Summerson, "The Structure of Law Enforcement in Thirteenth-Century England," *American Journal of Legal History* 23 (1979): 313–27; and his restatement of the argument with a particular eye towards Maitland, "Maitland and the Criminal Law in the Age of *Bracton*," in *Proceedings of the British Academy* 89:115–43.

16. C. 1 (presentation of benefices); C. 9 (property alleged to be in free alms); C. 15 (bringing debt cases within royal jurisdiction); C. 3 (jurisdiction over criminous clerks).

17. C. 4, 7, 8, 10, 11, 12.

18. G. O. Sayles, *The Medieval Foundations of England* (New York: A. S. Barnes and Co., 1961), 346.

19. Chap. 14.

20. See Henry de Bracton, *On the Laws and Customs of England*, ed. George Woodbine and trans. Samuel Thorne (Cambridge, Mass.: Harvard University Press, 1968), fol. 136. Assize of Northampton, c. 1; H. G. Richardson and G. O. Sayles, *The Governance of Medieval England from the Conquest to Magna Carta* (Edinburgh: University Press, 1963), 439–44.

21. R. F. Hunnisett, "The Origins of the Office of Coroner," *Transactions of the Royal Historical Society* 8 (1958): 86–104, at 93–94. The Pipe Rolls tell us very little about abjuration, *Three Rolls of the King's Court in the Reign of Richard I*, ed. F. W. Maitland (London: Pipe Roll Society, vol. xiv, 1891), 100–101.

22. Pollock and Maitland, *The History of English Law*, 1:138.

23. *Assize of Northampton*, c. 1. See also Sayles, *The Medieval Foundations of England*, 337.

24. Karl Shoemaker, "Criminal Procedure in Medieval European Law: A Comparison between English and Roman-canonical Developments after the IV Lateran Council," *ZSS KA* 85 (1999): 174–202; Hyams also takes up this point in *Rancor and Reconciliation*, 216–19.

25. Daniel Klerman, "Settlement and the Decline of Private Prosecution in Thirteenth-Century England," *Law and History Review* (2001), 19:1–65.

26. See Hyams, *Rancor and Reconciliation*, 159, on these points as well as for the forceful argument that a "feud mentality" continues to survive, though masked by the language of the nascent plea rolls. On this, see also T. A. Green, *Verdict According to Conscience* (1985); and Naomi Hurnard, *The King's Pardon for Homicide before AD 1307* (Oxford: Clarendon Press, 1969).

27. Assize of Clarendon, chap. 8.

28. Assize of Clarendon, c. 9 and Assize of Northampton, c. 8.

29. T. A. Green, *Verdict According to Conscience: Perspectives on the English Criminal Trial Jury, 1200–1800* (Chicago: University of Chicago Press, 1985), 32.

30. Naomi Hurnard, *The King's Pardon for Homicide.*

31. Pollack and Maitland, *The History of English Law*, 2:633.

32. *Britton*, ed. and trans. Francis Morgan Nichols (Oxford: Clarendon Press, 1865), c. 17.

33. But compare Hunnisett, *Medieval Coroner*, 41–42.

34. *Britton*, c. 17: "*a une croiz de fust en lour meins, deschaucez et desceyntz, a testes descovertes, en lour cotes senglement.*" Cf. *Fleta*, ed. and trans. H. G. Richardson and G. O. Sayles (Selden Society, vols. 72, 89, 99), (London: B. Quaritch, 1955), chap. 29: "Et discinctus et discalciatus, capite discooperto, in pura tunica, tanquam in patibulo suspendendus, accepta cruce in manibus recedat"; and *The Mirror of Justices*, ed. and trans. William Joseph Whittaker (London: B. Quaritch, 1895), 34: "deschauz, desceint, in pure sa cote ou chemise."

35. In Bracton's account:

> If after confessing the crime he chooses to abjure the realm [as opposed to putting himself to trial], he must select some port from which he can cross into another land, beyond the realm of England. . . . A reasonable number of days' journeys to the said port ought to be reckoned for him and he ought

to be forbidden to leave the king's highway, or to make stay in one place for two nights together, or to turn aside anywhere, or to stray far from the highway except because of some great necessity or to seek shelter. Let him always keep on the direct road to the port so as to be there on the day assigned him, and provided he is not hindered by a storm, cross as soon as he gets a ship and a wind."

Fol. 36a. (Thorne's translation).

36. *Fleta* (Richardson and Sayles), chap. 29.

37. 12 Ed. I (Statute of Wales), chap. 5 (1284).

38. John Hudson, *The Formation of the English Common Law* (New York: Longman, 1996), 158. While it is undoubtedly the case that sanctuary was available to fugitives before the Angevins, Hudson downplays the important procedural reforms to sanctuary and the increasing royal control over sanctuary process that began to appear only at the end of the twelfth century and that significantly altered the practice of sanctuary within the administration of English royal law.

39. Glos. ord. to C. 17.4.9: "*Sed nunquod poterit postea accusari iste de illo crimine?" By "poterit . . . accusari.*" The glossator was referring to a specific legal procedure, the *accusatio*, of the Church's penal law. The received gloss to Gratian's *Decretum* was produced by Johannes Teutonicus (1245) and later added to by Bartholomaeus Brixiensis (1258). Citations to the glossa ordinaria are to Decretum Gratiani: cum glossis d[omi]ñi Johã[n]nis Theutonici (Basel: Joannes Amorbachi[us], 1512).

40. On the *accusatio*, see Karl Blaine Shoemaker, "Criminal Procedure in Medieval European Law: A Comparison between English and Roman-Canonical Developments after the IV Lateran Council," ZSS *KA* (1999), 85:174.

41. Glos. ord. to C. 17.4.9.: "*Si non potest crimina remanebunt impunita: quod esse non debet. Et sic privilegium ecclesiae erit multis occasio delinquendi. Propter hoc dicunt quedam que a quolibet potest accusari postea, preterque ab illo que permisit impunitatem.*"

42. Ibid.

43. Ibid.

44. Ibid.

45. Ibid. In regard to the length of servitude for destitute sanctuary seekers, the gloss says elsewhere: "*Sed usque ad quod tempus serviet ei? Sit in arbitrio boni viri: ex quo lege non exprimitur.*" (But how long should [the sanctuary seeker] serve the creditor? It should be according to the judgment of good men: it is not specified in Roman law). Glos. ord. to C. 36.1.3, *in medio.*

46. Letter 152. See Chapter 2.

47. Ibid.: "*a societate tamen removemus altaris, ut poenitendo placare possint quem peccando contempserant, seque ipsos puniendo.*"

48. Daniel Lord Smail, *The Consumption of Justice: Emotions, Publicity, and Legal Culture in Marseille, 1264–1423* (Ithaca: Cornell University Press, 2003), 172–73, citing Sarah Blanshei, "Crime and Law Enforcement in Medieval Bologna," *Journal of Social History* 16 (1982): 121–38.

49. NA, JUST/1/951A, m. 3r.: "*Duo malefactores fugerunt ad ecclesiam de Haliwell et nescitur unde fuerunt nec nomina nota sunt et ibi cognoverunt latrociniis et abjuraverunt regnum.*"

50. NA, JUST/1/951A, m. 5d.: "*Quidam Williamus . . . et Radbertus . . . pro mala suspicione fugerunt ad ecclesiam et cognoverunt latrociniis et abjuraverunt regnum et extranei fuerunt.*"

51. NA, JUST/1/229, m. 14r. They may have been two married couples. In any event, the entry goes on to say the bailiff of the hundred failed to record their names. For this, he along with the village where this occurred were fined. Getting the names right was serious business. At Dorset in 1244, the coroner was amerced by the justices when he reported a murdered woman's name as Sybill, when the jurors said her name was Isabell. PRO, JUST/1/201, m. 6d.

52. E.g., NA, JUST/1/229, m. 14d; 1/614A, m. 2r; 1/230, m. 4d; 1/55, m. 21r; 1/4, m. 29d; 1/614B, m. 48d; 1/806, m. 17r;

53. NA, JUST/1/4, m. 30d.

54. Ibid.

55. For instance, a certain "*Emelota latronissa . . . fugit ad ecclesiam . . . per latricinio ibi abjuravit regnum coram coronotore.*" NA, JUST/1/174, m. 27d. Likewise, Juliana de Sautre who was "captured for stealing bread," "escaped from the custody of the sheriff . . . fled to the church of St. Paul and abjured the realm." NA, JUST/1/4, m. 27r. R. F. Hunnisett speculated that the number of women taking sanctuary and abjuring was very low: *The Medieval Coroner* (New York: Cambridge University Press, 1961). This would be consistent with later studies that paid more attention to the rates of female crime in the Middle Ages. See, e.g., Barbara Hanawalt, *Crime and Conflict in English Communities, 1300–1348* (Cambridge, Mass.: Harvard University Press, 1979), 115–17. As for English sanctuary practices, the rate at which women abjured alone might bear a careful study.

56. NA, JUST/1/56, m. 44d. Two married women fled together, along with a certain Galfredus and a certain Robert who were not their husbands. At 1/56, 46r, three women took sanctuary and abjured together.

57. NA, JUST/1/60, m. 29r.: "*Greta que fuit uxor Walteri Russel posuit se in ecclesiam de Eylesbury et cognovit se esse latrone et abjuravit regnum coram coronor-*

tore. . . . Juratores dicunt quedam Angus de London Alicia sua consors Willelmus le Potter et Henry de Winton filius Walteri posuerunt se in ecclesiam de Eylesbury et cognoverunt se esse latrones et abjuraverunt regnum coram coronortore."

58. NA, JUST/1/230, m. 4d; JUST/1/54, m. 19r;

59. When William de Knossyngton was captured for theft in Leicestershire around 1284, his brother Hugh helped him escape and they took sanctuary and abjured together. NA, JUST/1/457, m. 51d; In another instance, two brothers from Ireland fled to a church in Kent and abjured, presumably back to Ireland. JUST 1/369, m. 33d.

60. PRO, JUST/1/44, m. 11r.

61. *Yearbook of Edward I* (30–31), ed. and trans. Alfred Horwood (London, 1863, reprint. 1964), 526.

62. They did not need to claim sanctuary. Clerical status was sufficient to remove oneself from royal jurisdiction and ensure (in most cases) delivery to the church for discipline.

63. Cf. NA, JUST/1/635, m. 44d, where a clerk abjured after killing a woman; and JUST/1/635, m. 59r, where a parson abjured "*per diversis latrociniis factis.*"

64. NA, JUST/1/543, m. 67d.

65. NA, JUST/1/710, m. 35r.

66. Some treatise writers (*Britton*, chap. 17) did claim that abjuration could be denied if the fugitive remained in sanctuary more than forty days, but this case more likely turned on clerical status.

67. *Close Rolls Held in the Public Record Office, 1279–1288* (London: H. M. Stationery Office, 1900), 399.

68. Ibid.

69. Ibid.

70. NA, JUST/1/635, m. 44d.: "*volens sagitasse ad quandam metam . . . sagitavit quandam Annicia[m] . . . in hostia eiusdem Henri patris sui sub mamilla sinistra cum quadam pila.*"

71. Ibid.

72. NA, JUST 1/37, 36r.: "*Quidam Rogerus cappallanus furatus fuit unum chalone in ecclesia Sancti Trinitati et quia Episcopi Sarrisbury mandavit quod fuit exauctoritatus abjuravit regnum non habuit catalla.*"

73. *Statutes of the Realm* (London, 1819), 9 Ed. II, 1, c. 15 (1315–16).

74. For instance, Matthew Myre took sanctuary twelve years after the fact for killing Robert Robinson. *Sanctuarium Dunelmense* (London: Surtees Society, 1837).

75. NA, JUST/1/358, m. 23d. [the cite given is as revised by C. A. F. Meekings in 1950], see ms. cover] "*Hugo le Orp occidit Ricardum Fallonem quadam heschia*

et captus fuit et liberatus fuit Hugo le Windesoy tunc vicecomitatus et postea fregit gaolam de Rolham et fugit in ecclesiam Sancti Augustini et abjuravit regnum et cognovit mortem nulla habuit catalla."

76. NA, JUST/1/543, m. 59r. Smail noted the use of reflexive verbs in the records of sanctuary claims in Angevin Marseille as well, *The Consumption of Justice*, 171.

77. NA, JUST/1/369, m. 31d.

78. NA, JUST/1/635, m. 44d.: "*fugit versus ecclesiam de Creky et obviavit cuidam Williamo . . . apud Creky et ipsum ibidem de quodam cultello interfecit et incontinenti posuit se in ecclesia de Creky . . . cognovit se interfecisse predictum williamum et abjuravit regnum coram coronatore.*" Richard's mother and other associates were later hanged.

79. Ibid.

80. PRO, JUST/1/806, m. 3d.

81. Ibid.

82. Ibid. William Tyssington received a pardon for the death. His pardon is recorded in the *Calendar of Patent Rolls, Volume 3, 1292–1301* (London: H.M. Stationery Office, 1901), 6.

83. Sayles, ed., *Select Cases in the Court of King's Bench under Edward I* (Selden Society, vol. 89), (London: B. Quaritch, 136–71), 4:92.

84. *Close Rolls of the Reign of Henry III Preserved in the Public Records Office, 1247–1251* (London: H.M. Stationery Office, 1902–38), 6:181.

85. Ibid.

86. Ibid. That is, Copinus was given leave to acknowledge his offence and abjure the realm.

87. *Calendar of Patent Rolls, Volume 11, 1358–1361* (London: H.M. Stationery Office, 1916), 255.

88. NA, JUST/1/806, m. 18r.: "*et predictus Elyas captus fuit et ductus ad prisonam domini regis* [at Staffordshire] . . . *et ibidem in prisona occidit garconem gayolari et a prisona illa evasit et in fugiens ad versus ecclesiam.*"

89. Ibid.: "*insecuti fuit per gayolarum eiusdem prisonae et alios de villata de Staffordshire et decollatus fuit.*"

90. NA, JUST/1/635, m. 59r.

91. Ibid.

92. Ibid.

93. Ibid.: "*et ibidem attraxit anhelitum et revixit.*"

94. Ibid. Reginald Underwood's "post-resurrection" abjuration was "*extra legem et contra legem et consuetudines regni.*"

95. NA, JUST/1/117A, m. 68r. (emphasis added).

96. It is difficult to reconcile this, however, with the fact that the same entry records that some local tithingmen were charged with guarding against Alan's escape. Such a measure would have been inconsistent with the usual privileges of ecclesiastical liberties. A long tradition on the continent allowed sanctuary protections to bishops' houses and other private residences attached to a church or monastery.

One additional note: this roll entry marks one of the earliest occurrences in any English legal source of the word "sanctuary."

97. NA, JUST 1/562, m. 11d.: "*Ricardus prioria de Porilande receptavit Nigell . . . in domo sua . . . postquam . . . utlagetur et cum ballivis domini regis ad domo sua per capienda ipsum Nigell . . . tunc dedit ei clavem ecclesiae suae et statim posuit se in ecclesiam et ibi cognovit latrocinium et abjuravit regnum coram coronatore.*"

98. X. 3.49.6.

99. *Mirror of Justices*, 33–34.

100. *Decretum* C. 36.1.3.

101. NA, JUST/1/320, m. 27r. On sacrilege, see *Decretum* C. 17.4.20: "Gratian: It is sacrilege when someone violates something sacred, or takes something sacred from the sacred, or something sacred from the non-sacred, or the non-sacred from the sacred."

102. NA, JUST/1/44, m. 18d.

103. *Fleta*, c. 29.

104. X. 3.49.9.

105. Ibid.: "*et sic in capella predicta se tenuerunt et sagittantes et alia diversa facinora facientes quousque predictae comitates super ipsos vi et armata venerunt et ipsos ibidem decapitaverunt.*"

106. PRO, JUST/1/635, m. 9r.: "*felonice fregerunt domis hugonis le Wylde et Johannis le Messer . . . et bona sua ibidem depredati fuerunt per quod hutes levatum fuit et prosecuti fuerunt . . . usque Churlington . . . et ibidem posuerunt se in quandam capellam non dedicatam.*"

107. *Eyre of London, 14 Edward II (1321)*, ed. Helen Cam (London: Selden Society, 1924), 75.

108. Ibid.: "This is its tenor: 'Some persons, hoping to obtain ecclesiastical immunity and privileges and impunity for their excesses by the protection of the church, do not fear to commit homicides and mutilations of limbs in the churches themselves or in their cemeteries, which they would by no means have committed unless they thought they might find defense through the church in which they took refuge'" citing explicitly to *De munitate ecclesiarum cap. ult.* (X. 3.49.10).

109. *Yearbook of Edward I* (30–31), ed. and trans. Alfred Horwood (London, 1863), 541.

110. Ibid., 541–42.

111. NA, JUST/1/635, m. 30r.: "*Quodam contentio oriebatus apud Brampton iuxta Dyngele die Sabati proxima ante festum Sancti Lucae Ewangeliste anno regni Regis Edward filius Regis Henri xii in cimeterio ecclesiae de Brampton inter Williamum Hanred ex una parte et magistrum Ricardum . . . parsona ecclesiae de Brampton ex alita.*"

112. Ibid.: "*percussit dictum ricardum de quodam cultello in ventre ita quod in crastino post inde obiit.*"

113. Ibid. Walter had considerable land holdings, which were forfeited to the crown after his execution, but those holdings would have been forfeit if he abjured.

114. NA, JUST/1/543, m. 53r.

115. Ibid.: "*quousque predictus ricardus vir suis fuisset aquietatus per patriam . . . et cum idem ricardus domi venisset quedam Agnes Gaymer accessit ad eandem [uxorem] et fecit ipsam exire ab eadem ecclesia a custodiam eiusdem villata.*"

116. Sayles, *Select Cases in the Court of King's Bench Under Edward I*, 3:205ff.

117. *Calendar of Patent Rolls, Volume 10, 1354–1358* (London: H.M. Stationery Office, 1916), 18.

118. NA, JUST/1/54, m. 18r.

119. Ibid.

120. Even so, borrowing from standard practice in cases of royal pardon, the justices provided that "anyone could make an appeal against [the boy] if he wished." Ibid. It would appear that had the injured wrestler died, the boy would have had to abjure. In 1250, in the county of Norfolk, when a boy named "Gilbert wrestled with Basilia and, while wrestling, fell on her so that she died . . . he fled to the church, acknowledged his felony, and abjured." NA, JUST/1/562, m. 20r.

121. *Calendar of Close Rolls, 1234–1237* (London: H.M. Stationery Office, 1902–38), 3:225.

122. Ibid.

123. NA, JUST/1/358, m. 17r.: "*Walterus Molendarius de Codham fugit ad ecclesiam de Codham et abjuravit regnum et Adam de Greneford serjent' Hundredi et Borgia de Codham cognoverunt quod interfuerunt ubi abjuravit regnum et fecit eum abjurare sicut non cognovit aliquid latrocinio . . . quod deberet abjurare regnum et ideo in misericordia.*"

124. NA, JUST/1/37, m. 29r.: "*et ad judicium de Roberto de Heneford tunc coronatore quia fecit eum abjurare regnum pro tam parvo latrocinio scilicet pro blado . . . vi d.*" Cf. JUST 1/614B, 48r, where sanctuary and abjuration for small amount of barley raised no objections.

125. NA, JUST/1/85, m. 16d.: "*Juliana de Helwenham posuit se in ecclesiam fratrorum de monte Carmeli et cognovit de reciptasse Warrin virum suum postquam abjuravit regum per morte Radulfi de Denham . . . et Juliana modo venit et dicit quod dominus rex pardonavit ei sectam suam et abjuratione predictam et presentat cartam domini regis.*"

126. Ibid.

127. Ibid.

128. *Close Rolls Preserved in the Public Records Office, 1237–1242* (London: H.M. Stationery Office, 1902–38), 45. The roll states only that the king ordered inquiries to be made in the case.

129. Ibid., 6:149. In a manner that seems to have been fairly common, the pardon was issued with this condition: Henry must "find pledges to stand to right before the king's justiciars when they next come to the Tower of London in case anyone [presumably, the kin of the slain] wishes to speak against Henry in this matter."

130. *Calendar of Patent Rolls, Volume 2, 1307–1313* (London: H.M. Stationery Office, 1904), 425.

131. NA, JUST/1/60, m. 24r.

132. NA, JUST/1/568, m. 16d, "*Simon filius Thomi de Gwythorp posuit se in ecclesiam . . . et cognovit latrocinium et postea de ecclesia illa evasit . . . postea testatus est quod . . . William le Chapeleyn Johannem Belle Forthorn Alexus le Bebne et Johannem de Horburg qui ab eodem recepuint . . . decem solid' per auxilio et consilio ei preastando ad evadendum de predicta ecclesia ideo ad judicium de eis.*"

133. *Calendar of Patent Rolls Preserved in the Public Records Office, Volume 9, 1350–54* (London: H.M. Stationery Office, 1916), 495.

134. *Statutes of the Realm*, 9 Ed. II, st. I, chap. 10; note the 1327 petition to parliament complaining about disorders caused by overzealous guardians of sanctuary, *Rotuli Parliamentorum Anglie Hactenus Inediti,* ed. H. G. Richardson and George Sayles (London: Royal Historical Society, 1935), 108.

135. Ibid.

136. Sayles, ed., *Select Cases from the King's Bench Under Edward I*, 4:210.

137. The last detailed study of abjuration in England remains André Réville, "L'abjuratio regni: Histoire d'une institution Anglaise," *Revue historique* 17 (1892): 1–42.

138. *Close Rolls from the Reign of Henry III* (London: H.M. Stationery Office, 1902–38), 2:99: "*De coronatoribus mittendis usque Hornecastrum. —Mandatum est vicecommiti Lincon quod duos coronatores comitatus sui mittat usque Hornecastrum ad videndum quod quidam latro, qui se tenet in ecclesia de hornecastro et qui se confitetur esse latronem et malefactorem, ut dicitur, faciat assisam et abjurationem*

regni secundum consuetudinem terre et secundum libertates concessas W Carleolensi episcopo. Teste ut supra." See also ibid., 6:140.

139. NA, JUST/1/358, m. 20r, "*Walterus Bret indictatus de latrociniia fugit in ecclesiam de Broke et ibi se tenet adhuc et ideo mittantur milites ad eum . . . et postea predictus Walterus abjuravit regnum et elegit portum Doviae.*"

140. BL, *Egerton* ms. 2104A, fol. 220.

141. Ibid.

142. For example, NA, JUST/1/230. A typical entry: "*Lucas . . . fugit ad ecclesiam . . . per latrocinio et cognovit se esse latrone et abjuravit regnum.*" See also R. F. Hunnisett, "The Origins of the Office of Coroner," *Transactions of the Royal Historical Society* 8 (1958): 86–104, at 93–94. The Pipe Rolls tell us very little about abjuration, *Three Rolls of the King's Court in the Reign of Richard I*, ed. F. W. Maitland (Pipe Roll Society, xiv), 100–101.

143. NA, JUST/1/614B, m. 36r.

144. Ibid.

145. NA, JUST/1/274, m. 2r. See also JUST/1/274, m. 9d.

146. NA, JUST/1/369, m. 26d. But cf. JUST/1/369, m. 25d, where an abjuration before a bailiff passed without objection.

147. Ibid.; see also m. 29d.

148. This also is presumed by the thirteenth-century treatise writers.

149. NA, JUST/1/806, m. 2r.: " quia . . . dedit ei portum de Berwyk supra Tweed cum portum propinquiore dedisse debuisset ideo ad iudicium de eo." Berwick-upon-Tweed was significantly farther from Staffordshire, sitting about eight counties northward and on the border with Scotland, than several other suitable ports. See, however, the *Yearbook of Edward I* (30–31), ed. and trans. Alfred Horwood (London: 1863, reprint. 1964) Rolls Series, 508: "Note, that he who wishes to abjure the realm shall take a port assigned to him by the Coroner, and no other port."

150. NA, JUST/1/806, m. 26d. Recall Bracton's assertion that the fugitive should abjure "unshod and ungirt" in found at fol. 36.

151. *Wiltshire Crown Pleas, 1249*, ed. C. A. F. Meekings (Wiltshire: Wiltshire Records Society, 1961), 54.

152. *Rotuli Parliamentorum* (London, 1767–77), vol. 1, 14b.

153. *Close Rolls, 1231–1234* (London: H.M. Stationery Office, 1902–38), 2:38.

154. Ibid.

155. William of Newburgh, Chronicles of the reigns of Stephen, Henry II., and Richard I, ed. Richard Howlett (London: Longman, 1884–89), 2:466–73; the various accounts are also given in *English Lawsuits from William I to Richard I*, ed. R. C. van Caenegem (London: Selden Society, 1991), 2:686–94.

156. Newburgh, *Chronicles*, 2:46–473; Roger of Hoveden, *Chronica magistri Rogeri de Houedene*, ed. William Stubbs (London, Longman, 1868–71), 4:5–6.

157. Ralph de Diceto, *Imagines Historiarum*, in *Radulfi de Diceto decani Lundoniensis Opera Historica*, ed. William Stubbs (London: Longman, 1876), 2:143–44.

158. Gervase of Canterbury, *Chronicles*, in *Historiae anglicanae scriptores X*, ed. Roger Twysden (London: Jacob Flesher, 1652), 532–34.

159. *Chronicles*, 2:472–73.

160. NA, JUST/1/44, m. 18d.

161. Ibid.

162. NA, JUST/1/635, m. 75r.

163. *Calendar of Patent Rolls, Volume 2, 1281–1292* (London: H.M. Stationery Office, 1901), 143.

164. *Early Register of Writs*, ed. Elsa de Haas and G. D. G. Hall (Selden Society, vol. 87, 147), (London: B. Quaritch, 1970). I followed the translation given in the text, except that I have rendered "*immunitate*" as "immunity" rather than "sanctuary."

165. *Calendar of Close Rolls, 1337–1339* (London: H.M. Stationery Office, 1896–1913), vol. 4, 180; see also *Calendar of Close Rolls, 1296–1302* (London: H.M. Stationery Office, 1900), vol. 4, 267 and 372.

166. *Rotuli Parliamentorum*, vol. 1, 45a.

167. NA, JUST/1/562, m. 13d. The men did not appear and their pledges were amerced.

168. *Select Cases from the Coroners' Rolls, A.D. 1265–1413*, ed. Charles Gross (Selden Society, vol. 9), (London: B. Quaritch, 1896), 75.

169. NA, JUST/1/614A, m. 2r.

170. NA, JUST/1/1043, m. 7r.: "*Walterus Guyt occidit Williamum . . . et fugit ad ecclesiam et abjuravit regnum per malefactores suo quod cognovit et postquam exivit de ecclesia secuti fuerunt eum . . . usque Stirling et ibi ceperunt eum et reduxerunt . . . et ibi amputaverunt capum eius et ideo judicium de eis.*"

171. Ibid., Other instances of violence committed against abjuring felons appear at NA, JUST 1/457, 36r and 38d and *Select Cases from the Coroners' Rolls*, 37.

172. NA, JUST/1/568, m. 35d.

173. *The Calendar of Patent Rolls, Volume 10, 1354–1358* (London: H.M. Stationery Office, 1916), 202.

174. *Calendar of Patent Rolls, Volume 13, 1364–1367* (London: H.M. Stationery Office, 1916), 59.

175. *Calendar of Patent Rolls, Volume 10, 1354–1358* (London: H.M. Stationery Office, 1916), 98.

176. H. R. Luard, *Annales Monastici* (London, 1865), vol. 2, 311.

177. David Carpenter, "The Fall of Hubert de Burgh," *Journal of British Studies* 19:1,11 (1980).

178. Ibid.

179. *Close Rolls Preserved in the Public Records Office, 1231–1234* (London: H.M. Stationery Office, 1902–38), 25 and 45, where the king "recollects that when Hubert de Burgh had escaped from our prison to the church of St. John the Divine," Hubert had the assistance of "Richard Suward, G. Basset, and their accomplices." These men were subsequently outlawed "according to the law and custom of our realm."

180. Ibid.

181. *Close Rolls, 1231–1234*, 278, 328–29; *The Calendar of Patent Rolls, 1232–47*, 27; Roger of Wendover, *Flores Historiarum* (Rolls Series, 1889), 56–57.

182. Ibid.

183. This rendering of the canon rule is taken from a late fifteenth century manuscript. Robbins ms. # 12, Lyndwood, *Constitutiones provinciales*, fol. 91. However, Lyndwood's articulation has roots in earlier pronouncements; but cf. the ninth-century Anglo-Saxon law in *Alf.* 5.2, in *Gesetze* 1:51: "Advise the elder of the church not to give him any food."

184. Ibid., 443.

185. NA, JUST/1/1043, m. 20r.

186. NA, JUST/1/543, m. 66d.

187. NA, JUST/1/1043, m. 8r.

188. *Northumberland Assize Rolls* (Durham: Andrews and Co., 1891), 86.

189. Ibid., 338, 368.

190. But, cf. NA, JUST/1/568, m. 38r., where "the Bailiffs of a Liberty (in Norfolk) did not permit the coroner of this city to enter the [liberty] to view the aforesaid death and make inquiry according to the custom of the realm. Thus, to judgment concerning the Liberty."

191. NA, JUST/1/117A, m. 55d. Stone crosses serving as boundary markers for sanctuaries can be found at liberties in the north of England as well. Mazzinghi, *Sanctuaries*, 25.

192. NA, JUST/1/117A, m. 59d.

193. *Regesta*, vol. 2, no. 1083.

194. The text is reprinted in *English Lawsuits*, 1:141.

195. This thirty-mile abjuration rule is unusual, and sheds interesting light on the claim of the jury in Reading that John had only abjured the "fee of the abbot," a claim that the itinerant justices refused to honor.

196. Ibid.

197. *Sanctuarium Dunelmense et Beverlacense*, ed. James Raine (London: Surtees Society, 1837).

198. Krista Kesselring, "Abjuration and its Demise: The Changing Face of Royal Justice in the Tudor Period," *Canadian Journal of History* 34 (1999): 345–59.

199. Daniel Lord Smail, *The Consumption of Justice*, 170–72; 177–78. Kathryn L. Reyerson, "Flight from Prosecution: The Search for Religious Asylum in Medieval Montpellier," *French Historical Studies* 17 (1992): 603–26.

200. Smail, *The Consumption of Justices*, 171; see also Natalie Zemon Davis, *Fiction in the Archives: Pardon Tales and Their Tellers in Sixteenth-Century France* (Stanford: Stanford University Press, 1987), 11.

201. Reyerson, "Flight from Prosecution," 622.

202. Carlotta Latini, *Il Privilegio Dell'Immunità* (Milan: A. Giuffrè, 2002), 389–413. See Chapter 8.

203. William Chester Jordan, "A Fresh Look at Medieval Sanctuary," in *Law and the Illicit in Medieval Europe*, ed. Ruth Mazo Karras, Joel Kaye, and E. Ann Matter (Philadelphia: University of Pennsylvania Press, 2008), 18.

8. THE ROLE OF CANON LAW IN THE DESTRUCTION OF SANCTUARY

1. Bartolus, *In primam Codicis partem commentaria* (Turin, 1589), ad CJ. 1.12.1 "*qui sunt ad ecclesiis invite extrahi non possunt.*"

2. Azo, *Summa Codicis* (Lyon, 1564), folio 4, verso; Panormitanus, *Commentaria in tertium Decretalium librum* (Venice, 1617), f. 217, ad X. 3.49.6, noting his agreement with Bartolus.

3. R. H. Helmholz, *The Ius Commune in England: Four Studies* (Oxford: Oxford University Press, 2001).

4. A nice detailed survey of the early-modern debates over sanctuary in the Roman-canon tradition is Carlotta Latini, *Il privilegio dell'immunità: Diritto d'asilo e guirisdizione nell'ordine guiridico dell'età moderna* (Milan, 2002).

5. See, e.g., Pierre Timbal, *Le droit d'asile* (Paris: Sirey, 1939), 261ff. where the author finds civilian jurists leading the struggle against ecclesiastical immunities in Europe. And Ives, who finds a royal attack on sanctuary as a rehearsal for the English crown's eventual break with Rome: "Crime, Sanctuary, and Royal Authority under Henry VIII: The Exemplary Sufferings of the Savage Family," in *On the Laws and Customs of England: Studies in Honor of Samuel E. Thorne,* ed. Morris Arnold et al. (Chapel Hill: University of North Carolina Press, 1981).

6. Cf. the recent work of Richard Helmholz, where medieval canon law is found to be more restrictive of sanctuary privileges than the common law of

England: *The Ius Commune in England: Four Studies* (Oxford: Oxford University Press, 2001).

7. On the production of the *Decretum* in successive recensions, see Anders Winroth, *The Making of Gratian's* Decretum (New York: Cambridge University Press, 2002), especially Chapter 1.

8. *Decretum* C. 36, q. 1, d. a. c. 2.

9. *Decretum* C. 36.1.3.

10. Though by the thirteenth century, the glossators generally presumed a component of sexual assault. See, e.g., *Glos. ord.* to *Decretum* C. 36. q. 1. c. 3.

11. D. 87.6.

12. The following chart shows where the passages relating to sanctuary in Gratian's *Decretum* appear in the earlier collections.

	Gratian's Decr.	Ivo's Decr.	Panormia	Tripartitia	Burchard's Decr.
1)	D. 87.6	3.112, 118; 16.70		Orange	3.195
2)	C.17, q.4, c.6	3.104	2.81	sicut antiquitus	
3)	C. 17, q.4, c.7	3.113		si quis in atrio	3.196
4)	C. 17, q.4, c.8	3.122		miror quomodo	
5)	C. 17, q.4, c.9	3.123	2.75	Reum	3.194
6)	C.17, q.4, c.10	3.120		Frater	
7)	C.17, q.4, c.11	3.119		Ad episcopos	
8)	C.17, q.4, c.19	3.117; 6.370	2.76	Lerida	
9)	C.17, q.4, c.20	3.114			3.197
10)	C. 17, q.4, c.21	3.98	2.79-80		
11)	C.17, q.4, c.32	3.15; 16.68	2.74; 2.77	Metuentes	
12)	C.17, q.4, c.33	16.77		Uxor felicis	
13)	C.17, q.4, c.35	3.121	2.78	Toledo 12	
14)	C.17, q.4, c.36	3.107; 3.109	2.73	Orleans I	3.190–192
15)	C.36, q.1, c.3	3.108	2.72	Orleans I	3.191

13. C. 17. q. 1, c. 1ff.

14. C. 17. q. 1, c. 1–4.

15. C. 17. q. 4. c. 20.

16. C. 17. q. 4. c. 18.

17. C. 17. q. 4. c. 5.

18. C. 17. q. 4. c. 7.

19. C. 17. q. 4. c. 8.

20. C. 17. q. 4. c. 11.

21. C. 17. q. 4. c. 19.

22. C. 17. q. 4. c. 20.

23. C. 17. q. 4. c. 21. The *glossa ordinaria* adds: "likewise corporal punishment would be sustained" for sacrilege. *Glos. ord.* to C. 17. q. 4. chap. 21. The *Decretum* seems to limit the sanction for sacrilege to excommunication, C.17. q. 4. c.35.

24. *Contra*, Timbal: "Gratian does not insist on the confusion of asylum and immunity; . . . [in Gratian's text] the place of asylum is qualified as an *immunity*, but the law of asylum is not yet called an *immunity*." *Le droit d'asile*, 196 (emphasis in text).

25. C. 17. q. 4. chap. 6. (emphasis added).

26. Timbal, *Le droit d'asile*, 211.

27. However, the ordinary gloss to this passage did offer a helpful definition. A public thief was a "nocturnus depopulator agrorum." *Glos. ord.* to *Decretum* C. 17. q. 4. c. 6.

28. C. 14. q. 6. c. 3. (2nd recension).

29. Ibid.

30. Ibid.

31. Paulus de Castro, *In primam codicis partem commentaria* (Venice, 1593), fol. 24.: "*sed de jure canonico statutum est contrarium, quod pro nullo crimine, etiam ex quo veniat imponenda poena mortis.*"

32. Bartholomaeus Chassanaeus, *Consuetudines ducatus Burgundiae* (Lyon, 1732), c. 211, writing in the early sixteenth century and cataloguing earlier opinions.

33. Alciatus, *De praesumptionibus* (Venice, 1584), vol. 4, praes. 33, chap. 1.

34. Pierre de Belleperche, *Commentaria in Digestum Novum* (Frankfurt, 1571) *ad* CJ. 1.12.6 On Belleperche, see the recent book by Kees Bezemer: *Pierre de Belleperche: Portrait of a Legal Puritan* (Frankfurt: Klosterman, 2005).

35. Albericus de Rosate, *Dictionarium Iuris tam Civilis, quam canonici* (Venice, 1573), 222.

36. Ibid.

37. *Lettres secrètes et curiales, Jean XXII*, ed. A. Coulon and C. Clemencet (Paris: 1965) #4947: "non attenta reverential quam sancrosanctis ecclesiis jubet utriusque juris sanxio exhiberi, nec metuens ecclesiarum pblice ledere libertatem."

38. Azo, *Summa Codicis* (Lyon, 1546), folio 4, verso; Panormitanus, *Commentaria in tertium Decretalium librum* (Venice, 1617), f. 217, ad X. 3.49.6, noting his agreement with Bartolus.

39. *Lettres communes, Benoit XII*, ed. J. M. Vidal (Paris, 1903–11), #2107.

40. *Lettres communes, Jean XXII*, ed. Guillaume Mollat (Paris, 1921–47), #4708.

41. Ibid., #41318: "*Philippo R. F.* indulgetur ut in regno suo apostatantes a fide catholica vel haeretici ad ecclesias confugientes ut per immunitatem earum in apostasia vel haeresi hujusmodi defendantur, nullam tutelam propterea ab eisdem ecclesiis consequantur, sed locorum ep.is vel inquisitoribus haereticae pravitatis illarum partium super hoc requisitis, et de eorum assensu, ex dictis ecclesiis libere abstrahi valeant, etiam per brachium saeculare."

42. *Lettres communes, Urbain V*, eds. Michel Hayez, Bernard Barbiche, Florence Callu-Turiaf, and Yves-Marie Bercé (Paris, 1965), #5962. Alexander's letter is in the *Lettres secrètes et curiales de Jean XXII*, #756e.

43. *Lettres communes, John XXII*, #8623.

44. *Lettres communes, Clement V*, #5455.

45. Alciatus, *De praesumptionibus* (Venice, 1584), vol. 4, fol. 342, no. 33, chap. 1.

46. *Lettres secrètes et curiales, Clement VI*, ed. E. Deprez, J. Glenisson, and G. Mollat (Paris, 1910–61), #717: "*Rursus tu, et gentes tue asserere nitimini, de quo miramur admodum, si est ita, quod illi, qui ad ecclesias confugiunt, absque sacrilegio et fratione libertatis et immunitatis ecclesiae violenter exinde possunt extrahi, dum tamen vita et membra salventur eisdem.*"

47. *Lettres secrètes et curiales, Innocent VI*, ed. P. Gasnault and M-H. Laurent, (Paris: 1968} #589.

48. Johannes de Torquemada, *In gratiani Decretum commentarii* (Venice, 1578), ad C. 17, q. 4, chap. 35.

49. *Glos. ord.* to C. 17. q. 4. chap. 9: "*Si non potest crimina remanebunt impunita: quod esse non debet. Et sic privilegium ecclesiae erit multis occasio delinquendi. Propter hoc dicunt quedam que a quolibet potest accusari postea, preterque ab illo que permisit impunitatem.*"

50. Ibid., 577.

51. X.5.39.35.

52. *CJ.* 9.47.14.: "*non remitti poenam facile publice intersit, ne ad maleficia temere quisquam prosiliat.*"

53. Dig. 5.1.18; Dig. 46.1.70.5.

54. Dig. 16.3.31.

55. The anonymous text is entitled *Summa Induent sancti.* Fraher produced an edition of the text in the *Monumenta Iuris Canonici* (series A, Corpus Glossatorum, 1984).

56. Placentinus is one possible candidate because he warns against allowing wrong to remain unpunished (*maleficia remaneat impunita*)." *Summa Codicis ad Codex Justiniani* 3.35.

But it is possible that a precursor to Innocent's maxim appeared in a slightly earlier, Anglo-Norman source. In the early years of the twelfth century, Norman scribes set about compiling Latin texts that were more or less faithful attempts to set out the laws and customs of Anglo-Saxon kings. One of these twelfth-century compilations, the *Institutio Cnuti,* explained that "Christians ought not be put to death for a small thing; namely, for theft or for like things. [Nevertheless] they ought to be corrected in another mode *for the sake of others, so that no wrongs remain unavenged.*" II *Cnut* 2.1. Liebermann, *Die Gesetze der*

Angelsachsen (Halle: M. Niemeyer, 1898–1912; Aalen: Scientia, 1960), 1: 309–11. "*Interdicimus etiam, ne pro parva re Christiani morti tradantur, scilicet pro latrocinio aut pro talibus rebus,* sed alio modo corrigantur, propter alios, ne culpe inulte remaneant" (emphasis added). The non-italicized part was an Anglo-Norman interpolation, and it predated Innocent III's apparent revival of the maxim.

57. *Summula de criminibus,* incipit. An edition of this text has been produced by Fraher, "Tancred's Summula de Criminibus," *Bulletin of Medieval Canon Law* 9 (1979): 23, 29–35.

58. Tuetonicus, *Apparatus Glossarum in Compilationem Tertiam,* 3 Monumenta Iuris Canonici (Series A, 1980) *Corpus Glossatorum,* cited by Fraher, "The Theoretical Justification for the New Criminal Law of the High Middle Ages," 1984 *University of Illinois Law Review* 577, 580n14.

59. Hostiensis, *Summa Aurea,* fol. 339 (Lyon: Joann. de Cambray, 1556). The full phrase reads "*interest autem cuiuslibet, ne delicta remaneant impunita.*"

60. *Speculum iudiciale,* fol. 1 (Padua, 1479, incunable).

61. The basic works on this are Gaines Post, "A Roman-canonical Maxim 'Quod omnes tangit' in Bracton," in 4 *Traditio* 197 (1946); Peter Stein, *Regulae Iuris: From Juristic Rules to Legal Maxims* (Edinburgh: Edinburgh University Press, 1966).

62. *Tractatus de maleficiis,* fol. 2, dorso (Lyon, 1514).

63. Ibid.

64. C. 12.45.1.47.: "ad rei publicae utilitatem referendum est."

65. C. 12.53.1, no. 60. See also Walter Ullmann's study *The Medieval Idea of Law as Represented by Lucas de Penne,* chapter 7, "The Idea of Crime" (London: Methuen, 1946).

66. Mylerus, *De Asylorum jure,* fol. 37 (Stuttgart: J. G. Cottae, 1664), citing Tacitus, *Annals,* bk. 3.

67. Dig. 16.3.31.

68. Dig. 47.10.18.

69. Dig. 5.1.18.1.

70. X. 5.39.35.

71. de Penne, C. 10.16.3, no. 3.

72. Ibid. Cited in Ullmann, *The Medieval Idea of Law,* 143.

73. Fraher, "The Theoretical Justification for the New Criminal Law of the High Middle Ages," 582.

74. Ibid., 586.

75. Ibid., 582–83.

76. See Ullmann, *The Medieval Idea of Law,* 144.

77. *Glos. ord.* ad C. 17. q. 4. c. 9.

78. X. 3.49.6.: "*quid de illis fieri debeat, qui maleficia perpetrantes confugiunt ad ecclesiam, ut pro reverentia loci sacri debitas poenas valeant evitare.*"

79. Ibid.

80. Ibid.

81. Ibid.

82. Ibid.

83. Nicholas's rule appears in Gratian's *Decretum* at C. 17. q. 4. c. 6.

84. Ibid.

85. X. 3.49.10.

86. Ibid.

87. *Lettres communes, Clement V*, #5455.

88. *Lettres secrètes et curiales, Jean XXII*, ed. A Coulon and S. Clemencet, #3043.

89. *St. Albans Chronicle, The Chronica Maiora of Thomas of Walsingham*, ed. and trans. John Taylor, Wendy Childs, and Leslie Watkiss (Oxford: Oxford University Press, 2003), vol. 1, 237ff. and 273ff.

90. E. Perroy, "Gras profits et rançons pendant la guerre de Cent Ans: l'affaire du comte de Denia," in *Mélanges d'historie du moyen âge dédiés a la mémoire de Louis Halphen* (Paris: Presses Universitaires de France, 1951), 573–80. I am very grateful to Elizabeth Allen who shared with me two of her unpublished research papers relating to this historical episode.

91. *St. Albans Chronicle, The Chronica Maiora of Thomas of Walsingham*, ed. and trans. John Taylor, Wendy Childs, and Leslie Watkiss (Oxford: Oxford University Press, 2003), 1:241.

92. *St. Albans Chronicle, The Chronica Maiora of Thomas of Walsingham*, ed. and trans. John Taylor, Wendy Childs, and Leslie Watkiss (Oxford: Oxford University Press, 2003), 1:237ff. and 273ff.

93. See *Rot. Parl.* 3:37b; and the legislation enacted as 2 Richard II, stat. 2, chap. 3 (1379).

94. See *Rot. Parl.* 3:37b.

95. *Lettres Secrètes et Curiales de pape Jean XXII (1316–1334) relatives à la France*, ed. A. Coulon (Paris: Bibliothèque des Écoles Françaises d'Athènes et de Rome, 1906), #756e.

96. Rot. Parl. 3:321a; Thornley, "The Destruction of Sanctuary," 187.

97. See 1 Henry IV, chap. 15; 2 Henry V, 1:5; 9 Henry V, 1:7.

98. Thomas More, *The History of King Richard III*, ed. Richard Sylvester, 28–31 in *The Complete Works of St. Thomas More* (New Haven: Yale University Press, 1963), 2:26–31.

99. See Shannon McSheffrey's recent article "Sanctuary and the Legal Topography of Pre-Reformation England," *Law and History Review* (2009) 27: 483–514.

100. Peter Kaufman, "Henry VII and Sanctuary," *Church History* 53 (1984): 465–76. The manuscript is in the library of the Marquis of Bath, Longleat ms. 38.

101. *Rotuli Parliamentorum*, 3:503b.

102. NA, C 49 40/10 (1483).

103. NA, C/49/40/10 (22 Edw. IV) 1483.

104. Ibid.

105. Mazzinghi, *Sanctuaries*, 13; Thornley, "The Destruction of Sanctuary," 197.

106. Peter Kaufman, "Henry VII and Sanctuary," *Church History* 53 (1984): 465–76.

107. *Lettres secrètes et curiales, Innocent VI*, ed. P. Gasnault and M-H. Laurent, #589.

108. *Calendar of Entries in the Papal Registers Relating to Great Britain and Ireland, Papal Letters (A.D. 1431–1447)*, ed. J. A. Twemlow, W. H. Bliss, and C. Johnson (London: H.M. Stationery Office, 1893–1933), 9:282.

109. Ibid.

110. Thornley, "The Destruction of Sanctuary," 182.

111. 22 Henry VIII, chap. 14; 27 Henry VIII, chap. 19; 32 Henry VIII, chap. 12, in *Statutes of the Realm* (1810).

112. See Thornley, "The Destruction of Sanctuary," 200–201.

113. Thornley, "The Destruction of Sanctuary," 204n116.

114. J. Charles Cox, *Sanctuaries and Sanctuary Seekers*, 75.

115. 21 James I, chap. 28, sections 6 and 7.

116. Gervase Rosser, "Sanctuary and Social Negotiation in Medieval England," in *The Cloister and the World. Essays in Medieval History in Honour of Barbara Harvey*, ed. John Blair and Brian Golding (1996), already noted that confessional conflicts did not predict who would oppose or support sanctuary privileges.

117. Timbal, *Le droit d'asile*, 430–31.

118. *Bull. Rom.* (ed. de Turin), 9:424.

119. *Calendar of Entries in the Papal Registers Relating to Great Britain and Ireland, Papal Letters (A.D. 1431–1447)*, ed. J. A. Twemlow (London: H.M. Stationery Office, 1912), 11:580.

120. Robert Keilway, *Reports d'ascuns cases* (London: Printed for Charles Harper, et al., 1688), 191.

121. Ives, "Crime, Sanctuary, and Royal Authority Under Henry VIII: The Exemplary Sufferings of the Savage Family," in *On the Laws and Customs of England: Essays in Honor of Samuel E. Thorpe*, 301.

122. I. Thornley, "The Destruction of Sanctuary," in *Tudor Studies Presented to A. F. Pollard* (London: Longmans, Green & Co., 1924), 201.

123. X. 3.49.10.

124. *Calendar of Entries in the Papal Registers relating to Great Britain and Ireland, Papal Letters*, 11:580.

125. Ibid.

126. Ibid.

127. *St. German's Doctor and Student,* ed. T. F. T. Plucknett and J. L. Barton (London: Selden Society, 1974), 91:322.

128. Alciatus, *De praesumptiones*, fol. 342 (Venice, 1584).

129. Ibid.

130. Ibid.

131. Timbal, *Le droit d'asile*, 266.

132. Ibid., 440.

133. Ibid., 440.

134. The bull is known as *Cum alias* and can be found in *Bull. Rom.* 9:424.

135. Carlotta Latini, *Il privilegio dell'immunità* (Milan, 2002), 389–413.

136. Timbal, *Le droit d'asile,* 287–373.

137. CIC (1917), chap. 1179.

138. Peter Landau, "Traditionen des Kirchenasyl" in *Asyl am Heiligen Ort: Sanctuary und Kirchenasyl vom Rechtsanspruch zur ethischen Verpflichtung*, ed. Klaus Barwig and Dieter R. Bauer (Ostfildern: Schwabenverlag, 1994), 47, provides an overview to this issue.

Bibliography

MANUSCRIPT SOURCES

Berkeley, California: Robbins Collection of Civil and Religious Law, ms. 112, Lynwood, *Provinciale*.

London, British Library: Additions 10106, *Chronica de Regibus Angliae*; Egerton, 2104A, Cartulary of the Benedictine Abbey of Nuns of St. Cross at Harewell; Harley, 1708, Cartulary of Reading Abbey.

London, Kew, National Archive (NA): C 49/40/10 (Parliamentary petitions); KB 27 (King's Bench); JUST 1 (numerous) (Rolls of the Itinerant Justices); JUST 2 (Coroners' Rolls).

Paris, Bibliotèque National: Nouvelles acquisitiones latines, ms. 413.

Warminster, England: Longleat ms. 38 (Library of the Marquis of Bath).

PRINTED PRIMARY SOURCES

Aeschylus. *Oresteia*. Trans. Hugh Lloyd-Jones. Berkeley: University of California Press, 1979.

Albericus de Rosate. *Dictionarium Iuris tam Civilis, quam canonici*. Venice, 1573.

Alciatus, Andrea. *De presumptions*. In *Tractatus Universi Iuris*. 4 vols. Venice: Francesco Ziletti, 1584–86.

Alcuin. *Epistolae Karolini Aevi II*. Ed. Ernst Dümmler et al. Berlin: MGH, 1892–1925.

Ancient Roman Statutes. Ed. Allan Chester Johnson, Paul Robinson Coleman-Norton, and Frank Card Bourne. Austin: University of Texas Press, 1961.

Anglo-Norman Political Songs. Ed. Isabel S. T. Aspin. Oxford: Blackwell, 1953.

Augustine. *Sancti Aurelii Augustini Opera: Epistolae ex duobus codicibus nuper in lucem prolatae*. Ed. Johannes Divjak, *CSEL* 88. Vienna: 1981.

———. *Sancti Aureli Augustini tractatus sive sermones inediti ex codice Guelferbytano.* Ed. Germanus Morin. Zurich: ex Typographia Koeseliani, 1917.

Azo. *Summa Codicis*. Lyon: 1546.

Bede. *Bede's Ecclesiastical History of the English People.* Ed. B. Colgrave and R. A. B. Mynors. Oxford: Oxford Medieval Texts, 1969.

———. *Historical Works.* 2 vols. Trans. J. E. King. Cambridge, Mass.: Loeb Classical Library, 1930.

Beowulf. Ed. Burton Raffel. New York: Penguin Books, 1963.

Bracton, Henry. *De legibus et consuetudinibus Angliae. On the Laws and Customs of England.* Ed. George Woodbine, trans. Samuel Thorne. Cambridge, Mass.: Harvard University Press, 1968.

Calendar of Entries in the Papal Registers Relating to Great Britain and Ireland, Papal Letters, 1431–1447. Ed. A. Tremlow. London, 1912.

Carolingian Chronicles. Ed. Bernhard Walter Scholz. Ann Arbor: University of Michigan Press, 1970.

The Chronicle of Battle Abbey. Ed. Eleanor Searle. New York: Oxford University Press, 1980.

The Chronicle of John of Worcester. Ed. R. R. Darlington and P. McGurk. Oxford: Clarendon Press, 1995.

Chrysostom. *Homilia in Eutropium. PG* 52: 393.

Close Rolls of the Reign of Henry III Preserved in the Public Records Office. London, 1902–22.

Codex Theodosianus, cum perpetuis commentariis Jocabi Godefredi. Ed. J. D. Ritter. Leipzig: George Weidmann, 1736–45.

Collectio Vetus Gallica. Ed. Hubert Mordek. In *Kirchenrecht und Reform im Frankenreich: Die alteste systematische Kanonessammlung des früinkischen Gallien.* Berlin: W. de Gruyter, 1975.

Concilia Galliae a. 511–a.695. Ed. Charles de Clercq. Turnhout: Corpus Christianorum Series Latina (CCSL), 1963.

Corpus Legum ab imperatoribus Romanis ante Iustinianum latarum. Ed. Gustav Haenel. Leipzig: J. C. Hinrichs, 1857–60.

The Early Charters of Waltham Abbey, 1062–1230. Ed. R. Ransford. Woodbridge: Boydell and Brewer, 1989.

Early Register of Writs. Ed. Elsa de Haas and G. D. G. Hall. London: Selden Society, 1970.

English Lawsuits from William I to Richard I. 2 vols. Ed. R. C. van Caenegem. London: Selden Society, 1990.

Epistolae Romanorum Pontificum. Ed. Andreas Thiel. Braunsberg: E. Peter, 1868.

The Eyre of London, 14: Edward II A.D. 1321. 2 vols. Ed. Helen Cam. London: Selden Society, 1968.

Fleta. Ed. H. G. Richardson and G. O. Sayles. London: Selden Society, 1955.

Gesetze der Angelsachsen. Ed. Felix Liebermann. Halle: M. Niemeyer, 1898–1912; rpt. Aalen: Scientia, 1960.

Gregory of Tours. *Gregorii episcopi Turonensis. Libri Historiarum X.* 2 vols. Ed. Bruno Kusch and Rudolf Buchner. Hanover: MGH, 1951).

Hostiensis. *Summa Aurea.* London: Joann. de Cambray, 1556.

Die Irische Kanonensammlung. Ed. Herrmann Wasserschleben. Aalen: Scientia, 1966.

The Laws of the Earliest English Kings. Ed. F. L. Attenborough. New York: Cambridge University Press, 1922.

The Laws of the Kings of England from Edmund to Henry I. Ed. A. J. Robertson. New York: Cambridge University Press, 1925.

Leges Alamannorum. Ed. K. Lehmann. Hanover: MGH Legum, sectio I, 1888.

Leges Alamannorum et Baiwariorum. Ed. J. Merkel. Hanover: MHG Leges III, 1863.

Leges Burgundionum. Ed. L. R. de Salis. Hanover: MGH Legum, Sectio I, 1892.

Leges Henrici Primi. Ed. L. J. Downer. Oxford: Oxford University Press, 1972.

Leges Langobardorum. Ed. F. Bluhme. Hanover: MGH Leges I, 1868.

Leges Visigothorum. Ed. Karol Zeumer. Hanover: MGH, 1902.

The Letter of St. Clement of Rome to the Corinthians. In *The Apostolic Fathers.* Ed. Francis Glimm. Huntington, N.Y.: Cima Publishing, 1947.

The Letters of Pliny. Ed. William Melmoth. Cambridge, Mass.: Loeb Classical Library, 1915.

Lex Baiuwariorum. Ed. Ernst de Schwind. Hanover: MGH, 1926.

Lex Frisionum. Ed. K. A. and W. A. Eckhardt. Hanover: MGH Fontes Iuris Germanici Antiqui in usum scholarum XII, 1982.

Lex Romana Visigothorum. Ed. Gustav Haenel. Leipzig: B. G. Teubner, 1849.

Libanius. *Selected Works II: Selected Orations.* Ed. A. F. Norman. Cambridge, Mass.: Loeb Classical Library, 1977.

Mirror of Justices. Ed. William Whittaker. London: Selden Society, 1895.

Orderic Vitalis. *The Ecclesiastical History of Orderic Vitalis*, ed. and trans. Marjorie Chibnall. Oxford: Oxford Medieval Texts, 1968–80.

Orosius. *Historiarum adversum paganos.* Ed. C. Zangemeister. Hildesheim: G. Olms, 1967.

Pactus Lex Salica. Ed. K. A. Eckhardt. MGH Legum Sectio I, 1962–69.

Panormitanus. *Commentaria in tertium Decretalium librum.* Venice, 1617.

Pierre de Belleperche. *Commentaria in Digestum Novum.* Frankfurt, 1571.

Pleas Before the King or His Justices, 1198–1212. Ed. Doris Mary Stenton. London: Selden Society, 1967.

Pleas of the Crown for the County of Gloucestershire 1221. Ed. Frederic Maitland. London: Macmillan, 1884.

The Priory of Hexham, Its Chroniclers, Endowments and Annals. Ed. James Raine. London: Surtees Society, 1864–65.

Regesta Regum Anglo-Normannorum, 1066–1154. Ed. H. W. C. Davis. Oxford: Oxford University Press, 1913.

Reginald of Durham. *Libellus de admirandis beati Cuthberti virtutibus quae novellis patratae sunt temporibus*. Ed. James Rayne. London: Surtees Society, 1835.

Rotuli Parliamentorum Anglie hactenus inediti. Ed. H. G. Richardson and G. O. Sayles. London: Camden Society 1935.

Saint German. *Doctor and Student*. Ed. T. F. T. Plucknett and J. L. Barton. London: Selden Society, 1974.

Sanctuarium dunelmense et sanctuarium beverlacense. London: Surtees Society, 1937.

Select Cases from the Coroners' Rolls, 1265–1413. Ed. Charles Gross. London: Selden Society, 1896.

Select Cases of Trespass From the King's Courts, 1307–1399. Ed. Morris Arnold. London: Selden Society, 1985.

Servius Grammaticus. *Servii Grammatici qui feruntur in Vergilii carmina commentarii: Volume 1, Aenidos Librorum I–V Commentarii*. Ed. Georgius Thilo and Hermannus Hagen. Hildesheim: George Olms, 1961.

Socrates of Constantinople. *Historia Ecclesiastica, 2.25*. In *Die Griechischen Christlichen Schriftsteller*, vol. 1. Ed. G. C. Hansen. Berlin: Akademie Verlag, 1995.

Statutes of the Realm. London, 1810–1828.

Symeon of Durham. *Historia Ecclesiae Dunhelmensis*. Ed. David Rollason. Oxford: Oxford Medieval Texts, 2000.

Theodoret. *The Ecclesiastical History, Dialogues and Letters of Theodoret*. In *Nicean and Post-Nicean Fathers*, 2nd series. Ed. Philip Schaff and Henry Wace. Edinburgh: Continuum International, 1980.

The Theodosian Code. Ed. Clyde Pharr. Princeton: Princeton University Press, 1952.

Theodosiani libri XVI cum constitutionibus Sirmondianis. Ed. Theodore Mommsen. Berlin: Weidmann, 1905.

The Treatise on the Laws and Customs of the Realm of England, Commonly called Glanville. Ed. G. D. G. Hall. Oxford: Oxford University Press. 1965; reprint, Holmes Beach, Fla.: William W. Gaunt & Sons, 1983.

Tuetonicus. *Apparatus Glossarum in Compilationem Tertiam*. 3 Monumenta Iuris Canonici Series A, 1980.

Wulfstan's Canons of Edgar. Ed. Roger Fowler. London: Oxford University Press for the Early English Text Society, 1972.

Zonaras. *Epitome Historiarum*. Ed. J. Smith. Leipzig: Bibliotheca Scriptorum Graecorum et Romanorum Teubneriana, 1870.

Zosimus. *Historia Nova*. In François Paschoud, *Zosime: Histoire Nouvelle*. Paris: Les Belles Lettres, 1971.

SECONDARY SOURCES

Baker, John. "Criminal Courts and Procedure at Common Law, 1550–1800." In *Crime in England 1550–1800*, ed. J. S. Cockburn, 41–67. Princeton: Princeton University Press, 1977.

———. *An Introduction to English Legal History*. 2nd ed. London: Butterworths, 1979.

Beccaria, Cesare. *On Crimes and Punishments*. Ed. Richard Bellamy, trans. Richard Davies. New York: Cambridge University Press, 1986.

Beckerman, John S. "Adding Insult to *Iniuria:* Affronts to Honor and the Origins of Trespass." In *On the Laws and Customs of England: Essays in Honor of Samuel E. Thorne*, ed. Morris Arnold et al., 166–89. Chapel Hill: University of North Carolina Press, 1981.

Beyerle, F. "Zur Frühgeschichte der westgotischen Gesetzgebung." *ZSS GA* 67 (1950): 1.

Bindschedler, Rudolf. *Kirchliches Asylrecht (immunitas ecclesiarum localis) und Freistätten in der Schweiz*. Amsterdam: P. Schippers, 1965.

Bisson, Thomas. "Medieval Lordship." *Speculum* 70 (1995): 743.

Bloomfield, Morton W. "Beowulf, Byrhtnoth, and the Judgement of God: Trial by Combat in Anglo-Saxon England." *Speculum* 44 (1969): 545.

Brassloff, Stephan. "Zu den Quellen der byzantinischen Rechtsgeschichte." *ZSS RA* 25 (1904): 313.

Brown, Peter. *The Cult of the Saints: Its Rise and Function in Latin Christianity*. Chicago: University of Chicago Press, 1981.

Brundage, James. *The Medieval Canon Law*. New York: Longman, 1995.

Brunner, Heinrich. *Deutsche Rechtsgeschichte*. Leipzig: Duncker und Humblot, 1892.

Brynteson, William E. "Roman Law and Legislation in the Middle Ages." *Speculum* 41 (1966): 420.

Bulmerincq, August. *Das Asylrecht seiner geschichtlichen Entwicklung*. Wiesbaden: M. Sändig, 1970.

Busse, Wilhelm. "Die 'karolingische' Reform König Alfreds." In *Karl der Grosse und das Erbe der Kulturen*, ed. Franz-Reiner Erkens, 169–84. Berlin: Akademie Verlag, 2001.

Carpenter, D. A. "The Fall of Hubert de Burgh." *Journal of British Studies* 19 (1980): 1.

———. "King, Magnates, and Society: The Personal Rule of King Henry III, 1234–1258." *Speculum* (1988) 60: 39.

Carro, Jorge. "Sanctuary: The Resurgence of an Age-Old Right or a Dangerous Misinterpretation of an Abandoned Ancient Privilege?" *University of Cincinnati Law Review* 65 (1986): 747–78.

Caseau, Beatrice. "A Case Study for the Transformation of Law in Late Antiquity: The Legal Protection of Churches." In *Confrontation in Late Antiquity: Imperial Presentation and Regional Adaptation*, ed. Linda Jones Hall, 299–314. Cambridge: Orchard Academic, 2003.

Clanchy, Michael. "Law and Love in the Middle Ages." In *Disputes and Settlements: Law and Human Relations in the West*, ed. John Bossy, 34–57. New York: Cambridge University Press, 1983.

Collins, Sam. "*Domus Domini patet figura mysterii*: Architectural Imagination and the Politics of Place in the Carolingian Ninth Century." Ph.D. diss., University of California, Berkeley, 2005.

Constable, Giles. "Forgery and Plagiarism in the Middle Ages." *Archiv für Diplomatik* 29 (1983): 1–41.

Dann, R. "Über den Ursprung des Asylrechts und dessen Überreste in Europa," *Zeitschrift für Deutsches Recht und Deutsche Rechtwissenschaft* 3 (1840): 67.

Davies, Wendy, and Paul Fouracre. *The Settlement of Disputes in Early Medieval Europe*. New York: Cambridge University Press, 1986.

de Beaurepaire, Charles. *Essai sur l' asile religieux dans l' empire romain et la monarchie française*. Chartres: Biblioteque de l'Ecole des Chartes, 1853–54.

de Mazzinghi, Thomas. *Sanctuaries*. Stafford: Halden and Sons, 1888.

Doherty, C. "The Monastic Town in Early Medieval Ireland." In *The Comparative History of Urban Origins in Non-Roman Europe*, ed. H. B. Clark and A. Sims, 67–89. Oxford: British Archaeology Reports, 1985.

d'Ors, A. *Estudios Visigóticos II: El Código de Eurico*. Rome and Madrid: Cuadernos del Instituto Juríco Español, 1960.

Douglas, Audrey W. "Frankalmoin and Jurisdictional Immunity: Maitland Revisited." *Speculum* (1978) 53: 26.

Doyle, A. I. "The Work of a Late 15th Century English Scribe, William Evesham." *Bulletin of the John Rylands Library* 39 (March 1957): 313.

Dreher, Martin. "Die Ursprünge des Kirchenasyls und die Gesetzgebung Theodosius' II." In *Staatlichkeit und politisches Handeln in der römischen Kaiserzeit*, ed. Hans-Ulrich Wiemer, 177–216. Berlin: De Gruyter, 2006.

Drew, Katherine Fisher. "Another Look at the Origins of the Middle Ages: A Reassessment of the Role of the Germanic Kingdoms." *Speculum* 62 (1987): 803.

———. "Legal Materials as a Source for Early Medieval Social History." *Rice University Studies* 60 (1974): 33.

Ducloux, Anne. *Ad Ecclesiam Confugere: Naissance du droit d'asile dans les eglises (IV–milieu de V s.).* Paris: De Boccard, 1995.

Forster, R. H. "Notes on Durham and Other North-Country Sanctuaries." *Journal of the British Archaeological Association* 11 (1905): 118.

Fournier, Paul & Le Bras, Gabriel. *Histoire des collections canoniques en occident depuis les fausses decretales jusqu 'au decet de Gratien.* Paris: Recueil Sirey, 1931.

Fraher, Richard. "Conviction According to Conscience: The Medieval Jurists' Debate Concerning Judicial Discretion and the Law of Proof." *Law and History Review* 7 (1989): 23.

———. "IV Lateran's Revolution in Criminal Procedure: The Birth of *Inquisitio,* the End of the Ordeals, and Innocent Ill's Vision of Ecclesiastical Politics." In *Studia in honorem eminetissimi Cardinalis Alphonsi M. Stickler.* Rome: PAS, 1992.

———. "Preventing Crime in the High Middle Ages: The Medieval Lawyers' Search for Deterrence." In *Popes, Teachers, and Canon Law in the Middle Ages,* ed. J. R. Sweeney and S. Chodorow, 213–33. Ithaca, N.Y.: Cornell University Press, 1989.

———. "The Theoretical Justification for the New Criminal Law of the High Middle Ages: 'Rei Publicae Interest, Ne Crimina Remaneant Impunita.'" *University of Illinois Law Review* 1984: 577.

Frauenstädt, Paul. *Blutrache und Todtschlagsühne in Deutschen Mittelalter.* Leipzig: Duncker und Humblot, 1881.

Fruscione, Daniela. *Das Asyl bei den Germanischen Stämmen im Frühen Mittelalter.* Berlin: Böhlau Verlag, 2003.

Gamauf, Richard. "Ad statuas confugere in der frühen römischen Kaiserzeit." In *Das antike Asyl: Kultische Grundlagen, rechtliche Ausgestaltung und politische Funktion,* ed. Martin Dreher, 188–212. Köln: Böhlau Verlag, 2003.

Gaudemet, Jean. *La formation du droit seculier et du droit de l'eglise aux IV–V siècles.* 2nd ed. Paris: Sirey, 1979.

———. "Le bréviaire d'Alaric et les Epitome." In *Ius Romanum Medii Aevi.* Milan: Giuffrè, 1965.

Gescher, Franz. *Le droit d'asile. ZSS KA* 29 (1940): 466.

Gillingham. John. "1066 and the Introduction of Chivalry Into England." In *Laws and Government in Medieval England and Normandy: Essays in Honor of Sir James Holt,* ed. George Garnett and John Hudson, 31–55. New York: Cambridge University Press, 1994.

———. "The Beginning of English Imperialism." *Journal of Historical Sociology* 5 (1992): 392–409.

———. "Conquering the Barbarian: War and Chivalry in Twelfth-Century Britain." *Haskins Society Journal* 4 (1992): 67–84.

Godden, Malcolm. "Did King Alfred Write Anything?" *Medium Aevum* 76 (2007): 1–23.

Goebels, Julius, Jr. *Felony and Misdemeanor: A Study in the History of English Criminal Procedure.* New York: Commonwealth Fund, 1937.

Grafton, Anthony. *Forgers & Critics: Creativity & Duplicity in Western Scholarship.* Princeton: Princeton University Press, 1990.

Green, D. H. *Language and History in the Early Germanic World.* New York: Cambridge University Press, 1998.

Green, Thomas A. *Verdict According to Conscience: Perspectives on the English Criminal Jury Trial, 1200–1800.* Chicago: University of Chicago Press, 1985.

Gröll, Josef. *Die Elemente des kirchlichen Freiungsrechtes.* Amsterdam: Verlag P. Schippers, 1965.

Hall, David. "The Sanctuary of St. Cuthbert." In *St. Cuthbert, His Cult and Community to AD 1200*, ed. Gerald Bonner, David Rollason, and Clare Stancliffe, 215–236. Woodbridge: Boydell and Brewer, 1989.

Hallam, Henry. *A View of the State of Europe During the Middle Ages.* 2 vols. London: J. Murray, 1818.

Harding, Alan, "Early Trailbaston Proceedings from the Lincoln Roll of 1305." In *Medieval Legal Records*, ed. R. F. Hunnisett and J. B. Post. London: HMSO, 1978.

Harries, Jill. *Law and Empire in Late Antiquity.* New York: Cambridge University Press, 1999.

Harris, Troy. "Toward a Universal Standard: Free Exercise and the Sanctuary Movement." *University of Michigan Journal of Law Reform* 21 (1988): 745–60.

Heinzelmann, Martin. *Gregor of Tours (538–594): Zehn Bucher Geschichte: Historiographie und Gesellschaftskonzept im 6. Jahrhundert.* Darmstadt: Wissenschaftliche Buchgesellschaft, 1994.

Helmholz, Richard. *The Ius Commune in England: Four Studies.* Oxford: Oxford University Press, 2001.

———. *The Oxford History of the Laws of England: Volume I, The Canon Law and Ecclesiastical Jurisdiction from 597 to the 1640s.* Oxford: Oxford University Press, 2004.

———. *The Spirit of the Classical Canon Law.* Athens: University of Georgia Press, 1996.

Herman, E. "Asile dans l'eglise orientale." In *Dictionnaire de droit canonique.* Paris: Letouzey & Ané, 1990.

Hermann, Johannes. "Cod. Theod. 9, 45: De his, qui ad ecclesias confugiunt." In *Beiträge zur Rechtsgeschichte: Gedächtnisschrift für Hermann Conrad*, ed.

Gerd Kleinheyer and Paul Mikat, 271–82. Munich: Ferdinand Schöningh, 1979.

Hermanowicz, Erika. "Catholic Bishops and Appeals to the Imperial Court: A Legal Study of the Calama Riots in 408." *JECS* 12 (2004): 481–521.

Hinschius, Paul. *Das Kirchenrecht der Katholiken und Protestanten.* Graz: Akademische Druck- u. Verlagsanstalt, 1959.

Honoré, Tony. *Law in the Crises of Empire AD 379–455: The Theodosian Dynasty and its Quaestors.* Oxford: Oxford University Press, 1998.

Houlou, Andre. "Le droit penal chez Saint Augustin." *Revue Historique de droit Français et Etranger* 52 (1974): 5–29.

Hudson, John. *The Formation of the English Common Law: Law and Society in England from the Norman Conquest to Magna Carta.* London: Longman, 1996.

———. "Maitland and Anglo-Norman Law." *Proceedings of the British Academy* 89: 21–46.

Hunnisett, R. F. *The Medieval Coroner.* New York: Cambridge University Press, 1961.

———. "The Origins of the Office of Coroner." *Transactions of the Royal Historical Society* 8 (1958): 86.

Hurnard, Naomi. "The Anglo-Norman Franchises." *English Historical Review* 64 (1949): 289–323, 433–60.

———. *The King's Pardon for Homicide.* Oxford: Clarendon Press, 1969.

Hyams, Paul. *Rancor and Reconciliation in Medieval England.* Ithaca: Cornell University Press, 2003.

———. "Trial by Ordeal: The Key to Proof in the Early Common Law." In *On the Laws and Customs of England: Studies in Honor of Samuel E. Thorne*, ed. Morris Arnold et al., 91–126. Chapel Hill: University of North Carolina Press, 1981.

Ives, E. W. "Crime, Sanctuary, and Royal Authority Under Henry VIII: The Exemplary Sufferings of the Savage Family." In *On the Laws and Customs of England: Studies in Honor of Samuel E. Thorne*, ed. Morris Arnold et al., 290–304. Chapel Hill: University of North Carolina Press, 1981.

James, Edward. "Beati Pacifici: Bishops and the Law in Sixth-Century Gaul." In *Dispute and Settlements*, ed. John Bossy, 25–46. New York: Cambridge University Press, 1983.

Jordan, William Chester. "A Fresh Look at Medieval Sanctuary." In *Law and the Illicit in Medieval Europe*, ed. Ruth Mazo Karras, Joel Kaye, and E. Ann Matter, 17–32. Philadelphia: University of Pennsylvania Press, 2008.

Kantorowicz, Ernst. *Laudes Regiae: A Study in Liturgical Acclamations and Medieval Ruler Worship.* Berkeley: University of California Press, 1946.

Kesselring, Krista. "Abjuration and Its Demise: The Changing Face of Royal Justice in the Tudor Period." *Canadian Journal of History* 34 (1999): 345–59.

Keynes, Simon. "Crime and Punishment in the Reign of King Æthelred the Unready." In *People and Places in Northern Europe, 500–1600: Essays in Honor of Peter Hayes Sawyer*, ed. Ian Wood and Niels Lund, 247–288. Rochester, N.Y.: Boydell and Brewer, 1990.

Klerman, Daniel. "Settlement and the Decline of Private Prosecution in Thirteenth-Century England." *Law and History Review* 19 (2001): 1–65.

Koziol, Geoffrey. *Begging Pardon and Favor: Ritual and Political Order in Early Medieval France.* Ithaca, N.Y.: Cornell University Press, 1992.

Kulikowski, Michael. "Fronto, the Bishops, and the Crowd: Episcopal Justice and Communal Violence in Fifth-century Tarraconensis." *Early Medieval Europe* 2 (2002): 295.

Kunkel, Wolfgang. *Untersuchungen zur Entwicklung des römische Kriminal-verfahrens in vorsullanischer Zeit.* Munich: C. H. Beck 1962.

Kuttner, Stephan. "Ecclesia de occultis non iudicat: Problemata ex doctrine poenali decretistarum et decretalistarum a Gratiano usque ad Gregorium IX." *Actus Congressus Internationalis* 3 (1936): 225–46.

———. *Kanonistische Schuldlehre von Gratian bis auf die Dekretalen Gregors IX systematische auf Grund del' handschriftlichen Quellendargestellt.* Vatican City: Biblioteca Apostolica Vaticana, 1935.

———. "The Revival of Jurisprudence." In *Renaissance and Renewal in the Twelfth Century*, ed. Robert L. Benson and Giles Constable, 23–49. Toronto: University of Toronto Press, 1982.

Landau, Peter. "Die Bedeutung des Kanonisches Rechts für die Entwicklung einheitlicher Rechtsprinzipien." In *Die Bedeutung des Kanonisches Rechts für die Entwicklung einheitlicher Rechtsprinzipien*, ed. Heinrich Scholler, 23–47. Baden-Baden: Nomos, 1996.

———. "Traditionen des Kirchenasyls." In *Asyl am Heiligen Ort: Sanctuary und Kirchenasyl—vom Rechtsanspruch zur ethischen Verpflichtung*, ed. Klaus Barwig and Dieter R. Bauer, 56–83. Ostfildern: Schwabenverlag, 1994.

Langenfeld, Hans. *Christianisierungspolitik und Sklavengesetzgebung Romischer Kaiser von Konstantin bis Theodosius II.* Bonn: Habelt, 1977.

Le Bras, Gabriel. "Asile." In *Dictionnaire d'histoire et de geographie ecclesiastiques*, ed. Alfred Baudrillart. Paris: Institut Catholique de Paris de l'Académie Française, 1930.

———. "Canon Law." In *The Legacy of the Middle Ages*, ed. C. G. Croup and E. F. Jacob, 331–612. Oxford: Oxford University Press, 1926.

Liebs, Detlef. "Römische Juristen der Merowinger." In *Wirkung europäischer Rechtskultur: Festschrift für Karl Kröschell zu seinem 70. Geburtstag*, ed. Gerhard Köbler and Hermann Nehlsen, 635–66. Munich: Beck, 1997.

Linder, Amnon. "Constantine's Ten Law Series." *MGH Schriften* II (1988): 33.

Luther, Martin. *Tractatulus de his qui ad ecclesias confugiunt.* Ed. Barbara Emme and Dietrich Emme. Regensburg: D. Emme, 1985.

MacMullen, Ramsay. *Christianizing the Roman Empire.* New Haven: Yale University Press, 1984.

———. *Corruption and the Decline of Rome.* New Haven: Yale University Press, 1988.

Macrides, R. J. "Killing, Asylum, and the Law in Byzantium." *Speculum* 63 (1988): 509.

Magnou-Nortier, Elisabeth. "Etude sur le privilege d'immunité du IV au IX siècle." *Revue Mabillon Ligugé* 60 (1984): 465–512.

Maitland, Frederic, and Francis Montague. *A Sketch of English Legal History.* New York: G. P. Putnam and Sons, 1915.

Manfredini, Arrido Diego. "'Ad ecclesiam confugere, 'ad statuas confugere' nell'età di Theodosio I." *Atti di Accademia Romanistica Constantiana. VI Convegno Internazionale.* Perugia, 1986.

Markus, Richard. *The End of Ancient Christianity.* New York: Cambridge University Press, 1990.

Martroye, François. "L'asile dans la legislation imperiale du IV au VI siècle." *Memoires de la societe nationale des antiquaires de France* 75 (1918): 159.

Mattheas, Antonius. *On Crimes: A Commentary on Books XLVII and XLVIII of the Digest.* Ed. M. L. Hewett. Cape Town: Juta, 1987–94.

Matthews, John. *Laying Down the Law: A Study of the Theodosian Code.* New Haven: Yale University Press, 2000.

McKitterick, Rosamond. *The Frankish Kingdoms Under the Carolingians, 751–987.* New York: Longman, 1983.

McSheffrey, Shannon. "Sanctuary and the Legal Topography of Pre-Reformation England." *Law and History Review* (2009) 27: 483–514.

Meens, Rob. "Sanctuary, Penance and Dispute Settlement Under Charlemagne: The Conflict Between Alcuin and Theodulf of Orléans Over a Sinful Cleric." *Speculum* 82 (2007): 277.

Menochius, Jacobus. *De ivrisdictione, imperio et potestate ecclesiastica ac secvlari libri tres. Accessit liber quartus De immunitate ecclesiae, pro ad eam confugientibus.* Geneva: J. A. Cramer & P. Perachon, 1695.

Miller, William Ian. *Bloodtaking and Peacemaking: Feud, Law, and Society in Saga Iceland.* Chicago: University of Chicago Press, 1990.

Milsom, S. F. C. *Historical Foundations of the Common Law.* 2nd ed. Oxford: Oxford University Press, 1981.

Mommsen, Theodor. *Römisches Straftrecht.* Leipzig: Duncker und Humblot, 1899.

Morani, Moreno. "Sull'espressione linguistica dell'idea di 'santuario' nelle civiltà classiche." In *Santuari e politica nel mondo antico*, ed. Marta Sordi, 3–52. Milan: Università Cattolica del Sacro Cuore, 1983.

Myler von Ehrenbach, Johann Nikolaus. *Tractatus de jure asylorum tam ecclesiasticorum quam saecularium*. Stuttgart, 1663.

Norr, Knut Wolfgang. "Institutional Foundations of the New Jurisprudence." In *Renaissance and Renewal in the Twelfth Century*, ed. Robert Benson and Giles Constable, 299–338. Toronto: University of Toronto Press, 1982.

Oakley, Thomas. *English Penitential Discipline & Anglo-Saxon Law—Their Joint Influence*. New York: Longman, Green and Co., 1923.

O'Brien, Bruce Roland, Jr. "From *moðor* to *Murdrum*: The Pre-Conquest Origin and Norman Revival of the Murder Fine." *Speculum* 71 (1998): 321–57.

———. *God's Peace and King's Peace: The Laws of Edward the Confessor*. Philadelphia: University of Pennsylvania Press, 1999.

Oliver, Lisi. *The Beginnings of English Law*. Toronto: University of Toronto Press, 2002.

Olson, Trisha. "Of the Worshipful Warrior: Sanctuary and Punishment in the Middle Ages," *St. Thomas Law Review* 16 (2004): 473–549.

———. "Sanctuary and Penitential Rebirth in the Central Middle Ages." In *Boundaries of the Law: Geography, Gender and Jurisdiction in Medieval and Early Modern Europe*, ed. Anthony Musson, 277–300. London: Ashgate, 2005.

Pegge, Samuel. "A Sketch of the History of Asylum, or Sanctuary." *Archaeologia* 8 (1787): 1.

Pelikan, Jaroslav. *The Christian Tradition: A History of the Development of Doctrine*. 2 vols. Chicago: University of Chicago Press, 1971.

Pennington, Kenneth. "The Canonists and Pluralism in the Thirteenth Century." *Speculum* 51 (1978): 35–48.

Perdrizet, P. "Asiles gréco-égyptiens et asiles romans." *Annales du service des antiquités de l'Égypte* 20 (1920): 252–55.

Plucknett, T. F. T. *A Concise History of the Common Law*. 5th ed. Boston: Little Brown, 1956.

———. *Edward I and the Criminal Law*. New York: Cambridge University Press, 1960.

———. *The Legislation of Edward I*. New York: Cambridge University Press, 1949.

Pollock, Frederick, and Frederic Maitland. *The History of English Law Before the Time of Edward I*. 2nd ed. Boston: Little, Brown and Co., 1899.

Powicke, F. M. *King Henry III and the Lord Edward: The Community of the Realm in the Thirteenth Century*. 2 vols. Oxford: Oxford University Press, 1947.

Pratt, David. *The Political Thought of King Alfred the Great*. New York: Cambridge University Press, 2007.

Procopé, John. "Greek and Roman Political Theory." In *The Cambridge History of Medieval Political Thought*, ed. J. H. Burns, 21–36. New York: Cambridge University Press, 1988.

Pugh, Ralph. *Imprisonment in Medieval England.* New York: Cambridge University Press, 1968.

Reedy, William T. "The Origins of the General Eyre in the Reign of Henry I." *Speculum* 41 (1966): 688.

Réville, Andre. "L'*abjuratio regni:* Histoire d'une institution anglaise." *Revue Historique du Droit Français et Etranger* 50 (1892): 1–48.

Reyerson, Kathryn L. "Flight from Prosecution: The Search for Religious Asylum in Medieval Montpellier." *French Historical Studies* 17 (1992): 603–26.

Richardson, H. G., and G. O. Sayles. *Law and Legislation from Aethelberht to Magna Carta.* Edinburgh: University of Edinburgh, 1966.

Richter, Aemilius Ludwig. *Lehrbuch des Katholischen und Evangelischen Kirchenrechts.* Leipzig: Bernhard Tauchnitz, 1858.

Riggs, Charles H., Jr. *Criminal Asylum in Anglo-Saxon Law.* Gainesville: University of Florida Press, 1963.

Rissom, Geoffrey R. "A Germanic Concept of Nobility in the Gifts of Man and Beowulf." *Speculum* 53 (1978): 1.

Robinson, O. F. *The Criminal Law of Ancient Rome.* Baltimore: Johns Hopkins University Press, 1995.

Rosenwein, Barbara H. *Negotiating Space: Power, Restraint, and Privileges of Immunity in Early Medieval Europe.* Ithaca, N.Y.: Cornell University Press, 1999.

Rosser, Gervasse. "Sanctuary and Social Negotiation in Medieval England." In *The Cloister and the World: Essay in Honour of Barbara Harvey*, ed. John Blair and Brian Golding, 57–79. Oxford: Clarendon Press, 1995.

Ruedl, Hanspeter. "Ad ecclesiam confugere: Die kaiserliche Asylgesetzgebung in der Spätantike." In *Tradition—Wegweisung in die Zukunft: Festschrift für J. Mühlsteiger*, 133–45. Berlin: Duncker und Humblot, 2001.

Sawyer, Peter. "The Bloodfeud in Fact and Fiction." In *Tradition og historieskivning*, ed. Kirsten Hastrup and Preben Meulengracht Sorensen, 1–24. Aarhus: Universitetsforlag, 1987.

Sayles, G. O. *The Medieval Foundations of England.* Philadelphia: University of Pennsylvania Press, 1950.

Schott, Claus Dieter. "Der Stand der Leges-Forschung." *Frühmittelalterliche Studien* 13 (1979): 28.

Seckel, Emil. *Studien zu Benedictus Levita.* Hanover: Neues Archiv der Gesselschaft für altere deutsche Geschichtskunde, 1900.

Shoemaker, Karl B. "Criminal Procedure in Medieval European Law: A Comparison Between English and Roman-Canonical Developments After the IV Lateran Council." *ZSS KA* 85 (1999): 174.

Siems, Harald. "Asyl in der Kirche? Wechsellagen des Kirchenasyls im Mittelalter." In *Das antike Asyl: Kultische Grundlagen, rechtliche Ausgestaltung und politische Funktion*, ed. Martin Dreher, 263–300. Cologne: Böhlau Verlag, 2003.

———. "Zur Entwicklung des Kirchenasyls zwischen Spatantike und Mittelalter." In *Libertas: Grundrechtliche und rechtstaatliche Gewährungen in Antike und Gegenwart: Symposion aus Anlass des 80. Geburtstages von Franz Wieacker*, ed. Okko Behrends und Malte Diesselhorst, 139–186. Ebelsbach: Rolf Gremer, 1991.

Simpson, A. W. B. "The Laws of Ethelbert." In *On the Laws and Customs of England: Studies in Honor of Samuel E. Thorne*, ed. Morris Arnold et al., 318–33. Chapel Hill: University of North Carolina Press, 1981.

Sinn, Ulrich. "Greek Sanctuaries as Places of Refuge." In *Greek Sanctuaries: New Approaches*, ed. Nannos Marinates and Robin Hagg, 88–109. London: Methuen, 1993.

Smail, Daniel Lord. *The Consumption of Justice: Emotions, Publicity, and Legal Culture in Marseille, 1264–1423*. Ithaca, N.Y.: Cornell University Press, 2003.

Stengel, Wilhelm. "Asylon." In *Paulys Real-Encyclopädie der classischen Altertumswissenschaft*, ed. August Friedrich von Pauly and Georg Wissowa. Stuttgart: Metzler, 1884–1972.

Summerson, Henry. "Maitland and the Criminal Law in the Age of Bracton." *Proceedings of the British Academy* 89 (1996): 115–43.

———. "The Structure of Law Enforcement in Thirteenth-Century England." *American Journal of Legal History* 23 (1979): 313–27.

Theler, Johannes. *Asyl in Der Schweiz: Eine Rechshistorische und Kirchenrechtliche Studie*. Freiburg: Moller, 1995.

Thomas, Hugh. "Violent Disorder in King Stephen's England: A Maximum Argument." In *King Stephen's Reign, 1135–1154*, ed. Paul Dalton and Graeme White, 23–44. Rochester, N.Y.: Boydell and Brewer, 2008.

Thomassin, Louis. *Ancienne et nouvelle discipline de l'Eglise*. Paris: Chez François Montalant, 1725.

Thornley, Isobel D. "The Destruction of Sanctuary." In *Tudor Studies Presented to A. F. Pollard*, 182–207. London: University of London Board of Studies in History, 1924.

Trenholme, Norman. *The Right of Sanctuary in England: A Study in Institutional History.* Columbia: University of Missouri Press, 1903.

Ullman, Walter. *The Medieval Idea of Law: As Represented by Lucas De Penna.* London: Blackwell, 1946.

van Caenegem, R. C. *The Birth of the English Common Law*. 2nd ed. New York: Cambridge University Press, 1988.

———. "Public Prosecution for Crime in Twelfth-Century England." In *Church and Government in the Middle Ages: Studies Presented to C. R. Cheney*, ed. Christopher Brooks et al., 41–76. New York: Cambridge University Press, 1976.

———. *Royal Writs in England from the Conquest to Glanville*. London: Selden Society, 1958–59.

van Espen, Zeger Bernhard. *Jus ecclesiasticum universum*. Venice: Johannes Petri Gibert, 1769.

Veyne, P. *Le pain et le cirque: Sociologie historique d'un pluralisme politique*. Paris: Seuil, 1976.

Wallace-Hadrill, J. M. *The Barbarian West, 400–1000*. Malden, Mass.: Blackwell, 1996.

Wallach, Luitpold. *Alcuin and Charlemagne: Studies in Carolingian Literature and History*. Ithaca, N.Y.: Cornell University Press, 1958.

Weitzel, Jürgen. "Strafe und Strafverfahren bei Gregor von Tours und in anderen Quellen der Merowingerzeit." In *Recht in frühmittelalterlichen Gallien: Spätantike Tradition und germanische Wertvorstellung*, ed. Harald Siems, Karin Nehlsen-von Stryk, and Dieter Strauch, 109–26. Cologne: Böhlau, 1995.

Wentersdorf, Karl P. "The Situation of the Narrator in the Old English Wife's Lament." *Speculum* 56 (1981): 492–516.

Whitelock, Dorothy. "Wulfstan and the So-Called Laws of Edward and Guthrum." *HER* 56 (1941): 1–21.

Wilda, Wilhelm. *Das Strafrecht der Germanen*. Halle: C. A. Schwetschke und Sohn, 1842.

Wormald, Patrick. "Domesday Lawsuits: A Provisional List and Preliminary Comment." In *England in the Eleventh Century*, ed. Carola Hicks, 61–102. Harlaxton: Harlaxton Medieval Studies, 1992.

———. "Giving God and King Their Due: Conflict and Its Regulation in the Early English State." *La giustizia nell'alto medioevo* 44 (1996): 11–17.

———. "A Handlist of Anglo-Saxon Lawsuits." *Anglo-Saxon England* 17 (1988): 241–81.

———" 'Inter Cetera Bona Genti Suae': Law-Making and Peace-Keeping in the Earliest English Kingdoms." In *Legal Culture in the Early Medieval West*. London: Hambeldon Press, 1999.

———. "Maitland and Anglo-Saxon Law: Beyond Domesday Book." In *The History of English Law: Centenary Essays on Pollock and Maitland*, 1–20. New York: Oxford University Press, 1996.

———. *The Making of English Law: King Alfred to the Twelfth Century*. Vol. 1. Oxford: Blackwell, 1999.

Zimmermann, Andreas. *Das Neue Grundrecht auf Asyl: Verfassung- und volkerrechtliche Grenzen und Voraussetzungen*. Berlin: Suhrkamp, 1994.

Index

www.ingramcontent.com/pod-product-compliance
Ingram Content Group UK Ltd.
Pitfield, Milton Keynes, MK11 3LW, UK
UKHW041854031026
15587UKWH00006B/1226/J

9 780823 232680